Around the
in 20 Da

BERTRAND PICCARD

AROUND

IN 20

AND BRIAN JONES

THE WORLD
DAYS

The story of
our history-making
balloon flight

John Wiley & Sons, Inc.

New York • Chichester • Weinheim • Brisbane • Singapore • Toronto

First published in the United States in 1999 by John Wiley & Sons, Inc.

First published as *The Greatest Adventure: The Round-the-World Balloon Voyage of the Breitling Orbiter 3* in the United Kingdom in 1999 by Headline Book Publishing

Map illustrations by Paul A. Duffy, Letterpart Limited, Great Britain

This publication is designed to provide accurate and authoritative information in regard to the subject matter covered. It is sold with the understanding that the publisher is not engaged in rendering professional services. If professional advice or other expert assistance is required, the services of a competent professional person should be sought.

Library of Congress Cataloging-in-Publication Data

Piccard, Bertrand.
    Around the world in 20 days / Bertrand Piccard & Brian Jones.
      p.   cm.
    ISBN 0-471-37820-8 (cloth : alk. paper)
    1. Balloon ascensions. 2. Flights around the world. 3. Piccard, Bertrand. 4. Jones, Brian, 1947- 5. Balloonists—Switzerland.
    6. Balloonists—Great Britain. I. Jones, Brian, 1947- II. Title.

TL620.P523 A3 1999
629.133'22—dc21   99-046233

Printed in the United States of America
10 9 8 7 6 5 4 3 2 1

CONTENTS

DEDICATION

This book is dedicated to the team whose combined skills designed and built *Breitling Orbiter 3* and guided the balloon around the world. To commemorate their achievement, we quote from the fax which we sent to Control when we crossed the finishing line over Africa on 20 March 1999:

Hello to all our friends,
We can hardly believe our dream has finally come true. We almost got lost in political problems, in the slow winds of the Pacific, the bad headings over the Gulf of Mexico. But each time, with God's help and great teamwork, the balloon got back on course to succeed.

We are the privileged two of a wonderful and efficient team that we would like to thank from the bottom of our hearts, now that we are sharing with Breitling the results of five years' work.

ACKNOWLEDGEMENTS

So many people were involved in the round-the-world attempt that we cannot thank everyone individually. But we are grateful above all to Theodore (Thedy) Schneider, head of Breitling SA, whose unfailing generosity and enthusiasm sustained the project from first to last.

We should also like to thank Duff Hart-Davis for his help in preparing the text of this book.

Bertrand Piccard
Brian Jones

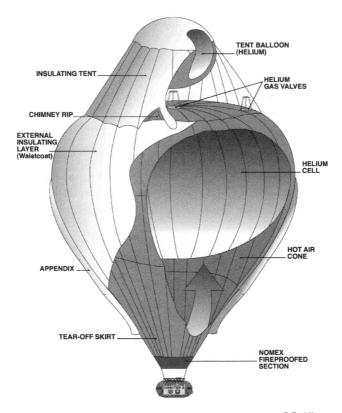

TENT BALLOON
(HELIUM)

INSULATING TENT

HELIUM
GAS VALVES

CHIMNEY RIP

EXTERNAL
INSULATING
LAYER
(Waistcoat)

HELIUM
CELL

HOT AIR
CONE

APPENDIX

TEAR-OFF SKIRT

NOMEX
FIREPROOFED
SECTION

© Breitling

A Rozier balloon works on a combination of gas and hot air, a principle invented by the eighteenth-century aviator Jean-François Pilâtre de Rozier. For take-off, the gas cell is partially filled with helium. As the balloon climbs, the heat of the sun and diminishing atmospheric pressure together make the helium expand. If the pilots want to level off or descend, they vent helium through valves in the top of the gas cell. At night, for extra lift, they burn propane or kerosene in short bursts, warming the air in the hot-air cone, which transmits heat to the helium. The two appendices, coming down either side of the envelope, are safety valves. If the balloon goes through its natural ceiling, either because it has ascended too fast, or because the pilots have pushed it up by burning, excess helium is forced out down the appendices, which are open at the bottom. The purpose of the relatively small tent balloon – also full of helium – is to hold the insulating tent clear of the top of the gas cell, and so minimize the transfer of heat into the balloon during the day, and out of it at night. The only way balloon pilots can steer is by climbing or descending in search of winds blowing in the direction they want. During their round-the-world flight Bertrand Piccard and Brian Jones depended heavily on the skilled predictions of their two weather experts in Geneva, who were constantly telling them the best height at which to fly in order to find the winds they needed.

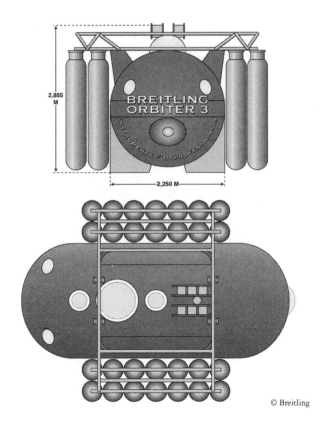

© Breitling

CHAPTER ONE

TAKE-OFF

BERTRAND

For everyone involved in the preparation of the *Breitling Orbiter 3* balloon, the winter of 1998–9 was a time of high anxiety and tension. My two earlier attempts to fly round the world had failed, one after six hours, the other after nine days; and our sponsors, the Breitling watch company, had made it clear that our third balloon would be the last: there would be no *Orbiter 4*. The race was on, as five other teams were making ready to launch in various parts of the globe. A round-the-world balloon flight was generally accepted as the last great challenge in aviation, maybe even the greatest, because it had to combine the power of technology with the unpredictability of nature.

We had little information about the Remax team, who were proposing to take off from Australia and fly a colossal balloon at extreme height in the stratosphere, but all the other starters were well known to us. In the United States Jacques Soukup and Kevin Uliassi each had a balloon under construction. Andy Elson, a former colleague of ours, was preparing the Cable & Wireless balloon for a launch in Spain; but our most dangerous competitor was the tycoon Richard Branson, whose *ICO Global Challenger* was nearing completion in Morocco.

After working on the *Orbiter* project for five years, I think I had become slightly obsessed with its importance. Hoping all the time that I might manage a tremendous achievement, I was driven on by a feeling of relentless pressure: even when I was cutting the lawn at home, I was thinking, 'Maybe it's foolish to be doing this rather than devoting more time and thought to some detail I may have forgotten.' Whenever I turned my attention to anything not connected with the balloon, I felt like a naughty child who had abandoned his homework to play in the garden.

After two failures I was well aware that the people around me didn't know whether to trust me or not. Scepticism increased still further when, in November 1998, I decided to change my co-pilot, asking Tony Brown, who had been going to fly with me, to stand down, and appointing in his place Brian Jones, the project manager.

Under Brian's calm and able direction, construction of the envelope and gondola had proceeded well at the Bristol firm Cameron Balloons. In purely technical terms we were well advanced: on 16 November the gondola, envelope and associated gear were loaded on to two forty-foot lorries and began the journey to our launch site at Château d'Oex, the ski village and ballooning centre 3,000 feet up in the Swiss Alps. We were ready to go at any time from early December – but we were held up by factors outside our control: the war in Iraq, which meant it was unsafe to fly over that country; the restrictions for overflying China; and – most important of all – the weather.

For the all-important task of finding and predicting wind patterns that would carry us round the globe, we had retained the services of two outstanding meteorologists, Luc Trullemans, a Belgian, and Pierre Eckert, a Swiss, who soon proved themselves absolute magicians. At first, though, we were all frustrated. Several times the met men telephoned to say that they saw a good weather slot coming up but that the winds would carry the balloon to Iraq or to prohibited parts of China – and so we had to pass up the chance of launching.

BRIAN

On 18 December tension increased dramatically when Richard Branson took off from Marrakesh. On this, his third round-the-world attempt, he was accompanied by the two other veteran balloonists, Per

Lindstrand and Steve Fossett – a formidably experienced team – and his equipment was as high-tech as money could buy. The chances of his succeeding seemed all too good. 'I know it's not a normal race,' my wife Jo wrote in her diary, 'but we felt as if we'd been left behind.'

The next week was tough going. We tried to concentrate on our own preparations, but one eye was inevitably on Branson's progress – and he did us no good when, without permission, he entered Tibetan air space and flew up over central China, explaining that it was impossible to comply with the authorities' instructions to land because of the vertiginous mountain terrain. Earlier in the year Bertrand had led a delegation to China, where he negotiated permission for balloons to cross the country using a precisely specified corridor; now it looked as though Branson had finished our chances, for the Chinese immediately banned all further balloon flights for the duration.

Then, on Christmas Day, we heard that Branson had been carried southwards by a low-pressure system over the Pacific, and forced to ditch in the sea near Hawaii. When his balloon landed in the water, the mechanism that was supposed to release the flying cables and separate the envelope from the gondola failed to operate, so the capsule was dragged along the surface by the wind at 20 mph. Fortunately the crew managed to escape and were rescued none the worse, but the gondola and envelope were lost to the sea.

Our feelings were mixed, to say the least. We regarded Branson as a friendly rival, but now he had increased our difficulties enormously, and it took nearly six weeks of intensive negotiation with the Chinese to win back the permission we had taken such trouble to gain. Not until the beginning of February 1999 did they agree to let us overfly the country, and even then they would only allow us to cross the southern part, below the 26th parallel. This meant that our weather men had a tiny target, 6,000 miles away, at which to aim.

Working from forecasts and computer models, Luc Trullemans and Pierre Eckert searched ceaselessly for a weather window that would give us the necessary track. What they had to do was predict, from existing patterns, the connections and interactions between different systems of wind that would give us the trajectory we needed – a task of astonishing complexity.

At last on Tuesday, 9 February, Luc spotted a possible slot for the following Sunday and Monday. On Friday the Breitling plane flew to Bristol to bring out the launch crew, and on Saturday, amid growing excitement, the gondola was fuelled up, the envelope was laid out on the launch field at Château d'Oex, and a tanker bringing the liquid helium set out from Paris on its eight-hour drive. (Because commercial vehicles are not allowed to drive in France at weekends, special dispensation had to be obtained for this journey.) But then, on Sunday, Luc and Pierre saw conditions worsening on the first part of the route, to North Africa, and to everyone's immense disappointment the attempt had to be called off. From that moment, the press and public stopped believing we had any chance of success.

It may be that in the long run Branson did us a service, for the Chinese ban made both Kevin Uliassi and Jacques Soukup abandon their attempts. This left only one immediate competitor, Andy Elson, who had flown with Bertrand in *Orbiter 2*. On the following Wednesday, 17 February, Andy and Colin Prescott took off in the Cable & Wireless balloon from Almería, in southeast Spain.

This created still greater stress in our camp. With another capable crew on its way and reports of good progress coming back, time seemed to slow to a snail's pace: every day that passed reduced our hopes of catching up, until finally our chance of winning the race appeared to have gone.

BERTRAND

A few months earlier, I had had a very strong intuition that this attempt was going to succeed, but now I was perplexed by all the problems confronting us. The weather was terrible, with a lot of unseasonable rain and avalanches claiming lives all over the Alps. February was drawing to a close – and normally the end of the month marked the end of the season for round-the-world ballooning attempts because thereafter wind patterns were not usually so favourable. Convinced that the weather window had closed, our team dispersed from the launch site at Château d'Oex, and I took my family to ski at Les Diablerets. Stefano Albinati called me from Breitling to suggest that we find a day for a press conference at which we would announce that our plans for the year were cancelled. We set the date as 8 March.

I was in despair. The next day my wife Michèle and I invited some friends to dinner in our rented chalet. To cheer me up they brought along some bottles of fine wine, and we had a happy evening. That was a decisive moment for me because it was a reminder that, whatever might happen, the most important thing was not to win success and glory but to have true friendship. Surrounded by close friends, it would be easier to cope with all the people who were sure to criticize yet another failure.

But, early next morning, the telephone rang. It was Luc, full of excitement. 'Bertrand!' he exclaimed. 'Listen. There's a really good slot coming up on the first of March.'

'You're joking,' I told him.

'Not at all,' he said, and he described what he and Pierre were seeing on their computers: over the western Mediterranean a big depression was forming, and they felt sure they could swing the balloon round the edge of it, anti-clockwise, so that after flying down over France and Spain we would be carried eastwards over Africa on just the trajectory they had been seeking.

I was amazed, because I thought our chance had already gone. Andy Elson was already seven days out, over the Sudan and heading for Saudi Arabia. But now Luc's call gave me a tremendously strong feeling that we were faced with a serious possibility. Before earlier flights we had established a system of alerts. If things were looking good, the first warning to stand by went out four days in advance. At launch minus three, the alert would be confirmed, and the launch team of eight would be called out from Bristol to join the pilots at Château d'Oex. At launch minus two the rest of the team would assemble. And so, on 25 February, our first warning went out.

BRIAN

My wife Jo and I had been in Château d'Oex since the middle of November, so when the team decided to disband it was a major undertaking, as well as a major disappointment, to pack everything up and head for home. The car was full to the gunwales, and we had just crossed the border into France when Bertrand came through on our cell phone phone and said, 'Brian — drive slowly! There's just a chance we may go.' Surprised and a little doubtful, we stopped near Mâcon, where we had something to eat.

Then Alan Noble, the flight director, phoned through and said, 'Maybe you'd better turn round.' Bertrand rang again, more cautious. 'Better *not* turn round yet,' he said, 'because then we won't be tempting fate.' After some debate Jo and I decided to carry on: the idea of unloading all our gear again in Château d'Oex was awful. We felt it would be better to drive home even if we had to fly back to Switzerland the next day. If we could touch base in Wiltshire, unpack everything and reload with clean clothes, we could somehow close a chapter and make a fresh start. We had this feeling, almost superstitious, that we should make a clean break. So we abandoned plans for a night stop in France and headed back to England as fast as possible.

We reached home at midnight – and in the event we had to turn straight round. By 10 o'clock next morning, Friday, we were boarding an aircraft at Heathrow, bound for Geneva, along with three members of the technical team – Kieran Sturrock, Pete Johnson and Bill Sly. Also on its way was the eight-man launch team from Cameron Balloons, driving a van from Bristol because they had to bring specialist tools with them.

On the plane the cabin crew were in such high spirits that one of them gave his entire briefing as a take-off of Sean Connery – doing it so well that you could easily imagine it was James Bond in charge of the public address system. Some of the passengers didn't realize what was going on, but others enjoyed it immensely.

Also with us was Brian Smith, one of the controllers who were going to monitor the flight from Geneva. Now he made the most of his status as a former British Airways skipper by sending a note up to the captain to inform him he had part of the *Breitling Orbiter 3* team on board. The response was immediate. We were all moved up from our economy seats in the back of the aircraft to Club Class, where we were plied with champagne. When the captain briefed the passengers, he said how pleased he was to welcome us on board. Later the cabin service director presented me with a teddy bear and asked me to take him round the world, suggesting that if the bear completed the circuit he might raise a lot of money at auction for a children's charity. I took the little brown creature, wearing his Union Jack T-shirt, and stuffed him in my bag. For obvious reasons we called him Sean.

Back in Château d'Oex, I called Alan, who was on his way out. I found him in a negative frame of mind. He was convinced that Bertrand and I were not really trying to go round the world. Rather, he thought, we were desperate to get the balloon into the air, just to make a flight of some kind. His sceptical attitude spread to the launch team, and I tried to gee the crew up by saying, 'Look – this is for real. Bertrand and I have been talking to our met people, and there's absolutely no way we're going to call a flight unless there's a significant chance of going all the way round.'

BERTRAND

It was strange to realize that maybe only five people were taking the alert seriously. Everyone else thought we were simply out to make advertising for Breitling by getting the balloon into the air for a few days. Brian and I, on the other hand, were perfectly clear that we would take off only if we had a really good chance. Luc and Pierre, our met men, were still insisting that the weather window was the best we'd had all year.

Alan remained cynical. 'If you'd had this slot at the beginning of the season, you'd never have taken it,' he told them.

'Of course we would!' they replied.

His expression softened slightly as he said, 'So you're really serious?'

'*Absolument!*' cried Luc. 'We're convinced.'

Preparations went ahead at a brisker rate. The gondola was sitting on its trolley on the floor of the workshop in Château d'Oex. Above it on one side was a gallery full of armchairs and tables, together with a kettle and a coffee machine. It was there, during the past three months, that we had held all our discussions and brainstorming sessions about how to solve technical problems and evolve the best possible systems. Now the place came alive again, and the atmosphere grew tense, as we analysed the weather patterns and debated whether to go or not.

By Sunday, 28 February, the gondola was out on the launch field, with the envelope of the balloon stretched out, but still wrapped, in a long sausage beyond it. Inside the workshop we all sat around and struggled to take the crucial decision. Some of us were sunk in the armchairs – which were covered in brown Dralon and had no castors, so that they were very low – and some were perched on higher seats, giving the whole gathering a slightly ridiculous appearance.

Should we carry on or not? I was completely *tiraillé* – torn apart inside. My longing to go was dragging me forward, but my fear of failure was pulling me back.

Brian and I both knew this was our last chance for 1999. We could cancel the launch and keep our balloon for next year – with the risk that somebody else would succeed during the summer in the southern hemisphere. On the other hand, we could take a chance and go. If we succeeded, we would become the first; but if the weather turned out less than perfect, we would fail, and have no balloon to make another attempt later.

So – at one moment I was saying to myself, 'It's too late in the season. Let's stop. Let's keep the balloon for next year.' A second later I was thinking, 'No, we can't do that. We *have* to take the risk and go. But only if the weather is going to be perfect – and how do we know that it will be?' Before the balloon had any chance to go round in circles, my mind was doing just that.

Alan and Don Cameron, head of the firm that built the balloon, were still far from positive. 'From the weather maps we've got,' they said, 'We just don't see how you can get round the world.'

'Of course you can't do it by looking at maps,' retorted Luc. 'You can only do it by working out trajectory calculations, because when the balloon is moving the weather will be moving as well. The high and low pressures are shifting all the time. It's not a static situation – it's dynamic.' He looked at Alan and said, 'You get them up there, and I'll get them round.'

The pressure on Brian and me seemed even heavier, and we knew we could not control fate, or the future. I said that when the time for a final discussion came, I would not push in any direction, but rather listen to everyone else's arguments. I strongly felt that if I kept quiet, fate would have a chance to declare itself and bring us all to the right decision.

At the crucial meeting we two hardly spoke. Luc and Pierre held the floor, confirming that the window still looked excellent. Even then Alan was doubtful, and he asked, 'How long do you think the flight will take?'

After a short conference the met men replied, 'Sixteen days.' Most of us had been thinking of a figure more like eighteen or nineteen, and for the first time Alan smiled, for sixteen was the figure he had been holding in his mind. 'If you say sixteen days, I say yes for the take-off. Any more, and you might not have enough fuel for safety.'

'I don't want you to fall out of the sky in the middle of the Pacific or the Atlantic,' he added. 'But now I think we can go.'

'All right,' I said. 'Everybody has to vote individually – because if we fail, I don't want anyone to start saying, "I was against it all along". And if we succeed, I don't want the ones who were against it claiming, "I was for it all the time".'

It was exactly 1 p.m. when we held a show of hands. The decision was unanimous: to take off. 'OK,' said Alan. 'Now we need to tell the technicians to go ahead immediately' – and he phoned them out on the launch field. After the severe disappointment of the cancelled take-off two weeks earlier, they had been awaiting our decision with some anxiety.

Earlier in the day Luc and Pierre had assured us that it was not going to rain in the immediate future, and the technical team had begun to assemble the envelope, attaching the Velcro and seventy-odd karabiners to cobble together the outer layer, which consisted of the top tent, the waistcoat and the hot-air cone. Then it started to drizzle, putting them in a dilemma.

During the winter a tremendous amount of snow had fallen and we had used a piste-basher to compact the covering on the launch field. On top of the snow the team had laid out immense square sheets of black polythene, meant for covering silage pits, to stop the balloon freezing to the ground. But heavy rain would be disastrous: if the envelope got soaked and the temperature fell below zero during the night, the fabric would freeze to the groundsheets and might have torn when the envelope started to inflate. Another problem was that Velcro does not seal properly when wet – a failing which had already been responsible for the deaths of two balloonists.

BRIAN

On the last day before take-off Bertrand and I kept away from the launch site as much as possible. We stayed together all the time, going shopping, walking about, sitting and talking over a coffee, all the while building our relationship. We wanted to escape from the pressure of the media and the public, and to be more relaxed for the take-off than Bertrand had been for *Orbiter 1* and *2*.

The gondola was already loaded, but in the supermarket we bought a few items of fresh food – bread, cheese, margarine and fruit. From the Hôtel de Ville, where we were staying, we got meals pre-cooked and vacuum-packed: salmon, chicken, emu steak and vegetarian burgers. The fresh food would last only a few days, but already on board were nineteen days' worth of dehydrated rations, as well as 150 litre-and-a-half bottles of water, stowed beneath the floor. Although Bertrand would have preferred carbonated water, we decided it was potentially dangerous as the escaping bubbles might produce more carbon dioxide than our breathing and saturate the filters in the cabin. In a last-minute drive to save weight we discarded some tins of mousse-type puddings, deciding we could do without them. We took no alcohol – not even a bottle of champagne to celebrate with, if celebration were called for. Our only luxury was two small tins of *pâté truffé*.

One factor to our advantage was that no other launches were in prospect. Earlier in the season, when several teams were preparing for take-off, Camerons had had to provide launch crews for all their balloons. Now that we were outside the normal weather window and everyone else had given up, there was no competition: we got the pick of the bunch, and the crew who came out from Bristol were the ones who had designed and built the envelope. Among them was Don Cameron himself, a canny Scot nearing sixty, founder and owner of the firm; with him came Dave Boxall, Gavin Hailes and Andy Booth, all of whom we particularly wanted to have at the launch.

On Sunday evening we had supper in the Hôtel de Ville, our last meal on earth – well, for some time at least. To put it like that sounds as if we were going to the guillotine – and that was almost how it felt. It was a strange time altogether. Then we went to bed for a short rest before the big day.

BERTRAND

According to the weather forecast, the morning of 1 March 1999 should have been fine. But before dawn the valley which cradles Château d'Oex was full of mist, and the sky was overcast. In the Hôtel de Ville Brian and I were both wide awake by 5 a.m., well aware that for the past twenty hours technicians had been working out on the launch field, a few hundred yards away, getting the balloon ready for take-off. After five years of preparation, of false starts and dashed hopes, the moment of truth was upon us.

I woke with a start, adrenaline already pumping, and immediately thought, 'What's happening on the field?' I grabbed the phone, called Alan Noble on his cell phone, and asked, 'How's it going?'

'Bertrand,' he replied, 'you should be asleep.'

WHAT?' Was everything over? Had they failed to inflate the balloon?

'You ought to be sleeping,' he repeated. 'We don't need you for two hours at least.'

'What's happening in two hours?'

'You're going. Everything's perfect. The balloon's standing up, almost fully inflated. There's no wind.'

'Alan!' I cried. 'I can't possibly sleep any more. I'm coming now.'

Immediately I felt a complete change in the physiology of my body. No more relaxation or trying to rest. I was one hundred per cent alert, ready to go. It was still dark, and when I went downstairs there was nobody in the restaurant except Brian, Jo, myself and one waitress, who had got up early to look after us. Brian ate a croissant, but I couldn't manage one because my mouth was too dry. Instead I had some muesli cereal and tea, but I was in such a state of nerves that when I went back to my room to brush my teeth and pick up my bag, I started to get stomach contractions and threw up. 'That's incredible,' I thought. 'Such a thing has never happened before. I've never been so afraid.' It made me realize that I was facing the most important moment of my life.

It so happened that 1 March was my forty-first birthday. The year before, I had taken off in *Breitling Orbiter 2* on my grandfather's birthday, and I had felt then that it was a sign of fate, that I was going to succeed. The intuition proved false: we failed. So now, on my own birthday, I thought, 'Maybe this is something I have to do myself, and not count on family fortune.'

BRIAN

I hardly slept at all. Jo and I were together, and there were a thousand things I wanted to say, but I just didn't feel like talking. I lay there wondering if she was asleep, and Jo – she told me later – did the same.

I felt just as nervous as Bertrand.

At 6 a.m. we drove the short distance to the launch field, passing quickly through the deserted streets of the village. The temperature was a couple of degrees below zero, and because of the mist we could see neither the stars nor the tops of the surrounding mountains, which rose three or four thousand feet above us. Then, as we turned on to the main road, our balloon came into view.

The sight stopped us dead. This was the moment about which we had been talking and dreaming for months – and now the reality came as a shock. In a blaze of arc lights the slender, towering envelope was gleaming brilliant silver against the black sky. One hundred and seventy feet high – tall as the leaning Tower of Pisa, not far short of Nelson on his column in Trafalgar Square, more than half the height of the Statue of Liberty – it rose like a colossal exclamation mark, emphasizing the vast scale of our undertaking. Escaping helium eddied round it in white clouds, like dry ice. At its base the chunky horizontal cylinder of the gondola, painted fluorescent red, was partially hidden by the double row of titanium fuel tanks ranged along each side. Men were swarming round it, some holding ropes, others manipulating hoses. The size of it was awe-inspiring. The volume of the envelope – the balloon itself – was 650,000 cubic feet, and the whole assembly, including the gondola and fuel, weighed 9.2 tons. This was the majestic giant in which we were going to commit ourselves to the sky.

'Can you believe it!' Bertrand exclaimed. 'That's ours!'

As we drove slowly towards it, with the balloon growing bigger and bigger in our eyes, my mind flew back thirty years to the launch of the Apollo 11 mission to the moon. In 1969 I had watched enthralled on television as the crew went aboard, and now I felt we were re-enacting the scene. I knew Bertrand had seen the Apollo launch live at Cape Kennedy, but now he was feeling such strong emotion that he didn't mention it. We were both wearing navy blue flying suits made of a soft, fireproof fabric, with the jackets which Breitling had specially created for us over the top. Our names and blood-groups were inscribed on chest-badges, and we carried survival knives strapped to the trousers of our suits. 'I think we look quite professional,' said Bertrand quietly as we approached the waiting crowd. 'If only these people knew how frightened we are inside!'

We parked our Chrysler Voyager next to the team's vehicles. The moment we got out, we were swallowed by the crowd, and to escape from all the people we had to run to the press conference in a building immediately beside the field. Word had gone round that the flight was on, and the room was full − but still there were only about a third as many people as at the launch of *Orbiter 2*. Then, there had been reporters standing on chairs and tables, trying to get a view. Now, after twenty-odd failures, very few people still believed that it was possible for a balloon to fly round the world, and it was difficult to find anything new to say. Alan made a brief speech. Then Luc and Pierre gave a meteorological briefing to the cameras. Bertrand was eager to get into the gondola and concentrate on our pre-flight checks, so he kept his remarks uncharacteristically short.

I had already noticed that when he and I appeared together he always spoke of flying with far greater eloquence than I could muster. Now I thought that something flippant would be best. 'Because this is Bertrand's birthday,' I said, 'we made a collection. Everyone was incredibly generous, Breitling particularly, but our difficulty was that we didn't know what to give him. We couldn't decide between a flight in a balloon and a round-the-world holiday trip − so, as a compromise, we thought we'd give him both.'

The Breitling publicity girls came up on to the platform, gave him a croissant with a single candle stuck in it (to represent a cake) and everyone sang 'Happy Birthday.'

Outside, the technicians were continuing their preparations. The tanker truck full of liquid helium, at minus 200°C, had arrived from Paris, and as the eighteen-man crew from Carbagas continued to inflate the balloon, under the orders of Roland Wicki, helium pouring through the vaporizers was making a continuous loud whistle. Firemen from Château d'Oex were helping to hold the envelope in position with ropes. Inside the cramped gondola Kieran Sturrock, our electronics specialist and master technician, was going through a long list of checks. The only fault he found was a slight leak from the cylinder of pressurized nitrogen which powered the valves used to release surplus helium from the top of the envelope. He tightened the connection as much as he could, though without quite managing to close the seal fully.

BERTRAND

The launch teams had started inflation at 3 a.m., and throughout the second half of the night everything went well. Then, as dawn broke, the wind began to blow. Gentle at first, it started to gust through the valley – the last thing any of us wanted. The balloon was already at its full height and beginning to sway about: any strong wind would be dangerous, as it might damage the envelope and dash the gondola against the ground. In the worst possible scenario, one of the tanks of liquid propane might split, explode and engulf the whole contraption in flames. It was clear that we had to take off as soon as possible.

The time came to say goodbye to our families – a moment we had both been dreading. Every time I set eyes on Michèle and our three daughters – Estelle (eight), Oriane (six) and Solange (four) – I wondered, 'Can it be right, risking so much in trying to go round the world?' I felt my conviction steadily diminishing.

At my earlier attempts the girls had started off full of confidence, but as more and more journalists asked them, 'Aren't you afraid something might happen to your daddy?' they began to be fearful. Then, after I had twice returned from failure not only alive but in good shape, they became confident again, and positively looked forward to further take-offs. So now they were happy enough. I took them in my arms and said, 'You see how wonderful this balloon is. This time we're really going.' That made them a little sad, especially Estelle, but none of them seemed really worried. More important to them was the fact that this was a Monday, and they were missing school.

For Michèle it was harder. But when I thanked her for backing me up so nobly through five years of struggle, she remained absolutely steady and only said, 'Be careful. I trust you not to take risks in an attempt to bring off something if it's impossible.'

Next I went to my father Jacques and thanked him for passing down such a great taste for adventure, for enabling me to meet all the fabulous people, astronauts and explorers with whom he had come into contact through all his underwater expeditions. Those men were the heroes of my childhood – giants who had come to our house for lunch or dinner and shown me how beautiful life could be if you explored the world and human nature. I thanked my father for giving me the energy with which to prepare for our journey round the earth. A telling photograph taken by Bill Sly, a member of the balloon team, shows both of us with tears in our eyes. We were not overcome or hysterical – just deeply moved; and although we were surrounded by cameramen taking pictures, both of us drew strength from those moments of intimacy, a private island in the middle of the throng.

I also went up to Thedy Schneider, head of Breitling; but, knowing that he doesn't like to talk a lot in emotional circumstances, I simply said, 'Thank you for trusting me.'

BRIAN

I, too, found the moment of parting incredibly difficult. I was anxious that I might break down in front of the cameras: I thought that if Jo could hold herself together, I would be all right, but if she began to cry, I would have a problem because I might not be able to speak. When I went up to her, in the middle of a mass of people, she was absolutely stoical: she stood there looking supremely confident. I felt very proud of her. When I gave her a kiss, she just said, 'Go do it' – and that was it. I thought, 'Thank God,' and turned away. Not until I saw a video film of the parting, months later, did I realize that as I moved off tears were streaming down her face.

BERTRAND

At 8 a.m. Brian and I climbed into the gondola, going in head-first through the rear hatch. We had made it an absolute rule that nobody would enter the capsule wearing outdoor shoes – a precaution designed to keep out any moisture that might condense on the portholes and obscure our vision as we climbed. So we approached in spare pairs of boots, and left them outside. The press had insisted that we stick our heads out of the hatch, and this we did, one at a time, while they took pictures. Then we took particular care to prepare the hatch correctly, so that we would not lose pressure as we climbed. My father came with a handkerchief to clean the seal minutely before we closed the clamp, as he had done so often before diving in his submarines.

BRIAN

All the time the wind was becoming more boisterous. High above us the silvery Mylar envelope was crackling and crisping, as if someone was wrapping a gigantic turkey in tinfoil. Hair-raising noises started to emanate from the gondola itself. Lashed beneath it was a raft of polystyrene blocks a foot thick to elevate the gondola and so hold the fuel tanks clear of the ground. As the balloon heaved and tugged, the smooth underbelly of the capsule started to rub on the polystyrene, and the screeching, creaking sounds were appalling. When the whole package began to lift clear of the ground and was jerked five or six feet into the air before being smashed down again, the onlookers thought the gondola itself was cracking and coming apart. The movement became so violent that the fire crew decided to lash our tether to their five-ton truck rather than risk the main strongpoint pulling out of the ground.

Inside, we were getting thrown about as we struggled to complete our pre-flight checks:

'VHF radios.'
'On.'
'Frequency one one nine decimal one seven.'
'Correct.'
'Altimeter pressure.'
'Set.'
'Fire extinguisher safety pins.'
'Removed.'
'Life-support system.'
'On.'
'Gas valve.'
'Open for check.'
'Two red lights.'
'OK.'

And so on for more than fifty items.

Concentration was difficult because of the noise and because stores and equipment kept tumbling out of the bunks on to the floor, blocking the narrow corridor along the middle of the capsule. Yet even when we were ready we had to stay anchored for a few more minutes: with the weight of us two on board the balloon needed more helium for lift-off, and the gas crew continued to pump. Bertrand was talking to Alan Noble on his cell phone phone, but for the moment we had handed over control to the ground crew and there was nothing we could do to help them.

My first tasks after take-off lay outside the gondola, so I climbed out through the top hatch and sat aloft, holding tight as we were thrown about. There was no danger of falling off because round the roof of the capsule ran the load frame, a heavy, double-decker rail about knee-high, which supported the load of the gondola and fuel tanks. We called this ring of stainless steel 'the playpen' because it gave a feeling of security, and beyond it were the titanium outriggers that carried the propane cylinders.

All round us spectators were crowding close, shouting with excitement, unaware of the danger they were in. If the balloon had split or been blown over, several of them might have been injured as the heavy fabric collapsed on them. Any one of our thirty-two propane tanks could have ruptured and exploded. If it had, there would have been an instant, devastating fireball. As it was, with the gondola being jerked around, one of the tanks got caught up on a cable: its lower end was dragged out of vertical alignment, and when it came free again it swung violently against the side of the hull. What with the wind, the shouts, the clashing of the tanks and the screeching of the polystyrene, direct voice communication was impossible.

BERTRAND

A hundred yards away across the packed snow, members of the Balloon Club of Château d'Oex had been preparing a hot-air balloon for take-off, with an experienced pilot in charge. Its aim was to ascend ahead of us and find out the state of the wind layers in the valley, as well as taking up journalists and photographers. The crew got it more or less inflated, but then, to our dismay, we watched them pulling it down again because the gusts had become too strong. When I saw that I thought, 'Now our problems are starting.' Brian's face turned paler and paler until it was white as a sheet.

In spite of the difficulties, neither of us considered calling off our own launch. I felt fatalistic. I knew the balloon could easily be ruined taking off in these conditions. If we sustained damage as we left the ground, we might have to come down again almost immediately – and a forced landing in the mountains would be extremely dangerous. First, we would have to find somewhere relatively flat, and then there would be a high risk of the propane cylinders exploding on impact. Nevertheless, we both felt there was no way back: we had to carry on. During an interview the day before I had said that if we didn't go, everybody would think us idiots; if we went, and failed, everyone would dismiss us as incompetent; and if we went and succeeded, everybody would say, 'Well, of course, it was perfectly simple.' So there was nothing for it but to take off and do what we thought was right.

For a while I too went up on top of the capsule. By then it was full daylight, and although the sky was still grey, the sun came burning through the mist and caught the top of the envelope. In the nick of time Luc and Pierre's prediction was proving right: the departure window they had forecast was above us, and the next front was already moving down from the north.

Three professional air traffic controllers from Geneva had volunteered their services for our flight, and two of them – Greg Moegli and Patrick Schelling – had established a control post in Château d'Oex itself. Their immediate task was to keep other aircraft away from the balloon's initial flight path, and Greg later described the operation as one of the craziest he had ever known. There were five helicopters, two airships and two fixed-wing aircraft circling the launch site; all the pilots were demanding permission to come as close as possible, and all were in a state of over-excitement.

On the ground the crowd had become enormous. At the last minute word had gone out that we really were on our way, and several thousand people had assembled. To one of them it seemed that the balloon had taken on a life of its own. 'It was like an animal,' she said, 'roaring to go.' Along with many others, she thought the fire engine was about to go round the world as well.

The plan had been that the ground crew would weigh us off, tell us when they were ready to cut the tether, and give us a countdown from ten to one. In the event none of that happened. Unable to risk disaster any longer, Alan simply waited for one more big bounce and at 9.09 a.m. local time – 08:09 Zulu time – at a moment when the balloon was rising, severed the rope with his Swiss army knife. Sky News later described the take-off as 'not so much a launch – more of an escape'. (Zulu time, designated by the letter 'Z', is the international term for Greenwich mean time. We remained on Zulu time throughout the flight.)

Just after we had lifted free, I climbed down into the cabin again and stood with my head out of the upper hatch, while Brian remained squatting on the roof. As we lifted away the noise was incredible. People were screaming at the tops of their voices to wish us good luck. They had waited months for this moment, and now they really let go. The intensity of their feeling brought tears to our eyes. The radio commentator was yelling so loud that he nearly swallowed his microphone, as if at the finish of some race. The bells of both churches, Protestant and Catholic, were ringing wildly. The fire engine's siren was wailing. The pent-up tension and excitement seemed to propel us into the sky.

BRIAN

We took off with a fair old jerk, and I had to cling tight to the rail of the playpen. For several hundred feet the babel of voices came with us, but Bertrand, sitting in the right-hand pilot's seat, shut the clamour from his mind as he began to monitor his instruments. From the view through the porthole in front of his head he could see that we were ascending, but only the instruments gave him our rate of climb.

We were both amazed by the speed at which we were rising. We seemed to be going up like a rocket. My first job was to cut free the polystyrene blocks, but when I looked down over the edge of the gondola we were already 500 feet off the ground, and I thought, 'There's no way I can ditch the blocks now, because on their way down they may plane away and kill somebody.' So the blocks stayed in place and came round the world with us. Abandoning that task, I lowered the antenna trays, the long trailing antenna unit for the satellite telephone – with its attached red anti-collision light and white strobe light – and the array of solar panels.

Very soon, only a thousand feet up, we hit the first inversion layer – a level at which cold air close to the snowy ground meets warmer air above. The balloon came up against the invisible barrier and stopped climbing. In open country that would not have mattered: the envelope would gradually have heated in the sun and we would have started upwards again. But the process might have taken some time, and here in the Alps delay was potentially dangerous because if we'd remained at the same height we would have started to drift sideways and might have been carried into the mountains. One early attempt to fly round the world, by Larry Newman in the *Earthwind 1* balloon, in 1993, failed after only an hour for that very reason. The crew could not manoeuvre fast enough and hit a hillside.

The way to restart a climb is to shed weight or use the burners, so Bertrand called out, 'One bag of sand!' and I started pouring the first fifteen kilos (33 lb) of ballast down through a light fabric tube designed to send the sand clear of the capsule and disperse it safely. A moment later he reached up through the hatch, grabbed me by one ankle and shouted, 'Look out – I'm going to burn!', warning me to keep clear of the propane jets. Blue flames roared six feet up into the hot-air cone, warming the helium in the gas cell above, and we started to climb once more.

Once through the inversion layer we accelerated again and I had to hurry through my tasks. We needed to shut the hatch and pressurize the gondola at around 6,000 feet above sea level – and we were going to reach that height in just a few minutes. As soon as I'd done everything, and double-checked that everything *looked* all right, I scrambled back in, and we both cleaned the seal, lifted the heavy ring-clamp into place and snapped it tight. Abruptly we were in complete silence.

We stood and waited anxiously. When Bertrand first shut the hatch after take-off in *Orbiter 2*, within twenty seconds he heard a whistling hiss which showed that the seal was not airtight and that he was losing pressure. The result was that for the first few days of the flight he was obliged to stay at relatively low altitude. So we listened again for any abnormal sound – but there was nothing: only beautiful silence. We looked at each other and grinned. The hatch was airtight. The balloon was climbing. We were on our way.

BERTRAND

After such a protracted build-up, it was wonderful to be airborne at last. But as we climbed away from Château d'Oex, among the snow-laden mountains, we paused briefly at a third and last inversion layer. Then the balloon suddenly seemed to shoot skywards. We'd been aiming for 200 feet per minute, but the variometer showed that our rate of climb was six times as fast — which was positively dangerous. An ascent as rapid as that could cause the envelope to burst as the helium in the gas cell expanded with heat from the sun and diminishing atmospheric pressure. In theory, the excess helium should be forced out down the appendices — two tubes of material three feet in diameter that ran from the gas cell down either side of the envelope to within a few feet of the bottom — but it was possible that the expansion of the gas was becoming too rapid for the tubes to discharge it fast enough. Even if the appendices were working normally, the balloon might eject a massive amount of helium through them, obliging us to compensate for the loss of lift by burning large quantities of propane.

'We need to vent,' I said. Swivelling the right-hand pilot's seat half round, I reached down behind me to operate the pneumatic system that controlled the valves in the top of the envelope. When I opened the knob of the nitrogen bottle and operated the pneumatic switches, the compressed gas went *whissshhh*, forcing its way up the narrow pipe that reached from the gondola right to the top of the envelope, where it pushed open the valves. Our natural inclination was to retain as much helium as possible because we had no reserve supply. But we soon found that one discharge was not enough: we had to vent again and again before we brought our climb under control.

By the time we finally got the balloon stabilized, we had already used up a third of the nitrogen that powered the pneumatic valve-opening system because of the leak that Kieran Sturrock had observed before take-off. That was alarming because it looked as though we would soon have to go on to the manual system, which consisted of a hand-pull on the end of a long wire; so we tried to economize by closing the nitrogen bottle off after every shot rather than leaving the pneumatic system live and the tube full, thus cutting the leak to a minimum.

We both kept thinking uneasily of other balloons that had burst in similar circumstances. The most recent was the *Global Hilton* balloon in January 1998, from which Dick Rutan and Dave Melton had managed to escape by parachute. Two weeks before that, *J-Renée* had split its envelope an hour after take-off in December 1997 because the pilot, Kevin Uliassi, had also been unable to vent helium quickly enough. At least he managed to fly the balloon down – which was more than could be said of Jean-François Pilâtre de Rozier 200 years earlier: rapidly expanding hydrogen burst his envelope, came in contact with smouldering straw in the burner, blew up and killed the inventor.

My mind was also on my grandfather, Auguste, and his first flight into the stratosphere in 1931. The similarities between that take-off and ours were uncanny. The balloon he built was enormous – nearly as big as ours – and he too was in a pressurized gondola. All his equipment was new and, like us, he had too much wind for safety. Before launch a rope became tangled in the winch that opened the gas valve, but nobody noticed it. The ground crew were supposed to wait until he gave them word to cast off, but the wind was so strong that they let go before he issued any command. His assistant suddenly said: 'That's odd – I'm seeing a chimney through the hatch.'

'Which part of the chimney?' my grandfather asked. 'Top or bottom?'

'Top,' came the answer.

To which the inventor replied, 'Obviously we're in the air!'

When he tried to slow their ascent by opening the gas valve, he couldn't do it because of the tangled rope, and his balloon hurtled upwards at a dangerous speed, climbing more than 50,000 feet in half an hour. When he closed his hatch he heard a tell-tale whistle – as we had in *Orbiter 2* – but he managed to seal the leak with a mixture of vaseline and hemp fibre.

As this memory flashed through my head I thought, I hope there are *some* similarities in each generation of our family but not that we turn out to be the same in everything!

Gradually our climb steadied. Pressurization was perfect, and at 08.28 Zulu we sent our first radio message to air traffic control in Geneva:

Geneva Delta. This is Hotel Bravo – Bravo Romeo Alpha. Good

morning. Overhead Château d'Oex. Passing 10,000 feet. Climbing to flight level two two zero. Heading one eight three degrees. Everything on board OK.

Back came the answer:

Good morning, *Breitling Orbiter 3*. I read you loud and clear. Report flight level two two zero. Good luck.

BRIAN

Our control centre had been set up in the comfortable, ultra-modern VIP lounge on the ground floor of the main terminal building at Geneva Airport. Led by Alan Noble, our controllers were working in pairs, each pair doing an eight-hour shift. Alan's assistant Sue Tatford was a formidable organizer, who made it one of her duties to confine the media to the press room next door and stop them bursting in. The second pair consisted of John Albury and Debbie Clarke (often known as 'Debs'), balloonists of wide experience, and among my closest friends. The third were Brian Smith (better known as 'Smiffy'), an airline pilot and, like myself, a balloon examiner, and his wife Cecilia ('C') – collectively 'the Smiffs', and again, good friends.

Alan and Sue were Cameron staff, but the others had volunteered their services free of charge. As a back-up – and a very efficient one, because she had worked as a controller for *Orbiter 2* – there was my wife Jo, who was not officially a member of the team now that I was flying, but nevertheless spent much of her time in the control centre, putting in a stint whenever there was a crisis or one of the regulars needed a break. The fact that everyone knew each other well was a great help, and meant that whenever a crisis blew up, the atmosphere remained that much calmer. Nevertheless, later in the flight when the balloon encountered difficulties members of the team sometimes stayed on long after their own shifts had finished. They could get meals in the airport's excellent restaurant, and when they needed to sleep they had rooms in the Holiday Inn, a two-minute drive away.

Smiffy and C found their initiation fairly traumatic. When I recruited them, they imagined that Jo and I would be working with them and would give them a hand. As things turned out, they were thrown in at the deep end. When they reached the control room after the launch they were, in C's own words, 'barely computer-literate', and they found themselves having to master complicated procedures at high speed. Alan and Sue instructed them but had no time to linger or repeat things – and after two days Smiffy felt so stressed that he was on the verge of quitting. His particular worry was that he and Cecilia were simply not competent enough to be left in charge at night. But soon his experience of airline flying and ballooning came together with his knowledge of meteorology and air control, and quite suddenly he found he was in his element.

From the balloon, soon after 10:00 Zulu, we reported to Control: 'We are heading for the Matterhorn. It would be a gorgeous picture if a plane could hurry up and make it there.' Alan, who had been taken by helicopter down to Geneva from the launch site, replied:

> Receiving your messages OK. Have spoken with Luc and passed position, speed, altitude. They will come back soonest with best cruise altitude. Was slightly alarmed that you had climbed 20,000 feet in little more than an hour. However, giving the Matterhorn good clearance sounds sensible.

The weather had turned out perfect, and our views over the Alps were dazzling. We sailed smoothly over the 14,000-foot peak of the Matterhorn and, next to it, Monte Rosa, with Italy beyond. On our other side we had Mont Blanc and all the French Alps. We flew straight over Les Diablerets, where Bertrand had skied so often, and the mountains, known to him by heart, in which he had done much of his hang-gliding.

Once we had crossed the Italian border, we felt comfortable enough to send a fax message – ostensibly from both of us, but in fact composed by Bertrand:

> It is now time for a tea-break to relax in front of an absolutely wonderful view of the Alps. Overflew Matterhorn, entering Italy five minutes ago. The take-off was a stressful moment with all that wind, and it is now so calm. Even for the third time, it is always the same emotion, to see the family and friends waving. We are specially thankful to all the people who allowed us to

jump into this incredible adventure. In this new world of our narrow gondola, we have the impression time has stopped.

BERTRAND

By the middle of the day Brian was worn out: weeks of ever-increasing stress and an almost sleepless night had drained him, so at 13:30 Zulu he turned into the bunk for a nap. With myself at the controls, *Orbiter 3* flew on southwards, slowly but smoothly, over Italy and France. In complete silence I watched the mountains file past the portholes. I knew I was taking the biggest gamble of my life, but for the first time in months, maybe even years, I was feeling fabulously well and confident. All our team had done their very best, and now, alone in the cockpit, I had no option but to trust the wind and the unknown.

CHAPTER TWO

ORIGINS

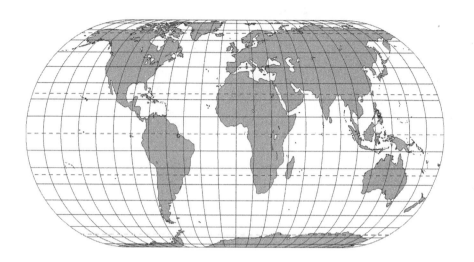

BERTRAND

To find the origins of the Breitling *Orbiter* project I have to reach back more than half a century, through two generations of my family, for both my father Jacques and my grandfather Auguste were pioneering scientists with a strong taste for exploration. Each was much honoured not just in his native Switzerland but throughout the world, and it was their challenging outlook on life, as much as their achievements, that gave me my taste for adventure.

My grandfather, a physicist, was a professor at the University of Brussels. Because he wanted to study cosmic rays, he invented the principle of the pressurized capsule and built a balloon that would carry him into the stratosphere, where the rays are not absorbed by the atmosphere as much as they are lower down. In 1931 he reached a height of 16,000 metres and a year later over 17,000 metres – almost 60,000 feet – becoming the first man to enter the stratosphere and, by the way, also the first to see the curvature of the earth with his own eyes. More than that, however, he proved that it was possible to fly at extreme altitude, above clouds, wind and bad weather, where planes would burn far less fuel in the thinner atmosphere. The principle of his invention was later used for pressurized aircraft and space capsules. In their day his flights were astounding achievements, and he returned to earth a hero, greeted like the latter-day astronauts when they came back from the moon.

Next he invented a submarine called the bathyscaphe, or deep diver, in which the principle of the stratospherical balloon was applied to ocean exploration. He made his first descent, to just over 10,000 feet, in company with my father. Then, on 23 January 1960, my father, together with Don Walsh, a US Navy officer, dived to the deepest part of the ocean – 11,000 metres, or seven miles down – in the Mariana Trench in the Pacific Ocean.

My father continued with the development of submersibles, building the world's first tourist submarine, with room for forty passengers. Next came a submarine designed to drift in the Gulf Stream, going with the current for 3,000 miles from Florida to Nova Scotia, rather as a balloon is carried by the wind. His aim was not that the craft should make rapid headway but that it should stay under water for a month at a time, keeping pace with the fish and other sea creatures borne by the stream.

This expedition was organized jointly with the Grumman Aerospace Corporation, which was opening an oceanographic department. In 1968, when I was ten, our family went to live at West Palm Beach in Florida for two years. Grumman was also building the lunar modules for the Apollo space missions, so that in Cape Kennedy we became good friends with several of the astronauts, as well as with Wernher von Braun, the head of the American space programme.

At a highly impressionable age, from ten to twelve, I witnessed every launch from Apollo 7 to Apollo 12, often watching alongside the astronauts who had manned previous missions. Better still, these heroic figures came for drinks and meals at our house, talked about their flights and gave me signed photographs. Seeing them not only on television and in the newspapers but also in the flesh, I felt I was at the heart of a pioneering movement that had caught the imagination of the entire world. Fired by the excitement of exploration, of breaking barriers and above all of witnessing a tremendous undertaking from the inside, I got such a taste for adventure that all the flying I myself did later seemed a natural consequence.

At the age of sixteen I became disheartened by the thought that mankind's last great adventure – the journey to the moon – had been completed and there was nothing left to do. Then in 1974 I saw a hang-glider, one of the first in Europe. Immediately I spotted a new opportunity and learned to fly. The physical challenge of hang-gliding thrilled me, especially when I started doing aerobatics; but soon I realized that the sport gave me something far more important than pure excitement in that it raised my level of awareness. The inherent danger forced me to concentrate absolutely, and that in turn enabled me to live intensely in the present moment, setting aside all thoughts of past and future and connecting me to myself. When I started doing aerobatics I found I scored much higher in exams, both at school and at university, because not only my mind but also my intuition and my confidence were functioning more efficiently. I flew not because I wanted to outstrip all rivals or emulate my illustrious forebears: it was more a matter of getting to know myself better. My most important discovery was that, once I was properly connected to my own inner resources, and really feeling inside my body that I was alive, I could achieve much more, not just in hang-gliding but in life also.

On my way home after a day in the air, every second of the flight, every thought and every emotion would live again in my memory, and the rest of the day seemed mundane in comparison. I saw that in normal life most people are on automatic pilot, using only part of their capabilities, but that if they could deepen contact with themselves they would become far more effective and efficient.

At that time there were no instruments to give a hang-glider pilot his speed. When I wanted to do a loop, I had only my own feeling to tell me precisely when to push on the control bar. If I pushed too early, without enough speed, the glider would stall as it came over and then tumble; if too late, the glider would stay in the dive, become too stressed and break. There was only one correct instant for starting a perfect loop, and the choice of it became obvious when my awareness was higher.

Many of the sports that became popular in the 1970s – wind-surfing, free-fall parachuting, snow-boarding, roller-skating – were of the same kind: because they made practitioners use their bodies as instruments, they gave people not only exercise and excitement but,

more importantly, a means of getting back to themselves through intuition and true emotion.

I owed much to my father, the scientist in the family, but I was also strongly influenced by my mother, the daughter of a Protestant priest, who studied music, psychology, oriental religion and philosophy. From early childhood I endlessly discussed ideas with her as we went for walks in the country. When I started flying, I was able to try out my new theories of self-awareness on her.

It was my exploration of human psychology, through hang-gliding, that brought me to medicine and led me to become a doctor. I saw that the people who feel bad in life are the ones who are not connected to themselves in the present moment: their connections are either to the past – in which case they tend to be depressives, always worrying about things that did not happen as they wanted – or to the future, in which case they often exhibit anxious behaviour. I realized that the present moment is the only one in which you can change something in your life, and is therefore all-important. I wanted to make use of the insights I had gained from hang-gliding by applying them as therapy in psychiatric medicine – not, of course, by pushing my patients to fly, but by teaching them to connect themselves to their inner resources and capabilities.

After five years' medical training at the University of Lausanne, I decided to take three years off to travel and try other forms of flying, including motorized hang-gliders and microlights. I then returned to Lausanne to complete my studies and went on to do eight years of postgraduate practice in psychiatry and psychotherapy. Throughout that period I kept up my aerobatic flying and began to specialize in a particular type of hang-gliding. During demonstrations at air shows a balloonist would take me up, dangling beneath the gondola, and launch me from a height of 6,000 or 7,000 feet. While I performed loops and spins and wing-overs, laying sky-trails with smoke boxes, loudspeakers on the ground would play the music of Jonathan Livingstone, sung by Neil Diamond. In due course I became European aerobatics champion.

During my postgraduate phase I learned hypnosis and realized that this was the medical equivalent of what I had been doing in the air. I was delighted to have found a link that enabled me to deepen my understanding of flight and medicine at the same time.

In all this flying I never felt I had to prove anything to my father or grandfather. Andy Elson, who became a rival balloonist in the race to be first round the world, often said that my only goal was to make myself as famous as them – but in fact it was much more than that. My profession was not to build submarines or balloons, as they had done: it was to be a doctor, and to explore the human condition – the mind and the soul – rather than the physical world. But it was true that I had harboured a spirit of adventure since childhood: I liked the style in which my heroes lived and worked, and the taste for exploration they had given me remained very strong.

By the age of thirty I had lost count of the number of times I had gone aloft under a balloon, pulled my release mechanism and glided down, making loops and spins. Yet I never considered flying a balloon myself, because the idea of allowing myself to be pushed by the wind, not knowing where I might land, seemed ridiculous. With my hang-glider I could control my descent precisely and land back on the spot from which I had taken off. Often the pilot of the balloon had to wait for two or three hours in the mountains before his team could rescue him, and I decided I would never go in for such an absurd sport.

Then, one evening in Château d'Oex at the end of January 1992, I was invited to a big dinner for balloon teams, and because I had been delayed by an interview I arrived late. When I came into the enormous room, I found hundreds of people starting to eat and only one seat unoccupied. I had no choice but to take it, and so found myself next to Wim Verstraeten, a friendly, round-faced Belgian, always smiling, who had dropped me from his balloon a couple of times.

Wim told me he had been invited as a pilot to take part in the first transatlantic balloon race, the Chrysler Challenge, due to be held in the autumn; he suggested that I, with my medical knowledge and wide experience of flying, would make a useful co-pilot and bring new skills to the enterprise. I scented a fabulous adventure, remembering how, in Cape Kennedy, I had met Charles Lindbergh, who in 1927 made the first solo crossing of the Atlantic in his single-engined *Spirit of St Louis*, and I accepted the offer immediately.

I realized that to go with the wind would be a fundamentally new experience and would call for a major mental adjustment on my part. Until then, in the air, I had always had the wind in my face: I had habitually fought it to overcome turbulence and control my progress. Now I would have to do the opposite and go wherever the wind took me. The idea seemed very strange. Nevertheless, I learned to fly a balloon and looked forward to the challenge – and before it came, fate seemed to send me a message.

That summer I flew to China with a party of doctors to study aspects of traditional Chinese medicine. Finding I had a moment of free time in Shanghai, I went into an antique shop, where I spotted a bowl of what looked like bronze medallions. One in particular took my fancy, and I asked the proprietor of the shop what the characters on it signified. He told me they were an ancient proverb meaning, 'When the wind blows in the same direction as your path, it brings you great happiness.' Fascinated, I bought the medallion immediately. Just as I was trying to accept the idea of flying with the wind, along came this mysterious sign, at precisely the right moment.

In August, when the crews gathered in New England for the start of the Chrysler race, I took the medallion with me, and at the press conferences Wim joked that we would win because his co-pilot had this magic talisman. In fact, we did win – not, of course, because the medal itself was magical, but because the ideograms on it had a magical significance. The teams who tried to fight against the elements ditched in the ocean but luckily were rescued. After five days and nights in a tiny, unpressurized gondola, Wim and I crossed the coast of Portugal and landed in Spain.

From that flight I gained not only a taste for ballooning but also an invaluable new friend. Because the forecasts from the official weather bureau proved hopelessly inaccurate, Wim made contact in mid-ocean with an expert working at the Royal Institute of Meteorology in Brussels, Luc Trullemans. He at once told us what to do to escape from the storms that had been dogging us. 'Climb above the bad weather,' he told us – and so we did. By going high, we harnessed some of the energy of the depression that had been making life so miserable and accelerated away ahead of it.

I came home thrilled by the experience, and found it amusing to tell people that Wim and I had won the race by trusting the winds rather than struggling to impose our will on the elements. We had gone with the wind and the weather, becoming friends of the Atlantic. All we could do to change direction was to fly higher or lower. At our ceiling altitude of 20,000 feet the winds carried us southeast, and when we went very low, only a hundred feet above the sea, they turned northeast.

Back in Europe, people asked us what we planned to do next. Almost as a joke we said we were going to fly round the world. When King Baudouin – then the ruler of Belgium – invited Wim and me to the Royal Palace to hear the story of the flight, he asked about future plans. I mentioned the idea of a round-the-world flight, and as soon as we left the palace I said to Wim, 'I have to tell you a story.'

During the 1930s my grandfather was invited by King Leopold (Baudoin's father) to talk about his flight into the stratosphere. After Auguste had described it the King asked what he would like to do next. The professor outlined his plans for a bathyscaphe, to which Leopold's response was, 'Well, that's really interesting. If you need any help raising funds, just ask me.' Back at the university, my grandfather related details of his audience with the monarch and said, 'Now that I've told the King about the bathyscaphe, I've got to go ahead with it.'

I turned to Wim and said, 'OK – so now we have to go round the world.'

CHAPTER THREE

ENTER BREITLING

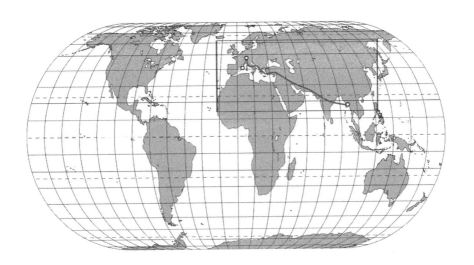

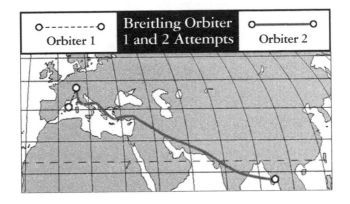

Breitling Orbiter 1 and 2 Attempts

Orbiter 1

Orbiter 2

BERTRAND

Who would finance our round-the-world attempt? Only a company passionately interested in aviation history, whose products were so good that I would be proud to advertise them.

The main sponsor of the transatlantic race had been Chrysler, the car manufacturer, but competitors had also been allowed to find personal sponsors for their own equipment. I happened to know Theodore (Thedy) Schneider, owner and chief executive of Breitling, the private company that makes high-quality aviation chronometers in Grenschen, in the German-speaking part of Switzerland.

From its start the firm had been associated with aircraft instruments, and its sponsorship of projects was directed towards powered flying machines. But when I approached Thedy, he responded immediately and gave Wim Verstraeten and me some help. I posted the Breitling logo in prominent places, and when we won the race the publicity was tremendous, with Breitling up alongside Chrysler in hundreds of photographs. Having asked for nothing, the watchmakers reaped a handsome reward.

At the beginning of 1993 I went back to the firm with an outline of my ambitious idea for a round-the-world attempt. Thedy's response was positive: if such a flight proved technically feasible, he would be part of it. I then approached the Swiss Institute of Meteorology (generally known as Météo Suisse), a weather office with experience of routeing ocean-going yachts around the world. At my request, thousands of computer simulations were performed to calculate the chances of balloons launched from different latitudes in Europe and North Africa at various seasons. The best advice was that we should launch in winter from somewhere 40 degrees north and fly at 10,000 metres. The computers reckoned the trip might take twenty days.

Armed with this information I went to the Bristol firm Cameron Balloons, who had built the entrants for the transatlantic race — and indeed made almost all the balloons that later attempted to fly round the world. After some study Camerons replied that they could have a pressurized gondola constructed out of carbon fibre and Kevlar, a combination which is lighter and stronger than steel, and that they themselves could make a really large envelope capable of lifting the capsule, its crew and enough fuel to keep the craft aloft for a three-week flight.

Actual construction of the gondola would be left to specialist manufacturers, but the general concept was mine, and I asked Camerons to use the system that had served my grandfather and father so well. The capsule would be a horizontal, pressure-tight cylinder, very similar to my father's last submarine. Inside would be a tank of liquid oxygen which would evaporate gradually, allowing the crew to breathe, along with lithium hydroxide filters to absorb the exhaled carbon dioxide.

Everyone agreed that the balloon should be a Rozier type, named after its inventor, the eighteenth-century aviator Jean-François Pilâtre de Rozier (see diagram on page viii). This type of balloon functions on a combination of hot air and gas. The main lift is provided by a large volume of helium in a gas cell. During the day, the heat of the sun causes the gas to expand and keeps the balloon aloft. At night the pilots burn propane or kerosene to heat the air in the hot-air cone, which in turn heats the helium, and so increases lift. Camerons saw that in a long-range balloon, insulation of the envelope would be all-important. The transatlantic balloons, being white, had heated up a lot during the day and cooled quickly at night; by giving the new envelope a waistcoat of aluminium-coated Mylar, the manufacturers would be able to slow these processes beneficially.

Probably one of my best ideas was to ask Camerons not only to construct our balloon – they were building for our rivals as well – but also to become fully involved in the flight itself. I wanted Alan Noble, one of their managers, to act as our flight director, as he had done during the Chrysler Challenge. Soon Alan became not just my privileged link with the factory but a good friend whom I could trust fully.

With a realistic proposal in front of them, the people at Breitling were keen to back the attempt whole-heartedly. And when they saw there was a chance of writing a new chapter in aviation history, they decided – if they could afford it – to be the sole sponsor and to make this the company's big project for the next few years.

As soon as Alan had come up with a costing, I went to see Thedy Schneider again. The moment the boss saw the figure, he said, 'Well, that's possible for us. Where do I send the money?'

'Thedy!' I said, slightly taken aback. 'I have no idea.'

'You must know,' came the answer. 'Now we've decided to go for it, we've got to move fast because there are others in the race. Where do you want the money sent?'

'Well,' I stalled. 'I can call Alan Noble.'

'Go ahead, then.'

Thedy handed me the phone. I dialled Camerons and explained the position. Alan, after a couple of double-takes, gave me an account number – whereupon Thedy wrote out a cheque for the first tranche. Within three days the money was at the factory in Bristol.

'We've got the cash,' said Don Cameron, 'but no contract. What do we do?'

'We have to work even harder, because these people are incredible,' Alan replied.

So the project got off the ground in the best possible spirit. Throughout the enterprise nobody ever considered Breitling to be mere sponsors: we saw them more as partners, members of the team, closely involved with every development. On my side, I never wanted money to come through me because I thought it was better that each partner should be responsible for his own speciality. Funds went straight to Alan at Camerons.

After leaving Thedy's office I drove for an hour towards home, but then stopped at a restaurant to recover from the intense emotion I was experiencing. I felt I had just been given the green light to start building my life's dream, and that in future nothing would be the same. The next years would be both very exciting and very difficult. I picked up the telephone and rang Wim. I explained that the project was on, and said I wanted to invite him officially to be my co-pilot on this incredible adventure. I told him how happy I was at the prospect of resuming the friendship we had built over the Atlantic.

That was in June 1995. For our weather team, I approached Météo Suisse, who produced Pierre Eckert, an expert on routeing yachts. To work with him I asked for the help of Luc Trullemans, from the Royal Institute of Meteorology in Brussels, who had given us such invaluable advice during the Chrysler race. The two are physically quite different – Luc tall, extrovert, smiling, enthusiastic and always eager to explain what he is doing; Pierre smaller, quieter, more serious in manner, not displaying his considerable ability, a keen cyclist and an ecological officer in local government. But when, at my invitation, they met for the first time in Château d'Oex they struck up an immediate rapport that demonstrated the international brotherhood of weathermen; and this pair, whom we came to know as 'the met men', proved out-and-out winners. Putting them together was a gamble that paid off magnificently. None of the other teams employed two weathermen: either they thought one was enough, or they feared that two would battle for supremacy. Our two, far from doing that, praised and complemented each other, so that the value of the pair became incalculable.

Luc had begun studying meteorology as a hobby, and only later made it his profession. He was never a pilot himself, but balloons entered his life when one landed in his back yard in Belgium: the pilot invited him to make the forecast for a meeting, and there he met Wim Verstraeten. Wim asked Luc to be his weatherman for his forthcoming flight over Mount Kilimanjaro in Tanzania, during the late 1980s, and that turned out a big success. Wim then sought Luc's help during the Atlantic flight of 1992 – and so it was that I met him after we had won the race.

For the Breitling flights Luc and Pierre had two principal sources of information. Pierre used ECMWF, the European Centre for Medium-Range Weather Forecasting, in Reading, England, and Luc got forecasts via the Internet from NOAA, the American National Oceanographic and Atmospheric Administration. These two organizations process observations from all over the world – from satellites, radio-balloons, aircraft, ships – and produce computer models that give forecasts for the next fourteen days. Much of the information comes from geostationary satellites, 23,500 miles out in space, which can observe the movement of clouds and so gauge the speed and direction of wind; also, by measuring infra-red radiation, they can give temperature profiles. Polar orbiter satellites, flying lower, analyse temperatures more precisely.

In planning our balloon flights the met men's main interest was in the wind forecasts, and from these – always moving ahead in space and time – they computed likely wind trajectories. The model that Luc used was particularly interesting because it derived from observations of the spread of fallout over Europe after the nuclear accident at Chernobyl. Working backwards, an expert deduced what the weather patterns must have been at the time to spread the radioactive particles as they did. The model was developed for use in forecasting should another nuclear accident happen, and it was used during the Chrysler Atlantic race. The balloon was taken as the equivalent of a single particle, blowing with the wind in different layers at various altitudes, and the model proved incredibly effective. All the other teams competing in the round-the-world race had access to the model, but we had an invaluable advantage in the form of two high-class brains working in synergy.

In Bristol, at a brainstorming session in the Princess of Wales pub close to the Cameron factory, someone suggested that our balloon be called the *Breitling Orbiter*, and everyone concerned adopted the name enthusiastically. Wim knew an Englishman called Andy Elson – a powerfully built fellow in his early forties, made rather dishevelled-looking by a straggling beard and the absence of one front tooth, but a skilled technician who had made the first balloon flight over Everest. Wim was convinced that Andy was the best engineer for high-altitude flight, so Alan commissioned him to take charge of the construction of our capsule on the general lines we asked.

It was Andy who introduced the idea of using kerosene fuel rather than propane. The great advantage of kerosene is that it is much lighter to transport. To carry enough propane on the first *Orbiter*, we would have needed a ton of titanium tanks. The synthetic rubber bags containing the equivalent amount of kerosene weighed only 100 lb.

Already I knew we were in a race. During the winter of 1995–6, while the *Breitling Orbiter* was still being built, Richard Branson and Per Lindstrand were in Morocco with their team, waiting for a favourable weather slot to take off in the *Virgin Global Challenger*. As it turned out they never got one, and they waited the whole winter without being able to launch. The only man who did get airborne was the American Steve Fossett, who took off from St Louis in America and flew alone in his unpressurized gondola for some 2,000 miles before coming down in Canada.

Now, in the winter of 1996–7, we had the same two competitors. Steve Fossett was making ready a new *Solo Spirit* near St Louis, and Branson was again preparing to take off from Morocco. To me, the strangest feature of Branson's gondola was its shape: a vertical cylinder, which would be very bad in the waves if he had to ditch in the sea, and with a sleeping space at the bottom – the coldest part. A further curiosity was that the atmosphere in his capsule was maintained by compressors, which were heavy and noisy and would use a lot of fuel.

Camerons had subcontracted the construction of our gondola shell to another company, Tods, but the first model did not survive the test process. When over-pressure was established inside, the capsule leaked badly at the points from which it was suspended, air forcing its way out. Tods immediately agreed to build another, but it was not ready until September 1996. This made the fitting of the equipment a rush, and when the gondola reached Switzerland it was still almost empty. Together with other technicians, Andy Elson had to prepare it at top speed, working under difficult conditions in a small hut at Château d'Oex.

We were eager to fly in December, but as the year drew to a close our craft was still not ready. On 7 January 1997, while we were still working, Branson took off from Morocco. This produced an atmosphere of desperation in the Breitling camp – but then came a big surprise. Next morning Alan rang me and said, 'If you switch on your

TV, you can watch Mr Branson's landing.'

I was astonished to hear that during the night the Branson team had hit some severe problem. This forced them to drop all their food and water and most of their fuel to avoid crashing before they came down in Algeria. The nature of the problem was never disclosed, but rumour had it that the balloon climbed too fast, went through its ceiling and lost so much helium that it could not stay airborne once the heat of the sun faded.

Once again the race was open, and when Luc and Pierre gave *Orbiter* a green light for the following Sunday, 12 January 1997, we took off from Château d'Oex. In retrospect I have to admit that the balloon was probably not ready. During the night before take-off we couldn't even load our food because the gondola was full of technicians: wires trailed everywhere and altogether the final hour before departure was a nightmare. Yet all the other omens seemed good. Thousands of people turned out to witness the take-off and the atmosphere was magical. In a short speech to the crowd I recited lines from a Belgian poet, saying that if the world is spherical, it is made that way so that love and friendship and peace can go round it. Because I had secured the support of the International Olympic Committee, our balloon was emblazoned with the five Olympic rings and the burners were ignited with the Olympic flame, brought specially from the Olympic museum. Our balloon was planned to be a symbol of peace linking all the countries of the world for two or three weeks. The weather was perfect, with not a cloud in the sky, and the wind at high altitude was ideal as it would carry the balloon at a good speed straight towards the jet stream.

Alas, all these hopeful auguries proved false. After only half an hour in the air one of the fuel tanks overflowed dramatically, sending a flood of kerosene across the floor of the gondola and contaminating our water reserve. By then the balloon was at 27,000 feet and flying beautifully at 60 mph, but Wim and I knew at once we could not stand the vapour, and we started to descend. Having taken off at 9 a.m., we ditched at 3 p.m. in the Mediterranean south of Marseilles. The disappointment was crushing, the frustration immense. As the capsule took salt water on board and we sat miserably on it in our survival suits and life jackets, a coastguard plane roared low over our heads, indicating that rescue boats were on their way; but our personal safety seemed relatively unimportant. We felt we had destroyed our dream. Although the gondola was towed ashore, everything in it was ruined. The envelope could not be recovered for two months, and by the time fishing boats brought it ashore it was smothered with algae and barnacles.

We flew home by private jet, with feet bare, clothes still wet, and carrying one square metre of the envelope which we had cut away for a souvenir. That same night I was back in my own bed, my dream shattered. But then in the morning Thedy Schneider rang and said, 'Cheer up! The world wasn't made in a day. Probably we'll need more than one attempt to go round it.' We agreed that there is only one certain way of never failing in life – and that is never to try.

At the debriefing in Geneva three days after the disaster, Alan Noble asked, 'Well – what's the form? Do we try again?'

'Of course!' Thedy told him.

'When can we start on a new balloon?'

'Ten seconds after you tell me how much it will cost.'

At the next meeting Alan came armed with a figure, and when he named it, within barely ten seconds Thedy said, 'OK, then. So we go!'

There were no recriminations about the failure of the fuel system, and we again commissioned Andy Elson to build a capsule. This time I was determined to be more closely involved in its construction, and I asked Wim, together with Breitling, to make a greater commitment – to come to Bristol more often to keep an eye on progress, and to take a more detailed interest so that both of us would be able to put right any defect that might manifest itself in flight.

During the year of *Breitling Orbiter 2*'s construction, our rivals were again hard at work. Steve Fossett, who had made a beautiful flight from St Louis to India, was building a new balloon. So was Branson. Two further challengers were the Americans Dick Rutan and Dave Melton, who were planning to take off from Albuquerque in New Mexico, and Kevin Uliassi, who was aiming to make a solo flight. But at Camerons it gradually became clear that Wim had too much work to do running his own balloon company in Belgium. Worried that he was not devoting enough time to our project and that he would never learn the gondola's systems thoroughly enough, Alan and I decided to take a third pilot – a partner who would be fully competent to fly the balloon while I was asleep and a technician able to carry out repairs if things went wrong. So it was that, in the summer of 1997, Andy Elson joined the flight team, and the gondola was modified to carry an extra crew member.

Then, in May, a new man appeared on the scene. He was a friend of Andy's and a highly experienced balloonist in his own right: Brian Jones.

BRIAN

My background was utterly different from Bertrand's. I was born in Bristol, where my father worked as a legal executive in a solicitor's office, specializing in matrimonial cases. My mother, who came from Wick, in the far north of Scotland, worked as a school secretary.

At home I was happy as could be, but by nature I was quiet and self-effacing, and this led to my being bullied at school, where rough treatment undermined my self-confidence and made me play truant. After doing that several times I felt dreadful shame hanging over me, and when I learned that the authorities had written to my parents, I was so scared that I ran away. Somehow I had formed the idea of walking to Scotland, and at the age of thirteen I set off northwards through Bristol. After seven hours, not far clear of the city, I went to sleep in a barn. There I was found by the farmer, who handed me over to the police.

As a member of the Boy Scouts I had very much enjoyed outdoor life, and in the Air Training Corps I developed a passion for flying; but, loathing school, I made a complete mess of my exams and left with only one O-level, in English. I took a job as a clerk with British Aerospace at Filton, in the northwest suburbs of Bristol. Soon, however, I realized that was a dead end, and I applied to join the Royal Air Force.

With a single O-level I had no chance of becoming a pilot – a minimum of five was needed – and the RAF offered me work as an administrative apprentice. I took the job and put myself into the force's equivalent of night school – the RAF Education Section. A year later, having passed the necessary extra four O-levels, I applied again for pilot training – only to be refused once more. Instead, I became a loadmaster, first on Hercules C-130 transports, later on Puma helicopters.

In seven years on Hercs I went all over the world and had numerous lively assignments, among them a mission to rescue the British Embassy staff from Phnom Penh during the Vietnam War. The Viet Cong were so close to the airfield that crew members were issued with bullet-proof flak jackets, and our pilot did what the Americans called a Ke Sanh approach, coming in high, at about 1,200 feet, until he was almost over the airfield, then tilting the nose steeply down, aiming for the piano-key markings on the end of the runway, with full flaps and gear down, to land with an almighty bang.

Twice, on separate training flights, we went round the world west-about, taking fifteen days to complete each circuit. On those trips the same aircraft and crew went the whole way: we would fly for eight or ten hours, then have a sixteen-hour break, with a longer stop-off in Hawaii.

During my helicopter service I did three tours in Northern Ireland, where we flew many sorties into the border areas known as bandit country — so dangerous that everything and everybody had to be moved by air. We would drop off army patrols and special forces, pick up prisoners and deliver food to outposts. On such missions the crew were always armed — the pilot with a rifle and pistol, and myself, alone in the back, with a machine gun and side arm. We never knew when the weapons might be needed.

When I left the RAF in 1977, at the age of thirty, I worked as a salesman and then as a sales trainer in the pharmaceutical industry before setting up my own wholesale catering equipment firm, Crocks, in Frome, Somerset, with the help of my sister Pauline. For a while the business did fairly well, and I also had two retail shops. But by far my greatest stroke of luck during those years was that I met my wife, Jo, who was a partner in a catering business — supplying food, rather than equipment — also in Frome.

Then in 1986 I was invited to fly in a hot-air balloon at a festival in Bristol, and immediately became hooked. I sold the shops, and with some of the capital bought a balloon of my own. By 1989 a major economic recession had set in. It hit the catering industry particularly hard, and because Crocks clearly could not provide a living for both of us, I left the business temporarily in my sister's hands.

Providentially, in that same year there was a major development in

British ballooning regulations. Until 1989 anyone holding a private pilot's licence had been allowed to fly a balloon, and there was no such thing as a commercial licence. Then the Civil Aviation Authority issued the first commercial licences, which meant that pilots could fly passengers for money. The result was that ballooning business took off.

Seeing a new opportunity, I began to fly commercially and also worked as a consultant for balloonists who wanted to carry passengers. I was already an instructor, and when I became a flight examiner and the National Training Officer for British instructors, my objective was to encourage higher professionalism in the sport. In 1994, together with Andy Elson and Dave Seager-Thomas, I set up a partnership, High Profile Balloons, which operated balloons for companies like the Royal Mail and Mitsubishi Motors. So, by the time I joined the Breitling project in May 1997, I had a good ballooning pedigree.

It was Andy Elson who invited me to take charge of planning for *Orbiter 2*. Things were not going well at Camerons, largely because Andy — though a competent technician — was not a great organizer, often promising to get something done but sometimes not quite managing it. Besides, he was somewhat temperamental. Being naturally calm, I found I could exercise a stabilizing influence, and saw many ways of improving procedures. Also, because I had done survival training in the RAF, I organized the training for the balloon pilots — and it was during one of the sessions at Camerons that I met Bertrand Piccard.

At first I was slightly in awe of this slender, intense-looking man, with his receding hair, high, intelligent forehead and penetrating blue-grey eyes, because it was he who had initiated the whole *Orbiter* project. However, I soon formed a favourable impression, noticing that he had time for everyone he met. If he came into a room full of people and two of them were important, he would shake hands with everybody else as well, whether they were secretaries or just someone holding the door open. Another great advantage for me, with my non-existent French, was that Bertrand spoke excellent English with a full command of technical terms.

It had already been agreed that during *Orbiter 2*'s flight I and Jo would act as the second pair on the control team in Geneva. When the workshop moved to Switzerland I became more and more closely involved in the preparations. During the build-up to launch I also continued to act as a soothing agent for the team. Before long, Andy and the others took to calling me 'Andy's user-friendly interface'.

BERTRAND

As with the first *Orbiter*, the project fell behind schedule. One deadline after another came and went. Andy had every technical detail of the capsule in his head but none of it was written down, and whenever I asked him if he was sure something or other would really work, he replied, 'Bertrand – trust me. I'm not a doctor!' The rest of us accepted his shortcomings because we were afraid that if we put too much pressure on him, he would walk out for good. Eventually we saw it was too late to call his bluff: we should have stood up to him earlier, but now all we could do was go with him.

Personal frictions exacerbated the technical problems. Andy began to say that Wim was not showing sufficient commitment, that he had not trained enough, and spent too much time talking on the telephone. At one point he said, 'If Wim flies, I don't.'

Because I was still indebted to Wim, I could not possibly stand him down. I told Andy that if I succeeded without Wim, I might well see my face in the newspapers but I would never again be able to look at myself in the mirror. Andy eventually agreed that he would take off with both of us, but only on condition that he and I alone flew the balloon. Wim, he said, could deal with communications and navigation.

In the extremely narrow confines of the gondola such bickering would be intolerable; we knew of many other crews who had come to grief through friction at close quarters. And so, to defuse the tension, I brought my psychological training to bear. All three of us talked through our lives and discussed our characters, deliberately highlighting our differences and finding ways to respect each other's peculiarities. By thus getting to know each other better, we built a good team spirit before take-off.

Once again our main competitor seemed to be Richard Branson, and we were constantly looking over our shoulders in the direction of Morocco. Time and again we received messages saying he was not ready to launch – but we were never quite sure how to take these.

There was always a suspicion that he was playing for time. One day in October 1997 his project manager, Mike Kendrick, rang Alan and asked us not to take off for the time being because Branson was about to go to China to negotiate rights of passage and did not want anything to prejudice his chances of gaining general permission for balloon overflights. Mike also suggested that Alan call Steve Fossett with the same message.

But Branson did not go to China, nor did we hear any more until a couple of months later when he inflated his balloon and prepared to take off. Unfortunately, because his weather slot was so small, he had to inflate during the day – a dangerous procedure in the desert, where violent, gusting winds almost always get up as hot air rises from the sand. The envelope took off without the gondola and flew on its own to Algeria, where it ruined itself on landing.

As for us . . . Andy, perennially optimistic, kept telling people we were ready when in fact we were not. 'Just a few bits and pieces to tidy up,' he would say, but the bits and pieces took two months to sort out. The result was that during all those weeks Branson was afraid we would go, and in the end this pushed him into attempting a premature take-off.

At last, in January 1998, our balloon really *was* ready – but when the gondola was lifted by a crane at the Château d'Oex launch field, some of the fittings which attached the main cables from the capsule to the load frame pulled out. The gondola fell back on the trailer and was damaged; the load frame, the burners and some of the pipes were bent, so take-off had to be postponed while repairs were made. After ditching in the Mediterranean in *Orbiter 1* I thought I could never feel more humiliated; but now, after this idiotic accident, our team looked even more ridiculous in front of the 270 journalists who had come to Château d'Oex.

Eventually, after our weathermen had found a good-looking slot, *Breitling Orbiter 2* took off on 28 January. As that was my grandfather's birthday, I thought it must be a lucky day for me. Little did I know that I would have to wait for my own birthday to take off on a successful flight. As soon as we reached 6,000 feet and closed the top hatch, we heard a hissing, whistling sound from the rear hatch. It was leaking. A combination of haste, bitter cold and exhaustion had led to the hatch being fitted incorrectly – and this meant that until we could get it properly sealed we would have to fly low, missing the fastest winds.

For me, history seemed to be repeating itself once too often: exactly the same problem had afflicted my grandfather when he took off for the stratosphere. However, he managed to seal the crack with a mixture of hemp and vaseline, while we tried in vain with a plastic bag and silicon sealant. So the first day of the flight was spoiled by anxiety – and on the second morning there was another shock when we found that we had somehow lost a third of our entire fuel supply. We never discovered quite what happened, but two of the six tanks, each containing 500 litres of kerosene, had emptied during the night. I felt really fed up with kerosene leaks, but I decided it would not be a good idea to express my disgust to Andy and kept to myself a promise that I would never fly again with that fuel system.

Only very fast and direct winds would carry us round the world with the fuel we had left. But because of the weather patterns we had to fly the balloon relatively low and slow for four days, during which Andy, accepting responsibility, went outside the gondola, hung below it on a rope above a 5,000-foot drop, removed the rear hatch and reset it correctly – after which it gave no more trouble.

By then I knew there was no chance of the flight succeeding, because the only strong winds were crossing the middle of China, and the Chinese were refusing all balloons permission to overfly their country. After more than a year of negotiations, to be baulked by sheer bureaucracy was infuriating, because as we approached the border we knew that up ahead of us there was a jet stream travelling at 160 mph, which would have swept us across the Pacific to California in only four days. But the Chinese remained adamant. There are international agreements allowing a civilian aircraft making an occasional flight to cross any country, but the small print says that every country is allowed, for safety reasons, to impose restrictions – and China imposed restrictions on the whole country for the entire year.

It so happened that the Vice-Prime Minister of China was in Switzerland during our flight, and every time he looked at television or a newspaper all he saw was 'CHINA REFUSES PERMISSION'. He felt he must do something, so he started faxing Beijing, but it was Chinese New Year and permission did not come through until we were over

In 1931 and 1932 Professor Auguste Piccard, inventor of the pressurized capsule, made the first two flights into the stratosphere (*Piccard Archives*).

In 1998 *Breitling Orbiter 2*, a similar shape and size to the stratospheric balloon, landed in Burma after a record flight of 9 days, 17 hours and 55 minutes (*Breitling*).

Brian Jones (*left*) and Bertrand Piccard during the construction of the *Breitling Orbiter 3* capsule, seen through the back hatch. On the far left is the liquid oxygen tank (*Gamma*).

Carbon monoxide detector

Oxygen monitor

Carbon dioxide/ propane/sulphur dioxide monitor

Breitling clock/stop watch

Warning light panel

External lighting

External video monitor

Flytec variometer

The central part of the instrument panel in the cockpit. To the left are the electrical systems, heating and life support controls and electrical fuses; to the right are the GPS, satellite telephone, remote camera controls, emergency systems and the gas valves (*Bill Sly*).

Some of the team during the assembly of the gondola in the workshop at Château d'Oex. From left to right: Brian Jones, Bertrand Piccard, Stefano Albinati, Thedy Schneider, Alan Noble, Pete Johnson, Kieran Sturrock, Joanna Jones and Roland Wicki (*Breitling*).

Final preparation of the equipment, before loading. Brian and Bertrand with Pierre Blanchoud (*Bill Sly*).

After three months of doubt and false alarms, the *Breitling Orbiter 3* capsule is finally brought on to the launch field (*Bill Sly*).

Like a ghost in the middle of the night, the silver-coated mylar of the *Breitling Orbiter 3* reflects the arc lights of the launch field, while the vapour of the liquid helium shrouds it in mist. An absolutely calm night was needed for this very difficult operation (above – *Annie Clement*; below left – *Edipresse – S. Féval*; below right – *Edipresse – P. Martin*).

The worst moment of the take-off: saying goodbye to loved ones. (Above left) Brian and his wife, Jo, in front of the cameras (*Yvain Genevay*).

(Above right) Bertrand and his father, Jacques, cannot hide the tears in their eyes as the moment of truth comes with the take-off (*Bill Sly*).

Bertrand, on his birthday, with Michèle and their three daughters, Estelle, Oriane and Solange (*Yvain Genevay*).

When the sun rises over Château d'Oex, the people can see the balloon for the first time. The envelope was so fragile it could not be inflated for tests; it could only be inflated once for the flight itself (*Breitling*).

Friendly rivals: (Above left) Steve Fossett takes off from the Busch Stadium in St Louis in *Solo Spirit* at the beginning of his round-the-world attempt (*Associated Press/St Louis Dispatch*); (above right) Richard Branson's *ICO Global Challenger* flying high above Mount Fuji on 24 December 1998; (left) Andy Elson's Cable & Wireless balloon ditches in the Pacific on 7 March 1999 – suddenly the route was clear for the Breitling team (both *PA*).

In the dangerously gusting wind, the *Breitling Orbiter 3* finally lifts off. After three months of waiting and doubt nobody believed it would, so the emotion is even greater on the launch field where thousands of people are waving and cheering (*Chas Breton*).

Still at a low altitude, the balloon will eventually climb to the same altitude as the jet plane flying above, at 30–35,000 feet (*Chas Breton*).

Burma (now called Myanmar) and almost out of fuel.

Without a full load of fuel *Orbiter 2* lacked the endurance to skirt China, and our mission was therefore doomed. Nevertheless, we pushed on – but at very low altitude to avoid being carried into the prohibited region – because we wanted to acquit ourselves as well as we could.

After the technical setbacks nothing further went wrong, and crew relationships turned out easier than they had been on the ground. However, Wim's lack of training on high-tech equipment meant that he could never be left alone in the cockpit, so Andy and I had to work alternate shifts. In that situation it was clearly useless to have a three-man team, and while the balloon was still airborne I privately made a second promise: that if ever a third *Orbiter* took off, I would have to change the crew.

Throughout the flight our morale was frequently bolstered by the messages that Brian Jones was sending up from the control centre. Always calm and good-natured, often witty, he kept everyone amused, and he did so much to lighten the atmosphere on board that I felt that in spirit he was with us in the gondola. One of his more memorable communications reached us over Afghanistan. 'Watch out,' he warned, 'because the people down there have very strange habits. At weddings the men dance round the tables firing weapons into the air. If you receive any invitations, please refuse and keep going.'

Because the higher winds would still have pushed us towards China, we flew extremely low – between 1,000 and 3,000 feet – for one day over Pakistan, three over India and one above the Bay of Bengal. As we sat out on top of the gondola, cruising at between 20 and 30 mph in complete silence, spices from cooking and incense from temples came wafting up, along with the faint shouts of children. This was emphatically *not* what we were meant to be doing: we were supposed to be flying fast and high, inside a pressurized cabin, in pursuit of our dream – and here we were, flying slow and low in the warm air, going nowhere.

But it was a magical experience. Having no goal any more we felt no stress, and once again I realized how important it is to accept whatever life brings. If we had fought against our situation, we would have suffered a lot: we might even have landed and gone home angry and despairing, blaming the entire world – especially China; but, by making the best of what had happened to us, we were choosing not to suffer. It almost seemed to me then that suffering involves an active decision: if you refuse to accept what life brings, you suffer, but if you accept your fate, you feel less pain.

Wim agreed with me, but Andy wanted to land: he had had enough of Breitling and its balloons. He had already found another sponsor for future projects in the form of the Scottish property magnate James Manclark, President of the Elephant Polo Association, who had promised to finance him a new balloon.

In faxes from the control centre Alan Noble urged him to keep going. He saw that a premature landing would bring ridicule on the whole enterprise and might put Breitling off a third attempt. Then, in a cleverly worded message he told us that the record we had to beat was the one set by the *Voyager* aircraft flown by Dick Rutan, who had circumnavigated the globe in nine days and one hour. A new endurance record was in our reach, and it was something really worth going for.

The idea put Andy in good humour. He settled down again with his pencils and ruler and returned to navigational calculations. When we landed in Burma we had indeed established a new duration record for any form of aircraft, un-refuelled and non-stop, of nine days and eighteen hours – or, to be precise, 233.55 hours. We had flown 5,266 miles. Even if we had failed in our ultimate objective and our success was more philosophical than technical, I felt happy and proud.

BRIAN

When we knew the balloon was going to land in Burma, a party of us set out from Switzerland to help recover the crew and equipment. Because there were no direct flights to Rangoon (renamed Yangon), Breitling hired a private jet, a Falcon 2000, and off we went, stopping in Bahrain to refuel. The party included Stefano Albinati (a professional jet pilot, who was flying the aircraft), Monika Pieren (the Breitling project manager), Alan Noble, myself and several members of the press.

We reached Rangoon before the balloon landed, but when we tried to organize a recovery helicopter, the Burmese military demanded £6,000 an hour to provide one. After prolonged negotiations we secured a better deal – Monika, a formidable negotiator, really came into her own, deciding what was a reasonable amount and offering only that. But the argument took so long that we only caught up with the balloon just as it was coming down safely to land in a dry paddy field some sixty miles north of the city. Immediately after touch-down it was surrounded by an enormous crowd of people who flocked to the scene from the nearby villages. Some of them, it was said, had gone down on their knees to pray to the huge silver shape as it floated over them.

When Bertrand and I met as he walked away from the gondola in high spirits, one of the first things he said was, 'I've made two promises – and if I don't keep them, you must remind me. I'm not flying again with kerosene, and I'm flying with a new crew. The spirit on board was good, but next time I want to get round the world.'

We had trouble hauling the envelope down because there was no way of releasing helium from the tent balloon in the top except by puncturing it – and it was floating way out of our reach. Resorting to military methods, we asked a soldier to fire a few rifle shots through it: he loosed off several rounds, but they seemed to make no difference. In the end we asked the locals to help us pull the balloon down – and they went berserk, ripping at the fabric, hacking at it with knives, until they effectively destroyed it. There was quite a wind blowing, and some hilarious scenes ensued when a bicycle got caught up in the cables and was dragged aloft, to the great consternation of its owner.

When the giant at last collapsed, the military carried off the trail rope, which you lower as the balloon is coming in to land to steady its approach, and much of the envelope. The crew and all the spectators disappeared, leaving me in charge. To my relief, a huge recovery truck soon appeared, and its crane lifted the gondola on to the back with no difficulty. It was during our drive into Rangoon that we ran into problems, for in the villages the top of the gondola kept catching on electric cables slung low over the road. By then I was feeling quite ill, having got a touch of sunstroke from working against time in a temperature of 110 degrees, so I slumped in the front seat while an intrepid local stood on the back of the truck and used a long bamboo with a fork on the end to hoist each wire clear of the burners. Again and again, as he let a cable go it hit a propane tank lashed across the back and there was a brilliant blue flash, causing one blackout after another. Especially when it grew dark our progress was spectacular. The sixty-mile journey back to the city took fourteen hours. Our local liaison man had to return to the villages next day with enormous handfuls of paper *kyats*, to pay for the damage we had caused.

At that time the Burmese authorities were very nervous about communications. No citizen was allowed to use the Internet, and every foreign telephone call, incoming or outgoing, was logged. The military were keen to get their hands on our gondola so that they could extract our communications gear, but we managed to spirit the whole thing away and hide it in the grounds of a factory until it could be crated and shipped off to Singapore.

CHAPTER FOUR

THIRD TIME LUCKY

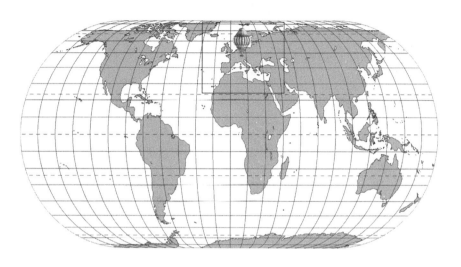

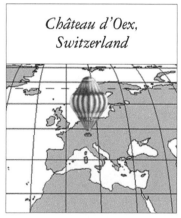

*Château d'Oex,
Switzerland*

BERTRAND

Back in Switzerland we were greeted as heroes, and within a couple of days Thedy Schneider had authorized the team to proceed with *Orbiter 3*. This time he appointed Stefano Albinati, who had flown the *Orbiter 2* recovery team out to Burma, to coordinate the project from Breitling's side. For this third attempt I decided on a two-man crew because I knew we could manage with two; carrying a third man would mean forgoing a lot of fuel as each man, his food, water, oxygen and personal equipment amounted to a burden of nearly 900 lb. I felt very sorry for Wim Verstraeten, but clearly a good friendship – even an important one – was not a sufficient basis on which to fly round the world.

Looking for a new co-pilot, we wanted someone who could devote at least half his time to the project over a period of a year. Our first choice was Tony Brown, a flight engineer on the supersonic Concorde. Tony, a stocky man in his fifties with a bushy moustache, managed to obtain leave of absence from his job, and with more than 5,500 flying hours to his credit he clearly had strong credentials. Yet all too soon I realized that he and I were going to have trouble working together.

When Tony joined us, everything was running smoothly and to schedule. But he seemed to feel he had to fight his way into the team.

It seemed to me that he thought I was playing the role of the chief too much; I wasn't giving him enough room, I was arrogant, and not taking enough care of him. For my part, I found that he brought with him some fairly rigid ideas. Although he was a good balloon pilot, he had never flown big distances; even so, he started explaining to me how to fly round the world. To come along, as we say in French, 'with your big shoes on', is not really the way to set about joining this kind of team project. But at least Tony and I could discuss our characters quite freely and acknowledge the fact that we had difficulty coping with each other, and we agreed we would have a go. That was between August and November 1998. But when we began technical training, my disillusion with him increased as it became clear that we could never combine our talents profitably.

I began to look with more and more interest at Brian Jones. I had seen how hard he worked and admired the ingenuity and constructive approach he brought to solving problems. His excellent aeronautical knowledge was enhanced by a strong sense of humour – and he was a very likeable person.

At the beginning of March 1998, immediately after his return from Burma, we appointed Brian project manager of *Orbiter 3,* in charge of the capsule's construction. Sometimes you feel a natural empathy for people even if you don't know them well. I felt drawn to Brian and saw that, besides having a calm temperament, he was extremely efficient. One thing I liked about him was the way he got things done. If we saw something going wrong with the preparation of the gondola, he would immediately write on the board, 'CHANGE THAT' – and he would follow up the instruction, which was directed partly at himself as an *aide-mémoire*, and partly at the technicians. He never prevaricated, but followed everything through from beginning to end. I myself tended to confuse people by putting up too many suggestions at once, and Brian always brought order into my rather haphazard creativity.

It was his idea that he should become our reserve pilot. At one of the first *Orbiter 3* meetings he said, 'You need a back-up, because there are only going to be two of you this time.' When everyone agreed enthusiastically, he suggested he should start to train with us on the gondola's systems – which he did. Later he made a tentative inquiry as to whether he too could have a flying jacket, like mine and Tony's. He never asked for one straight out, but I sensed that he was hankering after one. So I phoned Breitling and asked them to make another, explaining that once the project was over it would be Brian's only memento, the only thing to remind him that he had been reserve pilot. The firm responded quickly, and when Brian got his jacket he was delighted. Our relationship was starting to build, and I began to regret that he would not be on board when we took off.

On 16 November the gondola, envelope and associated gear were loaded on to two forty-foot lorries and set off for Château d'Oex. The crew went after them, settled in Switzerland and continued to prepare for the launch, which might take place at any time from the beginning of December to the end of February — the period during which global wind patterns are most favourable.

I started to look even harder at Brian and wondered why on earth I hadn't invited him to be my co-pilot in the first place. Later I realized I was not the only one feeling the strain. In her diary, Brian's wife Joanna wrote:

> The pilots seem very aggressive. It affects everybody. Living in Château d'Oex is not much fun any more. No one is clear what the problem is. It just becomes very tense.

On 23 November the tension between Tony and me finally erupted. We were doing technical training inside the gondola, and nothing was going right between us. Already, weeks earlier, Tony had said that if, once we were airborne, I did not let him take a big enough part in decision-making, he would find it a problem. Now I realized that what was proving an interesting psychological exercise on the ground could well become a dangerous antagonism during the stress of the flight and that we needed to resolve the problem quickly. So I deliberately increased the pressure of the training — and that night, during dinner at the Hôtel de Ville, the friction between us finally burst into flames.

When a heated argument broke out, and I insisted that I was not going to change good elements in the project just to please Tony, he snapped back with, 'All right, then. I won't fly. Fly with Brian.'

In my head I was saying, 'Oh yes! Oh yes!'

Tony turned to Brian and said, 'Brian – take my place.'

Brian, being a wise fellow, replied quietly, 'Don't bring me into this.'

After dinner I knew what I wanted, but not how best to achieve it. Pierre Blanchoud, our aeronautical adviser, urged me to take the decision. 'It's your project,' he said. 'You went to Breitling. You're the one who must decide.'

'Yes,' I replied, 'but that's why it's so difficult. If I make a mistake, the consequences could be disastrous.'

'All right,' he said, 'just go to sleep and see what the night tells you.'

Next morning I saw everything crystal clear: I wasn't going to fly with Tony, and I explained my decision to him. After breakfast we drove together to the workshop and shook hands, both feeling strong emotion. He told me he thought I had the ability to fly round the world, said how sorry he was we could not do it together and wished me good luck. I admired his stoicism and self-control. When I phoned Thedy to tell him about the change, he immediately asked why I hadn't chosen Brian in the first place. 'I'm sorry,' I said, 'but he didn't fly on Concorde – and the Concorde connection seemed to be interesting for the project.'

The newspapers made quite a meal of the switch – which was certainly a drastic move as it came so late in the project: if a suitable weather window appeared, we might need to take off within days. Journalists quoted Wim Verstraeten as saying that I could not sustain a friendship, was jealous of rivals and kicked out anyone who criticized me. People started attacking me for ditching pilots and for some of the technical decisions I had taken. I was also criticized for choosing to launch from Château d'Oex, where the weather was still bad. Switzerland was a good starting-point for anyone who had permission to fly straight across China, but because we now had permission only to cross the extreme south of the country, the choice no longer looked a wise one.

Andy Elson also weighed into the controversy. His plan to fly with James Manclark had not lasted long, but by then he was lining up to take off with another sponsor, Cable & Wireless, and he was preparing to launch from Spain as soon as possible. *Orbiter 3*, he said, had absolutely no chance of going round the world because it did not carry enough fuel. The auxiliary tanks on his own balloon, he boasted, contained more than our entire supply.

My only way of answering the critics was to complete a round-the-world flight. Appointing Brian in place of Tony gave me a feeling of tremendous liberation. I just hoped that I wasn't, once again, being blind. I had been blind about my first choice. Was I about to make another mistake?

BRIAN

When Alan Noble asked me to manage the *Orbiter 3* project soon after I had returned from Burma in February 1998, I lost no time in putting together a team, and I took an early opportunity to make an announcement about how I wanted all of us to work together. I stressed that I would try to protect them from any outside pressures, which always mount as a project progresses, and that in return I wanted their total commitment and loyalty. I also wanted no outbursts or bickering within the team, because they are so detrimental to morale, and I told everyone, 'Nobody walks out on this team. If anybody does walk out, you keep walking.'

Having known Tony for years, I could see from the start that he and Bertrand would have problems getting on with each other. One day as I was going through some paperwork in the office, I saw that Tony had insisted on having the term 'co-pilot' precisely defined. What did it mean, exactly? And why would Bertrand be captain, above him? All this was spelled out. I looked at Bertrand and said, 'This is complete bullshit!'

But my suggestion that the two pilots should have a back-up was a purely practical idea. My point was that either Bertrand or Tony could easily have an accident, right up to the moment of take-off, and if that happened there would be somebody ready to step in. At the launch of *Orbiter 2* the temperature was minus 16°C, and the field and gondola were covered with ice. Anyone could have slipped and broken an ankle.

Because I'm not a particularly pushy person, I was hesitant in inquiring about the flying jacket. I knew a third jacket hadn't been planned – nobody had thought about it – and I didn't *ask* for one. I just mentioned it to Bertrand and said, 'I'm a little disappointed that nobody seems to be taking me seriously as a reserve.' The jacket was just one example of this – but I didn't need to mention it again. He picked up on the idea immediately and, without saying anything more, went ahead. When a pilot's jacket appeared with my name on it, I thought, once again, 'Well – what a nice guy he is! He cares.'

At Camerons we had learned many lessons from the designs of the first two *Orbiters* and made whatever improvements we could devise. The gondola, though similar to its predecessors, incorporated a few such changes. It was made from two skins of woven Kevlar and carbon fibre, with a gel coating and foam insulation between them, like a bullet-proof waistcoat. One important innovation was the introduction of double-glazed, twelve-inch portholes, one on each side of the pilots' desk. The earlier gondolas had no portholes, and when the single-glazed hatches froze up the pilots couldn't see out at all.

We also had to design a new burner system because Bertrand stuck to his decision to switch from kerosene to propane fuel. For this we borrowed Pete Johnson, one of Camerons' best burner engineers, who joined the project full time. In other areas our star performer was Kieran Sturrock, first and foremost an electronics specialist but with a very good background in physics. Pete and Kieran made as highly efficient a pair as the met 'brothers' Luc and Pierre did.

As for the envelope, at 650,000 cubic feet its volume was fifteen per cent greater that that of the *Orbiter 2* balloon, and its shape was modified in an attempt to give it better insulation. In designing it we received much help from the École Polytechnique Fédérale de Lausanne, which ran numerous computer simulations on our behalf, investigating ways of reducing fuel consumption. Their conclusion was that to save fuel, the most important thing was to keep the balloon cool during the day.

So, on the shoulders, around the top of the gas cell, some of the Mylar was backed by a thin layer of high-density foam. The envelope was so large that more than twenty people were involved in its construction, which was highly complex. The outer skin was made of aluminized Mylar, a very light fabric strengthened with a mesh. Inside that was a second skin, and the two together gave the balloon a form of double-glazing and air conditioning. The aim was to stabilize the temperature inside the envelope as far as possible by controlling heat exchange, the idea being that during the day the envelope would reflect solar heat away, and at night the air gap between the skins would help conserve heat generated internally by the burners.

In daytime some solar heat would still penetrate the skins, which would make the balloon climb when warmth reached the gas cell and hot-air cone. To help get rid of excessive heat, Camerons placed small electric fans round the top of the hot-air cone. Each had its own solar panel, so that when the sun shone the fans would receive power and suck out the warm air. At night, when the balloon needed to retain heat, the fans would shut down because they no longer had any current.

The gas cell itself was made of nylon proofed with a laminated helium barrier. In putting the cell together, Camerons worked on a belt-and-braces philosophy: they punched thousands of holes in the expensive fabric and sewed the pieces together, then took other pieces of fabric and welded them over the seams. It was strange to reflect that *Orbiter 3* was the most sophisticated balloon ever built, yet it could never be fully tested on the ground. The envelope was so huge that it had to be made in pieces and, although Camerons ran computer simulations, until the whole contraption took to the sky nobody knew exactly how it would perform.

In a burst of unashamed nepotism I brought in Jo as project secretary, to do all the buying and back-up administration in the office. Once again I organized survival training for the pilots, and we majored on survival at sea because coming down in the ocean was obviously the likeliest danger the crew faced. Our equipment was geared to landing in water and included a survival suit and life jacket. The jacket had a personal survival pack attached to its base, containing a life raft, flares, water bags and energy sweets. We also had location aids – a heliograph, rocket flares and an EPIRB (emergency personal identification and rescue beacon), which talks direct to satellites. The idea was that a satellite would spot us, pin-point our position and start relaying messages to rescue-coordination centres. If all else failed – or if we had to bale out and parachute wearing only pyjamas – we would still be wearing Breitling emergency watches, which contain radio beacons capable of transmitting signals on the international distress frequency 121.5

MHz. Through that means alone, a passing aircraft or satellite should be able to locate us.

Bertrand had learned the drills the year before, so I took Tony Brown to the RAF test pilot school at Boscombe Down, and to the swimming pool at the Oasis leisure centre in Swindon. In the decompression chamber at Boscombe Down we went through drills for dealing with hypoxia, or shortage of oxygen, learning how to recognize oxygen deficiency, which reduces the victim's mental powers without him being aware of it.

In the presence of a doctor, with everyone wearing oxygen masks, the pressure in the chamber was reduced to the equivalent of 30,000 feet. One guinea pig would then remove his mask, and the rest would watch for tell-tale signs of oxygen starvation – bluing of the lips and finger nails – while he began trying to do simple sums or just write down his address. Although he did not realize it, his faculties would quickly start to fail. At one point Tony was concentrating so hard on counting backwards that he ignored the doctor ordering him to replace his mask. In tests the previous year Bertrand had gone quiet and confused, tending to look around with a vacant expression on his face. As for myself, having been in the chamber several times, I didn't take my mask off; but on earlier occasions I had started giggling, as if slightly drunk.

In the water the instructors made conditions as unpleasant as they could. The swimming pool was equipped with a wave machine and a water cannon which, together, could simulate moderate seas and heavy, cold rain. With water blasting at us, it was no easy task to remove our parachute harnesses, deploy the one-man life rafts, struggle into them and make them secure. We also went to Bristol Airport, where a box had been fitted out to resemble the inside of the gondola. The fire crew put us in and filled it with smoke, and we then had to rescue a dummy – an unnerving experience.

As I had done some parachuting in the RAF, I knew what it was like to be frightened jumping out of aeroplanes, and I abstained from further parachute training. Bertrand, of course, had done plenty of parachuting, but before *Orbiter 1* he did some free-falling to learn how to turn and stabilize descents.

In the team we put a lot of emphasis on crew relationships. 'Crew resource management', or the handling of human factors on the flight deck, has become an important subject in the airline industry. In the old days the captain ruled absolutely, and nobody would dream of criticizing him or questioning his decisions; but in the past ten years all that has been swept away, and it is now the duty of even the most junior person on a flight to speak up if he or she has something on their mind. The whole crew has to work as a team. On the *Orbiter 3* project we brought in a specialist to talk about the subject.

As the weeks went by, I could not help but be aware of the ever-increasing tension between Bertrand and Tony. I did what I could to smooth things over, keeping myself in the background, not letting my hopes of flying rise too high. I was in a bit of a dilemma. On the one hand, as manager of the project, I was trying to calm things down; on the other, as reserve pilot, I couldn't say too much in case the others felt I was trying to ease my way into the cockpit. Then the boil burst, and for a few days chaos prevailed.

When Tony left and Bertrand asked me if I would fly instead, I said, 'Of course.' Suddenly I realized why he had been staring at me so often during the previous few days. From the way he'd been looking at me I thought I must have had something hanging out of my nose! When I went back to our apartment at one in the morning, apprehensive about Jo's reaction to the news, she came out with a brilliant remark. 'There's only one thing that *really* worries me,' she said. 'What happens if the world really is flat?'

'The reserve is in the hot seat,' she noted, after that explosive dinner – and in fact, although nothing had been said to the media, I knew I was going to fly in Tony's place. That weekend we flew back to England so that we could break the news and say goodbye to our families.

My appointment as the second pilot was finally announced at a press conference in Château d'Oex on 9 December 1998. The fact that I was going to be in the air meant that Jo would have no one to partner her in the control centre, so John Albury and Debbie Clarke moved up into our place and Jo became first reserve. Bertrand and I pressed ahead with our training, and once again there was laughter in the workshop, which had become a very dour place.

When Branson took off on 18 December and ditched in the ocean six days later, for us the most fascinating thing about his debacle was that we knew it was coming thirty-six hours before he did. Luc and Pierre saw that he was in a very strong jet stream over the Pacific heading for America, but they felt sure from their computer models that a branch of the jet would take him to Hawaii. We could not understand why his advisers didn't tell him to fly lower to escape from the trap. If he'd come down from 11,000 metres to 6,000 or even 8,000 metres, he would have picked up a slower wind going in the right direction – but it seems that nobody passed him this vital information. But then if their computer projections suggested they were on the right path, they would not have realized the problem.

Branson's failure gave us confirmation that a jet stream is far from continuous. It consists of air that has been compressed between a cold front, a warm front and the tropopause – the layer of the atmosphere immediately below the stratosphere. If it has little space in which to move, it travels very fast; but when it has more space, it spreads out, slows down and splits. Branson inadvertently went out on a branch of the jet. Few people outside our team knew that he had tried to obtain Luc's services for his flight, offering the Royal Belgian Meteorological Service a year's salary for a month's work. Luc replied that he was working for us out of friendship and because it was his passion.

BERTRAND

In spite of all our setbacks during the winter – the bad weather, our aborted take-off in mid-February, the Chinese block, Andy Elson's launch on 17 February, the lack of suitable weather windows – I never gave up hope. Always, in the background, there were dozens of matters to be arranged besides the actual preparation of the balloon. Luckily, our relationship with the International Olympic Committee had remained perfect: we planned to carry a message of peace to all the countries we passed over, and the IOC warned their national Olympic committees that we were coming. The IOC also gave us much help in trying to obtain permissions – from China, from Iraq and from Iran. This last alone took two weeks' solid work because at first the Iranians said no, and we had to explain how important clearance was for us.

For everyone concerned, the time before take-off was immensely hectic. For me, it was the culmination of five years of hard work, of involvement and of hope. For five years I had nursed this dream in my heart and my head, and it was intensely painful to see hope nearly dying.

Through all our last-minute difficulties and doubts, my confidence was bolstered by the fact that I knew I had a first-class co-pilot, a partner with very high human qualities. Brian and I had talked together a great deal. We realized that we were very different kinds of people: our characters, backgrounds and families, our jobs, our experiences in life, our country and our language – all could hardly have been more different.

Yet in some things we were alike: we were both completely honest, with flexible characters, and we set a high store on good human relations. Neither of us would cheat. Neither of us would lie. This helped us to build a good relationship quickly, sometimes just by discussing our differences and joking about them. If we were both exactly the same, I said, it would be pointless having both of us on board. By cultivating our differences, we would be able to build a strong complementary partnership. The condition was that we had to accept and respect each other's idiosyncrasies – and that was how we founded a very strong friendship and respect for each other. By talking together constantly we got rid of the need to have one chief and one person obeying orders.

In the end, I think, we were three. There was Brian, there was myself, and there was Both-of-Us – and Both-of-Us was the one who always did the right thing at the right moment.

CHAPTER FIVE

HEADING SOUTH

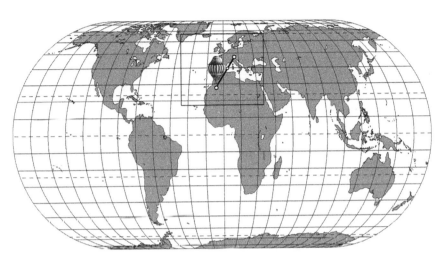

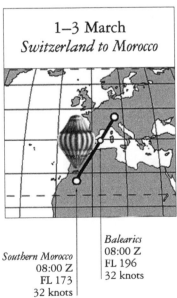

1–3 March
Switzerland to Morocco

Southern Morocco
08:00 Z
FL 173
32 knots

Balearics
08:00 Z
FL 196
32 knots

BERTRAND

During the first afternoon of the flight I kept the balloon between 20,000 and 22,000 feet. The sun was not heating the helium very much because the envelope's insulation was so good. To maintain altitude I had to burn propane quite often – and that wasn't a nice discovery. We had known from the start that we would have to burn at night, but if we had to burn during the day as well we would go through our fuel at an unacceptable rate. In time I realized that in fact it was better to have things this way round: with less efficient insulation, in daylight the balloon would have heated up more, climbed faster, and vented more helium through the appendices. That might have saved us a bit of propane, but at night we would have lost far more heat, radiated out through the fabric of the envelope into the darkness, and our overall consumption of fuel would have been far greater.

Brian slept for an hour and a half, from 13:30 to 15:00. He woke up with a headache, so I gave him some Ponstan, a relatively powerful, prescription-only analgesic, and at 17:00 he went back to bed for another ninety minutes. That was almost the only time we had recourse to the comprehensive first-aid kit, which I had stocked with every drug we could conceivably need, including morphine, for every imaginable body ailment – for the lungs, for the kidneys, for the blood, for haemorrhoids, for diarrhoea, for constipation. In the event, none of them was needed.

At sunset, when we were both again in the cockpit, our first real problems set in. For some reason the fax had gone out of action, and the antenna for the satellite telephone had frozen, so we could not use that either. But the worst worry was that we were using far too much propane. To maintain height, we had to increase our burning time even before dark fell because, as the sun went down towards the horizon, its power diminished. And now, at dusk, we hit another snag. The pilot lights – small, high-pressure flames that ignited the burners on top of the gondola – began to function erratically. They should have stayed alight all the time and ignited the burners automatically, governed by timers on the instrument panel. But they kept extinguishing themselves, and we had to use an electronic sparker to re-ignite them. This was exceedingly tiresome because one of us had to stand up repeatedly, go back a couple of steps and reach upwards to press the button on the burner control panel, mounted on the wall next to the fuel control unit in the ceiling of the central corridor.

In my little green notebook I recorded that we were having to burn for sixty per cent of the time: every ten seconds, a blast of six seconds from one of our double burners. We looked at each other and thought, 'We're really in the shit!'

No doubt the fax could be got going and the telephone would unfreeze. However, the fuel consumption was something else. If we had to rely on manual ignition, that in itself would be a nightmare. But the prospect of running out of fuel in a few days was infinitely worse. Calculations of consumption made on the ground had varied wildly: some had given us a maximum duration of twelve days, while others had put the figure at twenty-four. Now it looked as though our chances of making a full circuit were perilously slim. At the rate we were burning, we would run out of propane in less than a week.

So, after a period of calm, our workload exploded. We had to keep relighting the burners to control the balloon's height, while at the same time trying to reactivate the fax and talking on the radio to the air traffic controllers on the Côte d'Azur – a very busy area. We were in frequent contact with the control tower at Marseilles to tell them what we were doing: they, naturally, wanted us to maintain an even height, and there we were swooping up and down as much as 3,000 feet because the burners kept blowing out. We explained that we were having problems, and asked for a blocked flight level so that we could flop through the middle of it dolphin-wise until we could get the balloon stable.

I went to bed at 19:45, but it took me a long time to go to sleep because I was so used to the continuous, soft snoring of the kerosene burners which had been the hallmark of *Orbiter 2*. The sound was exactly like the steady roar of a commercial aircraft, and just as soothing. Now I had to get used to the intermittent, sharper roar of the propane burners. I seemed to doze off and wake up about two hundred times before I resorted to ear-plugs. Even then I remained uneasy, thinking about the dreadful amount of fuel we were getting through. At one point in the night I imagined I felt the balloon dropping, and I convinced myself that Brian had suddenly had to switch to the second pair of tanks, having exhausted the first. If we'd gone through one whole pair before half the first night was through, our chances were as good as finished. Everything had started so well, and now this first night was turning into catastrophe.

BRIAN

We originally planned to take twenty-eight tanks of fuel, arranged in fourteen pairs, with seven pairs on each side of the gondola. The right side was designated 'green' and the left side 'yellow'. But, midway through the project, Bertrand had the idea of adding four auxiliary cylinders, one at each corner, to give us extra range in case we had to sweep down over Africa at the start of the flight. That was exactly what we were doing now.

Every tank contained 250 lb of liquid propane mixed with ethane, a more volatile gas, to increase fuel pressure at high altitudes. Propane stays liquid at temperatures below minus 40°C. Above that, it turns into gas, which produces pressure to push the liquid out of the tank and to the burners. But at minus 50°C or lower – the sort of temperatures that prevail at high altitudes – the propane would not vaporize, and we needed the ethane, which does not liquefy until minus 89°C, to produce enough pressure.

Each pair of tanks was suspended on a strain gauge — a weighing device — so that at any time we should have had a good idea of how much propane was left in them. That was the theory. What we hadn't realized before we took off was that the strain gauges were highly susceptible to changes in temperature, and in the air, with the temperature varying widely, they became useless. At one stage a gauge would show minus forty kilogrammes, and at another moment it would shoot up to 200 — a complete nonsense.

Above us, on either side of the roof of the gondola, there were three burners, each regulated from its own control panel, and we had various options for bringing them into action. The No. 1 burner on each side could be used on its own; Nos 2 and 3 could be burned as a pair; or we could use all three together — and in an emergency we could use both sides simultaneously, with six burners running at once.

The prolonged burning on the first night made us fear that our stock of fuel was critically small. But because the strain gauges quickly proved unreliable, we had no way of calculating how much we were using, and all we could do was wait until the first pair of auxiliary tanks ran out. From their performance, we would be able to plot a rough graph and work out how far all sixteen pairs would be likely to take us. On the first and second *Orbiters* Andy Elson had been convinced that kerosene was the only fuel to use, but after the earlier disasters Bertrand had felt we must switch to propane because its technology was well known and it produced heat more efficiently than kerosene. So we had never been certain how long our tanks would last — and now suddenly we found that the bloody fuel gauges weren't working. The whole thing was turning into a fiasco.

At least the fax was back in action. During my stint at the controls I exchanged messages with Kieran Sturrock and Pete Johnson, the Cameron engineer who designed the burners. Both were still at the Hôtel de Ville in Château d'Oex, and they sent back minutely detailed instructions:

If you want to try adjusting the manual valve to give a small residual flame, here is how you do it. There is a cap head bolt in the end of the toggle lever. Find the right Allen key — it will be metric — and undo the bolt two or three turns (anti-clockwise).

Operate the toggle until it clicks to On, then adjust the screw until you get the small flame you want. Running on autopilot with a small residual flame like this may cause an alarm to go off.

Such thoroughness was typical. Kieran and Pete had been our star technicians throughout, involved in every aspect of the gondola's construction, and tremendously knowledgeable about its systems, as well as being enthusiastic about the enterprise in general. Now they were ready to field questions from us in the middle of the night and work on them immediately.

On the other hand, Kieran sometimes felt he was not getting the back-up he needed, and when he found that Alan had not responded to his instructions about repairing the fax, he fired off a blistering message to Geneva – although he did warn the startled recipients by telephone that his anger was directed at Alan rather than the team in general:

> What the fuck are you playing at in the Control Room? You are supposed to be responsible for the lives of two men in an experimental balloon, not running a social club. If we are only able to achieve the current level of service – two several-hour blackouts in thirty-six hours – you should be considering whether you need to abandon the flight before the balloon enters more unforgiving territory. If we are having problems, we should be looking for causes and solutions, not assuming they will go away.

Investigation revealed that the trouble was due to overloading at the earth station through which our messages were being routed and to a difference in the speed of the various modems being used. Once the problem had been identified, it was promptly sorted out.

At 22:20 I faxed Control:

> Hello whoever is down there. Brian in the seat. The launch was more than a little exciting. It was amazing the amount of valving we had to do to prevent the balloon climbing above FL 220. Both gas valves were open for over a minute at a time. Anyway, we are

up here now, Lord knows for how long. We'll get an opportunity for some calculations when the first pair of tanks are empty – please God not tonight. We're both a bit tired, but, as they say, if you can't take a joke, you shouldn't have joined. If Jo is there, lots of love.

In a few minutes I got a reply:

Hello, Brian, Wife here. Your message was perfectly timed. I have just entered the Control Room with John and Debs. I can't sleep, so will spend a couple of hours here and then disappear to the Holiday Inn. Back again tomorrow after breakfast. Your launch was a little more exciting than advertised! I think I have calmed down now.

What I hadn't mentioned was that, as a joke birthday present, I had given Bertrand a tiny black-and-white toy football, which I presented to him, carefully gift-wrapped, as soon as we were clear of the mountains. When anyone tapped the wretched thing, it played that awful song '*Olé! Olé! Olé! Olé! We are the champs! We are the champs!*' four times over – and when Bertrand first heard it, he laughed, 'Oh no! It's too early! We mustn't tempt fate.' Nevertheless, we hung the ball on its string from one of the lights in the cockpit, and occasionally, when we bumped into it or touched it by mistake, it started to sing – whereupon we would cry, 'Not yet! Wait!' Once it had started its routine there was no way of stopping it except by removing its batteries.

BERTRAND

When Brian shook me awake at 01:45 on the morning of 2 March, my first words were, 'Did you really switch to the second pair of tanks?' 'No, no,' he reassured me, 'we're still on the first.' Immediately I felt hopeful again, and I was further cheered by the fact that our progress precisely matched the met men's forecast. We were flying at 22,000 feet, on a heading of 210 degrees, and making 25 knots – exactly what Luc and Pierre had specified. Soon we turned even more to the west, on 222 degrees, but again it was according to plan.

Brian went to sleep, and I flew for the rest of the night. In the early hours of the morning I found I needed to burn for only twenty-five per cent of the time, with the burners coming on in four-second bursts every sixteen seconds. At first light, even after our very heavy consumption during the first hours of darkness, the first tanks were still not empty, and I thought, 'This is fantastic. We probably have at least sixteen days of flying after all.'

Before dawn broke we were over the Balearic Islands – Mallorca and Menorca – off the east coast of Spain. It was a beautiful moment, with no clouds anywhere, a full moon reflected in the sea and lights shining from the black islands far below.

I realized how different this flight was from the previous attempts. On *Orbiter 2* I had felt much more philosophical. At an early stage, when we knew we would not be able to go round the world and the flight had become aimless, I accepted the feeling of being carried by the winds, of not having any goal. Now that I saw our ultimate target was within reach, I became much more tense, concentrating hard on every aspect of the balloon and its performance. It was strange to reflect that *Orbiter 3* was the most sophisticated balloon ever built, yet this was its maiden flight. Camerons had run through computer simulations of how it would perform, but it could never be fully tested on the ground, and nobody had known how it would behave when it took to the sky.

The telephone was still not working, but at 06:15 the sun came over the horizon behind us on our left, and I shut the burners down. I carried out the sunrise checks, switched on the solar array and cut the strobe and the red navigation light. Then at 08:00 Brian woke up, made himself breakfast and came into the cockpit, where we spent the whole day together.

BRIAN

Anyone with a tendency to claustrophobia would have been horrified by the dimensions of the capsule in which we had sealed ourselves for the duration. The gondola was in essence a short tube with rounded ends, sixteen feet from nose to tail, and seven feet in diameter. To cut down noise and condensation, all its inside surfaces were padded with knobbly white fireproof foam insulating material. The biggest single space was the cockpit at the front, where there was just room for both pilots to sit side by side on comfortable, high-backed rally-type seats taken from a car. In front of these was a desk with a straight inner edge and a curved outer rim to fit the half-dome of the nose. The surface of the desk was cut from a sheet of transparent acrylic, so that we could see down through it and out through the forward hatch in the lower part of the nose. Facing each seat, at head height, was a twelve-inch porthole for forward vision, and the black instrument panel was mounted across the nose above the table, between the pilots.

Immediately behind the right-hand seat, partitioned off, was a tiny kitchen shelf, no more than two feet square, with a wash-basin set in its working surface and a little water heater in the form of a rectangular metal box mounted on the bulkhead. Apart from two miniature kettles, designed for use in cars, the water heater was our only cooking apparatus. For the first few days of the flight, while our fresh food lasted, we would switch it on, let it warm up for half an hour, and then lower one of the bags containing pre-cooked meat or fish into the water.

Behind the kitchen area was the starboard bunk, with storage spaces above and below. Because we had decided in advance to use only the bunk opposite for sleeping, this one was permanently covered by our survival kit – parachutes, life rafts, immersion suits and so on – which was laid out for immediate use in the event of an emergency. The central corridor, about two feet wide, was just high enough to allow us to stand upright. We are both of medium height – Bertrand 5 ft 10 in, myself one inch shorter – but anyone taller would have had to stoop. The sleeping bunk on the port side of the corridor was seven feet long but only two feet wide, with less than that from the bunk to the rack above. When the curtain was drawn across the inner side to shut the bunk off from the passage, the occupant was enclosed in a space not much bigger than a coffin.

Each bunk had a foam-rubber mattress and a built-in harness – an extra safety feature which we incorporated after Steve Fossett's spectacular crash in the Coral Sea the previous summer. In the middle of the night, at around 28,000 feet, his balloon was ruptured by violent winds and slashed by hail in a storm cloud. Finding himself hurtling downwards, he turned his propane burners on at full power and lay flat on his back in his bunk to minimize damage from the impact on hitting the sea. This almost certainly saved his life, but by the time he emerged from the floating gondola the envelope had caught fire, and he was almost asphyxiated by toxic fumes when the blazing remains of the balloon collapsed on top of him. By then he was holding his life raft in one hand and his emergency beacon in the other, but he was in such trouble that, instead of switching the beacon on, he pressed the test button by mistake. This meant that it gave out only two or three bleeps – but, by a miracle, he was directly underneath a satellite, which picked up the transmission, and he was rescued.

We decided that, if we found ourselves descending out of control, we would do the same as Steve had, and strap ourselves in as well. All the storage spaces were packed tight with food, clothes and equipment; the only other open area was at the back, where a small toilet was tucked into one corner and, on the other side of the rear hatch, stainless-steel cylinders of liquid oxygen and nitrogen were secured to the wall. (The nitrogen was for re-pressurizing the gondola and fuel tanks – operations that might have become necessary at high altitude.) In such cramped quarters there was almost no possibility of getting physical exercise – but the view from the toilet was spectacular.

A breathable atmosphere was maintained by the life-support system, which drew oxygen from the tank and circulated it round the gondola, while lithium hydroxide filters absorbed the carbon dioxide given off by our breathing. A tube carrying air enriched with oxygen passed along the upper wall of the sleeping bunk on its way to the cockpit, and the person in the bunk could get more fresh air by opening a hole in the tube, which sent a gentle breeze over one's face.

We had three oxygen systems. The main cabin system produced a constant flow, taking oxygen from the liquid oxygen (lox) tank and injecting it into the air to produce a breathable atmosphere. (It was also possible to connect a mask to this system.) Then we had a system which delivered 100 per cent oxygen (under pressure if needed) through masks connected to our flying helmets, which we would don if the cabin pressure failed. Finally, we had oxygen on our parachutes – because if you bail out at 30,000 feet without special breathing apparatus you are liable to suffer brain damage.

Detectors showed the percentage of oxygen in the air, which we could adjust via the normal lox system, and other monitors continuously measured levels of carbon dioxide, sulphur dioxide and propane in the cabin. A series of warning lights came on if pressure inside the gondola rose too high, as well as showing if the gas valves at the top of the envelope were open or closed, and if the burner pilot lights were working normally. If our living conditions were fairly basic, our equipment was as high-tech as money could buy. Electric power came from twenty solar panels, each three feet wide and eighteen inches tall, which trailed below us on a long line in an array like a four-sided kite so that, no matter what heading the balloon was on, some of them were always facing the sun. The moment the sun came over the horizon every morning, *bang!* − they sprang to life instantly, and we could see the charge coming through on the instruments.

Electric power was stored in five car batteries under the floor of the cockpit. In case they failed, we also had dry lithium batteries designed to last seventeen days. In fact the power system proved highly efficient: the only time the panels failed to charge the batteries fully was late in the flight when, in the jet stream, we were surrounded by cirrus cloud which partially obscured the sun, and in the second half of the night we had to switch to the lithium battery supply.

Our most valuable single instrument was the global positioning system (GPS), which continuously showed the position of the balloon on a small moving map, and gave us our heading and our speed. The instrument's black-and-white screen was only three inches by two and a half, and often it covered the whole of the country below us; but it had a zoom facility to enlarge details. When we saw from our maps that an airfield or a navigation beacon was coming up ahead of us, we could dial in and get an instant reading, telling us that beacon X, for example, was 255 miles away on a bearing of 085 degrees. The GPS display also had a line showing what our trajectory would be if we held our present heading: as we climbed and descended, heading east, we could see the line changing direction, a little to the north or a little to the south. This made it possible to aim directly at chosen targets. At the bottom of the screen was a digital read-out of speed, direction, altitude and position. As back-ups, we had two more GPS in our main and spare laptop computers, and we could call up the figures on the computer screens if necessary. There was also a hand-held GPS in our survival pack.

Two radar transponders automatically gave out our identity, altitude and position to air traffic control centres along our route. The controllers would ask us to 'squawk' a number – say 5555 – and when we punched that in it told them who we were. An orange light flashed on our transponder unit whenever a radar station was interrogating it to check our identity. For voice communication we had VHF (short-range) and HF (long-range) radio and a satellite telephone. Bertrand often used the satphone to talk to Luc and Pierre in French, so that he knew exactly what our weathermen were thinking. But most exchanges with the control centre went via one or other of our two Capsat fax transmitters. We would tap messages into a laptop computer (provided by Devillard in Geneva) and transmit them through satellites; replies from Control came up on our screen, and although we could not print the messages because we had no printer on board, every one was retained on the computer. Bertrand, being no sort of a typist, tended to send very short messages, whereas I went in for longer missives.

Alan Noble had insisted on this system because it reduced the possibility of error. Radio or telephone messages could be garbled or misheard, but with the fax everything was clear. On the whole it was extremely efficient, but sometimes, when we were directly beneath a satellite, the balloon would create its own cone of silence, blocking the antenna and cutting transmission. Whenever a message came up an orange light would flash, and – especially when we had sent down an important question – we were like children eagerly waiting for the answer in the post. In case of failures, almost all our equipment was duplicated or triplicated.

Our instruments included two altimeters – one standard, with revolving hands like a clock, and the other electronic, which gave a read-out in red digits. There was also a radio altimeter, which worked only at 2,500 feet or below by sending a beam straight down, and was for landing in low visibility. A variometer gave us our rate of climb and descent. To make a complete record of the flight, a barograph was automatically taking a reading of altitude every few seconds. This instrument was sealed by an official observer before take-off, and we had no access to it while we were in the air.

We also had four video cameras, two mounted outside the gondola, one mounted inside, and another inside which could be either mounted or hand-held. By putting digital video recordings on to our laptops with a digital Logitech camera we could send clips by satellite telephone back to Control.

BERTRAND

We relied heavily on all this sophisticated equipment; but even more we depended on the expertise of the team supporting us from the ground – not least our met men. I don't think Brian or I realized how hard those two were labouring on our behalf. They were supposed to be alternating in twelve-hour shifts, but frequently they overlapped each other. Luc never went to bed before one o'clock in the morning because he had to wait for the latest weather model, which came in over the Internet at midnight; and he was always up again at six or seven, back in the control centre, to analyse the night's models. Because there was no spare desk space, he worked throughout the flight with his laptop perched on a little round coffee table which he had commandeered from the restaurant – and whenever there was the slightest chance of a celebration, he nipped next door for a glass of champagne with the girls in the press room.

Another vital element of support came from the three air traffic controllers who had volunteered their services for the duration of our flight: Greg Moegli, Patrick Schelling and Niklaus Gerber – known collectively as 'the balloon Mafia'. All had full-time jobs at Swiss Control, the official air traffic control organization at Geneva Airport, but they were working on flexible timetables and arranged to cover for us whenever they could take time off. Their role was to obtain clearance for the balloon from air traffic control centres round the world. Every centre had to be alerted to our approach either so that other aircraft could be directed to keep clear of our likely track, or so that we could change height to avoid busy flight paths.

Every commercial pilot has to file a flight plan before take-off, giving the route he is proposing to fly, but ours was extremely unusual in that we did not know exactly where we would be going. The plan filed by Greg – who incidentally bears a startling resemblance to Luciano Pavarotti – gave a grandiose outline of our route:

> Château d'Oex, Switzerland – crossing the Alps – Nice – the Balearic Islands – Morocco – Mauritania – Mali – Niger – Chad – Sudan – Saudi Arabia – Oman – India – Burma – South of China – Pacific Ocean – California – crossing USA – crossing Atlantic Ocean – Canaries – intended landing in North Africa east of 10 degrees lat.

In the box for 'Estimated duration of flight' he had put '20 days' and under 'Aircraft colour and markings' he had entered 'Envelope silver grey, capsule red, name *Breitling Orbiter 3*'. Normally each country updates the plan and hands it on to the next as an aircraft leaves its FIR, or flight information region, but because the track of the balloon could not be forecast exactly, Greg and his two colleagues sent out their own updates. These they passed to the communications centre at Swiss Control, where a team of more than thirty people put them in the correct form and sent them out over AFTN – the Aeronautical Fixed Telecommunications Network.

Our trio also made hundreds of telephone calls to clear the way for us and smooth our path. For twenty-four hours every day during the mission they were receiving coordinates of the balloon's position and passing them to the relevant centre. Every day, on a spread-out map of the world, they put in markers with details of our latest track, height, speed and position. One of their main objectives was always to reserve a block of vertical air space around the balloon so that there would never be any danger of collision with commercial traffic. Often they had a hard time explaining to local controllers that the balloon was sixty metres high, weighed nine tons, and was not flying level like an airliner but going up and down. Normally, they asked for a separation of at least 2,000 feet.

The prime aim of Luc and Pierre's strategy was to send our balloon out on a trajectory which, after maybe ten days and 6,000 miles, would bring it to precisely the right spot on the southwestern border of China. An inexperienced observer might well have questioned the wisdom of their tactics at the very start of our journey as, instead of launching us eastwards, they had sent us southwest, down across the Mediterranean and on over North Africa. We appeared to be heading in the wrong direction – but the met men knew exactly what they were doing.

Satellite imagery had shown them a big depression centred over the western end of the Mediterranean. Because the winds around an area of low pressure always blow in an anti-clockwise direction, they knew that the balloon would swing round the periphery of the depression, heading (in succession) southwest, south, southeast and finally east as the winds ejected us from the low and took us away over the Sahara.

The only way we could alter course was by changing altitude – by going up or down in search of winds that would push us in the direction we wanted. We could climb by burning propane, and descend by venting helium or by letting the balloon cool and sink on its own. To help us maintain the track we needed, Luc and Pierre were constantly advising us on the height at which we should fly, and we kept telling them what winds we were actually finding. Hundreds of routine messages passed back and forth in standard aviation terminology. 'Flight level two three zero' meant 23,000 feet, 'flight level two eight zero' 28,000 feet, and so on. Thus at 10:25 on the first day, as we were still climbing after the launch, I had reported on height, wind direction and speed:

FL [flight level] 214 has a track 171 [degrees] m [magnetic] at 20 knots. FL 240 has a track 180 at 18 knots.

Back came the answer from Control:

Have spoken with Pierre. He says FL 210 is good for daylight hours but will probably advise FL 180 for tonight.

Twenty knots is about 23 mph. With some 25,000 miles ahead of us, that seemed a painfully slow rate of progress.

The balloon tended to revolve slowly as it flew. As far as we could tell, the gentle rotation was caused by the variation in wind pressure on the upper and lower sections of the 160-foot-high envelope: the currents hitting the top of it were often different from those striking the bottom. Sometimes, having turned clockwise for a few hours, it would suddenly start going the other way. But the movement was never fast enough to be disconcerting: on the contrary, it meant that different views kept coming past the portholes.

Already, on the morning of Day Two, Control was passing up requests from journalists for telephone interviews, and we told them we would be happy to comply whenever we were not too busy. At 10:17 I reported that we were burning slowly to try to rise above a layer of mist and get out into true sun. Three minutes later, when I saw we were doing 43 knots on flight level 232, I asked, 'Is it too fast for Luc?', and something of the extent of the met men's knowledge is revealed in their reply:

> Try to stay at FL 240, which should have a track of 235 magnetic, until 12 Zulu, and 225 magnetic between 12 Zulu and 18 Zulu. The speed should vary between 40 and 50 knots. We will run a longer forecast in the beginning of the afternoon to evaluate the possibility to overfly more exotic regions (we suppose you know Mallorca already). There are no weather hazards on your track. We just see some clouds over the northern coast of Algeria with tops at FL 150. Stay at FL 240 – no higher. Best regards – Luc and Pierre.

BRIAN

Throughout Day Two the burners continued to give problems, but by trial and error we more or less mastered them, setting the timers so that the residual flame from one burn ignited the next, and our consumption of fuel came down to a reasonable level. A greater worry was the build-up of ice on the fuel-control unit, in the ceiling next to the top hatch. Round the upper hatch, set into the shell of the gondola, was a penetration plate – a wide metal ring with connectors in it, through which passed the control taps that activated the fuel system. The metal conducted cold from the atmosphere, so that during the night moisture from our breath in the cabin air froze on to the unit, and to get at the controls we had to scrape it away. In one fax we described it as 'a horrible job, worse than painting a ceiling'. Ice had also formed in thin sheets on the envelope of the balloon – probably inside the hot-air cone – because propane gives off a large volume of water when it burns. Later I complained to Alan:

> We're getting little showers of ice onto the gondola, very disconcerting. It's like someone trying to get in. Did you notice anybody caught in the rigging when we took off?

From the start Bertrand and I had a marvellously open relationship. He had always insisted on complete candour, and early in the flight he insisted once again, 'Brian – if I do anything you don't like, you must say so. Or if I start to smell and have bad breath, for goodness' sake tell me.' It was the same with our sleeping arrangements. We agreed that whenever either of us felt seriously tired, we would talk about it frankly, decide who was the more exhausted, and that person would go to bed while the other remained on duty. But an open system like this works only if nobody cheats – and in our case, it was out of the question to cheat, as it was not in our characters, and in any case we were both striving to reach the same goal.

In normal flight during the day the balloon was absolutely steady – so much so that often we had no sensation of moving. If the life-support fans were running, circulating air, they made a noticeable hum, but at other times there was complete silence. After our first rather disturbed twenty-four hours it was easy to sleep, and on the foam rubber mattress we both slept really well. I found it more comfortable to sleep naked, but Bertrand wore pyjamas with short legs and sleeves. Some people thought we were crazy to undress at all: if anything suddenly went wrong with the balloon, the person in bed might be at a severe disadvantage. But if something had gone wrong at altitude, we couldn't have baled out in our day-clothes any more than if we were naked or wearing pyjamas. We would have had to dress up in survival suits. The point was, we hoped we were in for a three-week marathon, and the best way of getting through it was to make life as natural as possible. So we undressed and cleaned our teeth and behaved as much as possible as if we were at home.

Although we shared a duvet, each of us had his own sleeping bag made from a sheet. Bertrand also had a special pillow which came from the Town and Country Hotel in Bristol, where he had often stayed. He had been so comfortable there that he asked Sue Tatford to go and get one of the pillows for him. She felt ridiculous making such a peculiar request, but the hotel gave her a pillow with good grace – and here it was now, trying to get round the world in a balloon.

In our domestic habits we were very gentlemanly: whenever I got up, I would clear the bed and leave it ready for Bertrand, and he did the same for me. On one occasion he even left a chocolate on my pillow. In matters of personal hygiene we took equal care. There was no question of having a shower, but when we got up or went to bed we would generally have a complete rub-down with wet wipes (the kind you use for washing babies) and neither ever complained that the other was becoming smelly. In fact there was practically no dust or dirt in the gondola: the few clothes we had remained remarkably clean, and we wore the same things for four or five days.

A regular pattern of life quickly developed. We each wanted eight hours' rest, and Bertrand, who preferred to sleep while it was dark, would turn in during the early evening and sleep through the first part of the night. I would wake him a few hours before sunrise, and then go to sleep myself until about the middle of the day. This suited me, as I didn't have to get up and dress in the coldness of the night. Usually when I woke Bertrand I made him a cup of tea while he made the bed for me; he would drink the tea and some orange juice as he flew the balloon while it was still dark. Then, as dawn broke two or three hours later, he would get his breakfast.

When I woke up in the middle of the day, I got my own breakfast, and at the end of the afternoon Bertrand made his dinner. We tended to spend the afternoons together, until sunset – and Bertrand was kind enough to describe those as 'really nice moments'. If we were flying slowly, they seemed really long, but if we were travelling fast they passed all too quickly.

As for food – for the first few days we lived like lords. We would put the water heater on for half an hour, drop a bag in for twenty minutes, and then eat hot fillet steak, emu meat, chicken or salmon with knives and forks off plastic plates. We also had apples, bananas and nuts, and water or orange juice to drink. We kept no fixed meal times, but ate whenever we felt like it. Because the kettle took twenty-eight minutes to boil for a hot drink, and because there was only room in the heater for one portion of food, we had to plan meals well in advance, and usually we ate at different times. This was not only because one of us was always on a working shift: separate meals had another advantage in that if there had been anything wrong with the food, only one of us would have been affected. Also, we tended to want different things.

Food was stored in spaces under the bunks. Bertrand had found some very light but strong boxes made of corrugated plastic which we modified so that they would slip perfectly into racks. There was another space under the floor at the rear which we used as a fridge, keeping the butter, cheese and orange juice down there because the temperature was about zero, even when the cabin was warm. Slim as he is, Bertrand has a much bigger appetite than I have, and he seemed to eat twice as much. But food never bothered me. I had to eat to stay healthy, but I never felt particularly hungry. I tended to have breakfast when I woke up – muesli at first, later *panettone* (an Italian-style fruit cake) – and after that I would eat once in every twenty-four hours. Bertrand always gave himself a tremendous breakfast: a large beaker of muesli-type cereal with powdered milk, orange juice and sometimes *panettone*.

Although the main role of the water heater was to warm up our packets of pre-cooked food, it also provided hot water for washing. We could move the drain tube about over the tiny sink to rinse our hands. From the sink the water drained into plastic bottles, and whenever one was full we would empty it down the toilet. Under the sink was a space in which we stored our plates, cups, tins of powdered milk and so on.

The toilet was a pan with an airtight cover on top and a valve at the bottom, and when we had something to dispose of, we would drop it in the bowl, seal the lid, close the cover and open the valve. The pressure trapped in the toilet blew the contents downwards and out of the gondola. The bowl was coated with Teflon so that nothing would stick to it, but Bertrand had learned from previous experience that the most efficient method of disposal was to line the bowl with a plastic bag. Having found some French supermarket bags which were a perfect fit, he bought several rolls, and whenever we needed to answer a major call of nature we used a new bag. We didn't seal the bags – just folded the top over. Then, as we opened the valve, they'd go out *bang!,* very fast, and we imagined that most of the contents would vaporize.

We were concerned that every time we emptied the loo we would be using up some of our pressure, so when we just wanted to pass water we used red plastic pee-bottles, and it was the duty of anyone who had a bowel movement to empty the full bottles into the bag before discharging it.

The performance was something to which I hadn't much looked forward, but when the time came I found I was taking a close, clinical interest. 'Bertrand,' I said, 'your pee's too dark. You're not drinking enough' – and he was delighted I was looking out for him so well. Our garbage went into dark grey plastic bags, which were stored near the toilet. We were fairly careful about where we dropped anything – but it was with some reluctance that we rejected the idea of attaching to each offering a label saying 'Virgin Atlantic Airline'.

BERTRAND

Life was altogether very comfortable. The gondola was warm during the day, and we had wonderful, constantly changing views. Between 20,000 and 24,000 feet the outside temperature was minus 35°C, and the moisture from our breath condensed on the hatches. At night it froze, but then in the day, when the sun came on it, it melted again.

For as long as we were heading south we had twenty-four hours between sunsets; but when we turned east and eventually started travelling at 100 knots, there were only twenty hours between one sunset and the next – so, with eight hours' sleep apiece, we had only four hours together, and it seemed a very short time. We got the impression we weren't seeing enough of each other.

We were very careful to record as much information as possible. The previous two flights had produced almost no data, and when we were planning the third trip Brian had insisted that as much technical data as possible should be preserved. Not only had Kieran Sturrock designed automatic data-logging sensors, but we also had special technical log books, which were supposed to be filled in every hour or two, giving fuel state, readings from the life-support system monitors, outside temperatures and so on. Not being much of a typist – using three fingers only, increasing by one in each successive Breitling balloon – I recorded personal impressions in longhand in a green notebook, but Brian preferred to tap his thoughts into the laptop.

Many people who have never flown a high-tech balloon imagine that the pilots have little to do. In fact we were almost always busy or asleep – and although we both took a book along, neither of us opened it throughout the twenty days of our flight.

We were carrying, as a talisman, a copy of Guy de Maupassant's novel *Une Vie* (A Life), which he had given to Jules Verne, author of *Around the World in Eighty Days*. Verne was so fond of the book that he had it finely bound in leather, with his initials inscribed on the cover in gold, and the copy had been lent us as a good-luck token by the original owner's great-grandson, Jean-Jules, who works full time to promote the spirit of his ancestor. As he said, he felt we were the only balloon team who embodied the true love of adventure that character-ized his great-grandfather: seeing that we were neither money-grubbers nor record-hunters, he was keen that something which had belonged to Jules Verne should go round the world with us.

It so happened that he had made the presentation at a moment when I was racked by doubts – about my previous co-pilot, about the flight, about the wisdom of the whole enterprise. The ceremony was held in the Jules Verne restaurant in the Eiffel Tower in Paris; and when I opened my heart to Jean-Christophe Jeauffre, founder and organizer of the Jules Verne Adventure Association, asking whether he thought I was right to risk so much – my family, my job, my nice life – he gave a robust answer. 'It's not a question of whether or not you have a *right* to fly,' he said. 'You have a *duty*. Mankind needs people to do things like this. People are going to dream with you. The fact we're giving you this unique book shows how much we trust you.' I found his words very moving, and returned to Switzerland with my energy restored, sud-denly seeing everything clearly. In other words, that book was one of the crucial factors that got *Orbiter 3* into the air and me out of the ocean of doubt in which I had been drowning.

During the afternoon of Day Two we reached a speed of 49 knots – our fastest yet – and we eagerly watched the GPS in the hope that we would hit 50. Then Alan phoned to say, 'Slow down! Slow down!', and we descended gently from 24,000 feet to 16,000. There our speed fell to 31 knots, and when we entered Moroccan air space we were doing only 25. Our controllers knew that it was psychologically difficult for us to reduce the pace, but the met men could see from their weather patterns that it was the only thing to do. Alan kept saying, 'Don't worry. If you go any faster, you'll head up to the Black Sea, and you'll never reach China at the right point.'

The only real frustration for us was when we got orders we could not understand. If any puzzling instruction came up, we would fax back asking for a report on the general situation so that we could appreciate all the factors involved. We hated the idea of the balloon being remote-controlled. Quite soon Geneva realized it was best to give us several different indications. The first was the general weather pattern, with the forecast track, and the second the track that, ideally, they would like us to achieve. Sometimes the two matched, sometimes they didn't. The best occasions were those when we could even improve on what the met men were forecasting by finding a wind heading a few more degrees in the direction they wanted us to fly – in which case we would call Control and ask, 'Shall we take it?' To which they would reply, 'That's great! That's perfect! Go for it!'

Then we would work to hold the ideal track, going up and down as necessary. If we started to lose our heading, we would try to work out why, and maybe climb or descend a little. The clouds rarely gave any indication of direction or speed because generally they just sat there outside the portholes, coming with us. The only way to fly the balloon accurately was to keep an eye on the GPS, which gave us our track degree by degree and our speed knot by knot. By logging our heading, speed and altitude, we created a wind profile, and our log accumulated dozens of entries indicating fine changes: 'Flight level 157, 185 degrees, 24 knots. Flight level 160, 180 degrees, 23 knots.' In only 300 feet of height variation the wind could change by five degrees – an enormous difference considering the distance that lay ahead of us.

On the evening of Day Two we were still making only 25 knots, and we passed slowly over Almería, where Andy Elson had taken off twelve days before us. Before our own launch Luc and Pierre studied his track closely, comparing it with their computer models. Again and again they said, 'We think he's going to do this' or 'We think he's going to do that' – and their predictions were proving extremely accurate. Already he was over India, thousands of miles ahead of us.

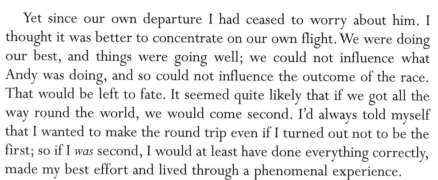

Yet since our own departure I had ceased to worry about him. I thought it was better to concentrate on our own flight. We were doing our best, and things were going well; we could not influence what Andy was doing, and so could not influence the outcome of the race. That would be left to fate. It seemed quite likely that if we got all the way round the world, we would come second. I'd always told myself that I wanted to make the round trip even if I turned out not to be the first; so if I *was* second, I would at least have done everything correctly, made my best effort and lived through a phenomenal experience.

We left the Mediterranean a little east of Gibraltar, and entered Moroccan air space as the sun went down in a blaze of glory to the right of our track. As usual, the balloon was revolving slowly, once every two or three minutes, so the spectacular red sunset came past one porthole after the other. Evidently we flew over a prohibited area, for later we heard that Control had received a mild complaint from the Moroccan authorities. The message ended: 'It's OK this time, but please don't do it again.'

During the afternoon Brian had slept for two hours, again suffering from a headache, and I continued flying for the first hours of darkness. Then at 20:00 I went to bed and Brian took over. In my diary I noted that I slept deeply for five hours, and then spent two hours relaxing and dozing.

BRIAN

I spent much of the night grappling with an intermittent electrical problem with the burner override control. The system was supposed to cut the burners automatically if propane failed to ignite and spurted up into the envelope unburnt, or if the burners became too hot – indicating that a tank was almost empty – resulting in vapour rather than liquid propane coming out of the nozzles. When the burners kept flaming out, the only thing I could do was to isolate the safety systems – which meant that if the burners received gas but failed to ignite it, a cloud of vaporized, unburnt fuel would go up into the hot-air cone. When it did light, there was a loud *ba-boom!* and the whole balloon shook, sending a shower of ice rattling down on top of the gondola.

The situation became fairly fraught, especially when there were two or three consecutive detonations. Sitting in my seat trying to regulate the burners, I would suddenly realize that they had failed to ignite – whereupon I would have to leap up and hit the sparker button before a second charge of unburnt fuel went up into the envelope. (Bertrand, when he was in the hot seat, was so delighted to have efficient burners for the first time that he would have flown right round the world by manual control if necessary: the failure of the automatic systems irritated him far less than me.)

That night we also had the first problems with our variometer, officially known as the Flytec. Most of our other instruments were duplicated, but we only had one variometer to measure our rate of climb and descent, and now it went berserk, telling us that we were descending or ascending at high speed when in fact the balloon was flying level. We relied on the Flytec so heavily that its erratic behaviour caused us serious concern, so I faxed the control room and asked them to contact the manufacturers, describe the fault and request advice. Fortunately, during a pressure test before launch, Bertrand had investigated a hissing sound and identified its source as the Flytec coupling among the mass of wires and plastic pipes behind the instrument panel. So now he knew straightaway how to locate and un-couple the variometer and send some shots of pressurized cabin air down the static tube that connected it with the outside atmosphere. The trouble lay not in the instrument itself, which was of very high quality; the problem seemed to be that water condensed in the extension pipe which we had added. Although we cleared it for the time being, the malfunction recurred every couple of days, and the instrument continued to behave erratically every now and then.

Every couple of days we had to change the carbon dioxide filters, which were called 'scrubbers' because they cleaned the air. I explained to Bertrand that 'scrubber' is slang for prostitute, and we began to include the word in our messages: 'Bertrand says he's just changed the scrubber because it was dirty,' or, as Bertrand himself faxed, 'I've changed the scrubber because I wanted somebody new to talk to.'

On the evening of Day Two several Swissair pilots called us to wish us well, and the sound of friendly voices coming out of the night was immensely cheering. Then at 20:00 the first pair of fuel tanks finally gave out. They had lasted two days and a night, exceeding our expectations, and their performance was a great encouragement.

BERTRAND

We changed shifts at midnight. Brian went to sleep, and after a few hours over Morocco I was rewarded by one of the most magnificent sights I had ever seen. 'Absolutely incredible view of the Atlas mountains, with a full moon,' I faxed at 04:48.

> Everything is black, except patches of snow that are gleaming white. The effect is to emphasize the relief, as if in an extra three-dimensional picture. It's like looking at a daylight scene through very strong sunglasses. Except for the white areas, the landscape is entirely black: the brilliance of the moonlight makes the peaks seem much closer to us than they really are. Far in the distance the lights of Marrakesh are glittering.

We were still heading southwest, away from the direction we ultimately wanted – but that remained the met men's strategy. The balloon was flying well, and I was having to burn for less than a quarter of the time: three and a half seconds every sixteen seconds. I had shut down all the automatic alarms and was monitoring all the burners very carefully.

That morning, while I was still on duty, a big event occurred: my first visit to the toilet. As I have said, the view from the seat was fantastic, and as nobody was flying close to us we didn't need curtains over the window. Unfortunately my session ended in fiasco as the lavatory became jammed, and I had to go through the elaborate flushing routine two or three times, closing the lid with the rubber seal and then opening the valve at the bottom. I was really embarrassed: the last thing I wanted to do was to block the system, specially the first time I used it – and there I was, rushing back to the cockpit to make sure our altitude was stable before returning to try the procedure again. At last it went *tsssschhh,* and everything was gone.

Sunrise over the Atlas was superb. The mountains were mostly dark red, with no snow any more, because we were farther south – though white summits still showed on the northern horizon. It was rather alarming to find that during the night large icicles had formed around the bottom of the envelope and the cables were sheathed in ice. When the sun came up the ice began to melt, so that water dripped on to the gondola, only to freeze again immediately, hazing over our view through the portholes.

On the whole the portholes stood up to the harsh conditions extremely well: they were double-glazed and had silica-gel crystals in the space between the two pieces of acrylic to mop up any moisture that might creep in. The hatch covers, on the other hand, were only single-glazed, so they attracted moisture, which froze solid every night. They were our simple dehumidifying system, drying the air in the cabin. Two or three times a day we would sponge up whatever water had collected and squeeze it into the sink, and thence into a storage bottle. (Somebody calculated that in three weeks two pilots would breathe out a total of forty litres of water.)

My report of the glorious sunrise evidently put Alan in a good mood, and he faxed from Control: 'Bertrand: Good Morning. Aren't these Cameron balloons good? The IOC has asked you to start sending out the Peace message.'

I replied:

Dear Alan, Sorry if you are jealous, but I think I have a date with a nice air traffic control Moroccan woman who keeps on calling me with a sweet voice. She loves to have me loud and clear, and always asks me about my position.

For the IOC peace messages (the ones signed by the pilots), please wait until we have passed Libya, because I don't want that country to believe it's a provocation. We could start to send them from Egypt. But the message signed by Mr Samaranch can be sent already now to the countries we have over-flown and will overfly in the next few days. Please call the IOC to explain that.

Later Alan became slightly alarmed by my report of ice because of the extra weight the balloon might be carrying, and wondered if we could fly lower for a while to get rid of it:

We are suggesting you might like to descend tomorrow to perhaps 10,000 feet to let the ice melt and dry the balloon. You will also be able to go for a walk and get some fresh air. If you agree, it would be good to let the balloon go down naturally shortly before dawn. Then spend a couple of hours at low level before returning to altitude. The meteo gurus say this will not affect your track, and the loss of speed is expected to be small.

BRIAN

For most of Day Three we continued to head southwards at what seemed a desperately low speed. We had to be very patient because everything seemed to be taking such a long time. When we had the problem with the Flytec, for instance, we struggled with it for hours. If we faxed Control, it might be twenty minutes before a reply came because the messages had to pass through a ground station which was often busy.

Naturally we were itching to turn east and accelerate, and at last, in the evening, we began to swing round, degree by degree, as Luc and Pierre had predicted. At 22:30 we were at 17,700 feet on a heading of 115 degrees, though making only 22 knots. Every hour the fax automatically sent down details of our position, and on the half hours in between we reported manually to indicate to Control that we were still alive. We did this because in theory the balloon could fly for the rest of the day with both pilots dead and the automatic system functioning before it sank slowly towards the ground for lack of heat from either sun or burners.

It did not help to know that Andy's balloon was so far ahead – but it seemed to us that he was advancing even more slowly than we were. Control had started passing us reports on his progress, and that night – the fourteenth of his flight – he was somewhere north of Bangkok. 'When Luc comes in, please ask him for an update and opinion on Andy's balloon,' I faxed. 'Seems to me that Bangkok is a pretty good position for avoiding China completely.' Until then we had thought that our only chance of winning the race would come if Andy was carried up against the closed Chinese border. In fact, although it took him a long time, he managed to avoid China altogether.

Minor technical problems continued to plague us. The system that monitored the air in the cabin set off an alarm when it began to show a sulphur dioxide content of 0.4 parts per million. I thought the gas might have been given off by the lithium batteries, but because I wasn't sure, I consulted Control. The query was passed to Kieran, who suggested taking out the battery packs and passing our hand-held warning unit over them one by one. 'Once you have isolated the culprit, it needs to be bagged and sealed until it can be dumped. The alarm is set at a low level, so no cause for concern at the moment.'

That encouraged me to turn off the alarm system for the time being, but I must have been feeling combative, because I reported, 'If the second-stage alarm activates, the only way to deal with the ear-piercing noise is to put the fire axe through the speaker.' In the end the episode degenerated into farce: we took the instrument out, reset it, waved it around over the batteries and couldn't find anything – yet over the top of the bunk it started registering again. We began to think that something in human wind might be setting it off – so we faxed down and asked, 'Could it be the fact that we were farting in bed that set it off?' The answer came back: 'Possibly'. In self-defence I felt bound to point out that 'it was Bertrand in the bunk at the time of the alarm. Mine are distinctly Eau de Givenchy.'

Another annoyance was that the plug on one of our kettles, which fitted into a 12-volt socket designed for a car cigar-lighter, had overheated and melted, and later in the night I contacted Kieran to discuss the feasibility of rewiring the kettle through the switch for the water heater. In the end this was what I did, causing Bertrand to admire my skill with a soldering iron, and surprising myself when it worked first time.

BERTRAND

When I went to bed that night the noise of the burners was absolutely regular, like somebody snoring. Every sixteen seconds there was a four-second burn – a soothing rhythm. But whenever the balloon started to climb too much, Brian had to cut the burners for one or two firings – and that moment was always uncomfortable because it broke the pattern. I kept waking up and thinking, 'No burners! Has Brian gone to sleep in the cockpit? Have we got a problem?' Then the sound would start again and I knew everything was all right. The noise became so deeply engrained in my subconscious that when we were back on earth after our landing, for two weeks I would often wake up in the middle of the night with a feeling of terror, thinking the burners had shut down. When I switched on the light, I realized I was in my own room and went back to sleep with a smile.

BRIAN

Soon after midnight I got a fax from Pierre Eckert – still at work in the Swiss Météo office – that banished all small irritations: a marvellous confirmation that he and Luc had us where they wanted us:

> The turn to eastern direction happened quicker than expected, but in accord with the latest version of the numerical model. We also reached the latitude we were looking for with exactly the timing we discussed last Sunday, before your take-off.
>
> Starting from now, you should have headings between 90 magnetic and 100 magnetic at all levels above FL 180 – I suggest that you stay at FL 180 (or below if you do not lose too much speed) until you go down for de-icing and your jug of fresh air. Anyhow, the later perspectives are good. I think we will bring you to FL 240 as soon as the ice has melted. Your trajectory then is to the east and stays at around 25 [degrees of latitude] north to the Red Sea. Oman should be reached by Saturday.
>
> I am presently on a night shift and start to be pretty tired. The weather over Geneva is active. I just gave a storm warning. On your track I see no problem. By the way, how many camels did you see for the moment? Best regards, Pierre.

CHAPTER SIX

FRESH AIR OVER AFRICA

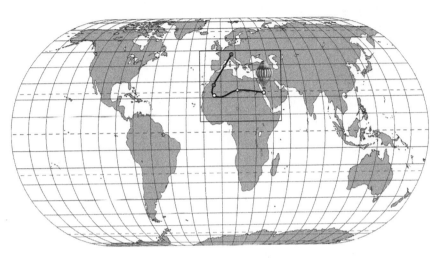

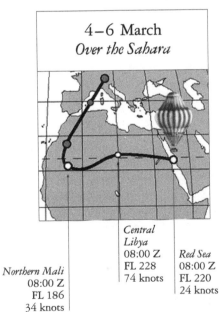

4–6 March
Over the Sahara

Northern Mali
08:00 Z
FL 186
34 knots

Central
Libya
08:00 Z
FL 228
74 knots

Red Sea
08:00 Z
FL 220
24 knots

BRIAN

At 01:44 on the morning of 4 March I faxed John Albury at Control to make quite certain there would be no misunderstanding about the manoeuvres ahead:

> I must talk to Bertrand when he wakes up, but I have the following thoughts. Towards the end of darkness tonight we descend to low level to lose the ice. Then let the sun get to work and climb to 24,000 feet. I'm inclined to retain the polystyrene blocks under the gondola for some protection in case we have to land with tanks still fitted, but probably to get rid of the yellow-side auxiliary tanks. The ice is quite amazing – large icicles all around the base of the skirt (reminds me of a lady I once knew). Most of the time there are small showers of it falling on the gondola, I assume because the envelope is flexing—
>
> Have you given Debs one on that very comfortable couch yet? Or shouldn't I ask?
>
> I think I'll sign this Bertrand in case I'm in trouble.
>
> Love, Bertrand (don't we all?).

BERTRAND

When I took over from Brian before dawn, the view was fantastic, with the moon shining on the Sahara and a million stars glittering above. Several times I doused the cockpit lights so that the stars would show up more brightly. I realized we were following the old route of the Aéro-Postale – the first commercial airline to deliver mail – which used to fly from Paris, via Toulouse, to Dakar in Senegal, and on across the South Atlantic to Brazil. Those pilots – Jean Mermoz, Henri Guillaumet and above all, Antoine de Saint-Exupéry – were the real pioneers of commercial flying. In *The Little Prince* Saint-Exupéry wrote about the very places we were passing over, so I couldn't help wondering which of all those million stars was the star of the little prince.

Back in the right-hand pilot's seat, I read through the messages which had come in while I was asleep. Essential technical information from the ground was spiced with jokes, especially now that our first video report had gone out on Swiss television, CNN and other stations, and friends were sending personal messages. I was much moved to find that Michèle had sent this fax:

Je suis maintenant au centre de contrôle avec les enfants, et nous sommes très heureuses de nous sentir ainsi plus près de toi et de te suivre mieux des yeux – sur les cartes et du coeur – en pensées et informations partagées avec toute l'équipe d'ici. Nous sommes ravies de savoir que tout continue de bien se passer pour vous. Transmets à Brian toutes nos amitiés et dis-lui qu'il est très photogénique with his American hair cut. *Les enfants sont très confiantes dans votre vol et leurs prières vont aux vents pour la réussite de votre projet et l'aboutissement de votre rêve. 'Bonjour Papa' de Solange – 'J'espère que tu réussiras' d'Estelle, baisers – 'J'aimerais que tu réussisses ton tour du monde et je te donne trois baisers' – tapes avec l'index d'Oriane. Salutations de Sandro Haroutounian qui nous prépare notre dîner ce soir au restaurant de l'aéroport. Nous vous embrassons tous les deux. Michèle & Co.*

I am now in the control centre with the children, and we're very happy to feel closer to you, following your progress better with our own eyes on the maps, as well as with our hearts, sharing all the thoughts and information of the team here. We're thrilled to know that everything is still going well for you. Give Brian our best love, and tell him he is very photogenic with his American haircut. The children are very confident about your flight and say their prayers to the winds for the success of your project and the fulfilment of your dream. 'Good morning, Papa,' from Solange – 'I hope you'll succeed,' from Estelle, kisses – 'I would love you to succeed in going round the world, and I give you three kisses' – taps with her forefinger from Oriane. Greetings from Sandro Haroutounian, who is preparing dinner for us at the airport restaurant this evening. We embrace you both. Michèle & Co.

It was wonderful for me to know that my family had seen what a fantastic job the team in the control centre was doing. But to hear from Michèle like that was also a good way of discharging emotion. When Brian and I were alone together, our emotions remained perfectly stable; but when a loving message came straight from my wife and children, it went like an arrow to the heart.

Michèle had bought a big map of the world with the idea that she would stick a pin into it to mark each day of our progress – exactly as my mother had done for my brother Thierry, my sister Marie-Laure and me when our father was drifting for a month in the Gulf Stream. But the spread-out globe looked so vast that she was afraid that a few pins over Europe and Africa, each an inch apart, would worry the children. So she put the map back in the cupboard and waited until we were nearly across the Pacific; then she fixed it on the wall in the corridor at home, with all the retrospective pins in position, and said to the girls, 'Look – there's the world, and this is where Brian and *Papa* have got to already. There's only Central America and the Atlantic to go.'

As the sun came up on Day Four, it shone through the frozen porthole, creating an extraordinary effect. With one hand I held the video camera to film it and with the other I scratched away the ice, making strange patterns, until at one point the shapes on the glass looked exactly like the earth seen from space.

Light revealed the spectacular, dark red colours of the desert.

Somebody had warned us how boring it would be to fly over the Sahara, with nothing to see for days on end, but the reality was quite the opposite. The views that unfolded below us were absolutely fabulous. Every hundred kilometres there was something new – different colours, different shapes, different sand, different rock. For me, the desert was alive: I suddenly realized that the mineral part of the earth is just as alive as humans, animals, trees and plants. The light was alive, the sand was alive; far from being empty, the desert was full of potential. Most landscapes have already been shaped and finished by a combination of natural forces and man, so there is little scope for change. The desert, in contrast, is right at the beginning of evolution, full of the possibility of life.

It struck me that all normal life derives from a thin layer of humus formed on desert. If you have water, you can make trees grow, and the falling leaves make humus. We tend to think that the earth itself is humus, but that is completely wrong. Humus is a miracle – a thin layer spread over the surface of the desert. On that brilliant morning I saw that all life is a miracle – and that the whole planet could be a desert, like Mars. Flying over the Sahara, we could almost have been above another planet.

That first day over the desert was a completely new experience. I opened my notebook, picked up my pen and wrote:

> The desert below looks like the bottom of the sea, with the same kind of shapes. Now and then we see incredible reliefs formed by rocks sticking out of the sand, some like the spines of gigantic dinosaurs, which stretch for kilometres. So much variation of shape and colour, between yellow and black, with every shade of red, and one area of bright, coppery blue, which looks almost as if it still contains water.
>
> In front of such an immense void, such an amount of nothing, I can imagine that people would be moved to write. I think of Saint-Exupéry, running the sand through his fingers beside his aircraft after he had been forced down by engine failure, and writing great books. It is very arrogant to think that there is nothing here. It's only our human mentality which makes us suppose that, because there are no men, there is nothing. If we

really think, we realize the desert's full – full of sand, full of air, full of dryness, full of colour, full of light, full of dunes – and that's why it's full of potential. It's full of emptiness – and to see emptiness for once is wonderful.

I spent hours staring at the desert, writing, feeling its strangeness. For me, that was one of the most beautiful passages of the flight.

BRIAN

The desert had the same effect on me – and there was the surprise factor as well. We expected the Caribbean to look like a picture postcard, and we knew how dramatic northern India might be, but we never dreamed that the desert would be the most spectacular sight of all. Because it was so unexpected, its beauty came as all the more of a revelation.

Still in the early hours of the morning, we swung back on to a southerly heading, and asked Control for reassurance. Shouldn't we be turning east and climbing to catch the jet stream, rather than going down to de-ice? In his first message of 4 March Alan confirmed:

We don't have a met man here yet, but my understanding of the situation is that height, speed and track are not critical at this time, but will become more critical within the next few days. Therefore now is a good time to de-ice, sinking naturally with the dawn. While you are at low level and with a good view of the ground [it] might be a good time to drop the empty cylinders.

Unlike the main battery of twenty-eight propane cylinders, our four auxiliary tanks had no automatic release mechanism, and the only way to drop them was to go outside the gondola and cut them free. Hence the need for an EVA, or extra-vehicular activity. In our planning we had hoped that only one EVA would be needed – and clearly, it had to take place over a totally remote area, where the falling tanks couldn't do any damage, and at a moment when there were no clouds below us to obscure our view of the ground. Ideally, we needed to make the drop at a time when we weren't travelling too fast, because to go down low and then come up again could lose us several hours of valuable progress. If we'd descended at a time when we were doing 100 knots, we would have lost a lot of time. Apart from dropping the tanks, we wanted to get rid of as much ice as we could – most of all the coating that was partially obscuring the portholes.

The idea of an EVA was exciting, and as we prepared for it, letting the balloon descend gently to 10,000 feet, our adrenaline was flowing; but when we opened the top hatch and climbed out, we found it was lovely just to sit out in the fresh air on top of the gondola and enjoy the feeling of being completely still. Anyone susceptible to vertigo would have been in severe trouble, for one looked straight down through two miles of air to the sandy wilderness below. Luckily we both have a good head for heights, and although there was a safety harness, neither of us felt any need to put it on.

The ice was prodigious. Some of it was already melting and water was pouring down off the envelope, though any drips that fell on to the propane tanks froze again immediately. Stalactites ten feet long dangled from the skirt, joining it to the gondola. In theory there was a small risk of being hit by falling lumps, but the accretion of ice inside the envelope seemed to consist of only very thin sheets, which were melting before they fell.

Kieran had suggested that our ignition problems on one side of the burner system were due to an electrical short on one of the detectors. It turned out that he was correct in his diagnosis, and I set to work fixing the fault, while Bertrand attacked the icicles with a fire axe and knocked the coating off the cables. As he laid about him he felt like a boy again, smashing the icicles around the eaves of the family chalet. Then his parents used to say it was a shame to break such beautiful things, but now he hit out with abandon, sending ice cascading downwards. As he said, it was probably the first time that ice had rained on the Sahara in several thousand years.

We were travelling at only 25 knots and seemed not to be moving at all. It was very warm, and just to breathe fresh air was a delight. Above us the sky was cloudless, and below us an infinity of sand and rock stretched away as far as the eye could see. With the burners shut down, there was not the slightest sound to spoil the silence. On the rugged bars of the load frame and its outriggers we felt perfectly comfortable.

When I lay on my front and reached out over the back right corner to cut the white nylon tape to free one of the auxiliary tanks, Bertrand did hold me by the ankle — but that was the extent of our security precautions.

Having set up our cameras to record the event, we did a countdown and I tried to cut the tape with a knife. When it proved too tough, I resorted to a pair of powerful bolt-croppers — and away the tank went, tumbling end over end, glinting in the sun. We watched it all the way to the ground, and in the final few seconds of its descent we saw its black shadow hurtling to meet it at the point of impact. A puff of sand showed where it slammed into the desert. We speculated about what might happen to it, deciding that if it remained on the surface it would probably crumble away in time, after years of bombardment by sandstorms; but if it buried itself in the sand it might lie there for a couple of millennia before some archaeologist dug up the mysterious object.

With the four tanks gone, there remained a good deal of pipework — flexible hoses with couplings on them. Our advice had been to save as much weight as possible by slinging them away as well, but they were expensive gear, and we looked at each other and thought, 'These are too good to jettison. You never know — they might come in handy.' So we kept them — and thank God we did, because later in the flight we had a fuel problem and found we needed them.

There were a couple more constructive jobs to be done outside. Having repaired the burners, I fitted a second aerial for our telephone, while Bertrand cleaned the outside of the portholes. He made up a window-cleaning kit by taping together a telescopic boat hook and a radio antenna with a sponge on the end. And there he sat, 10,000 feet up in the air, applying his improvised window-cleaner with immense pride.

In our high spirits we were just like two schoolboys. As I filmed my partner at work, I commentated, 'I'm now filming Bertrand trying to clean some bird doo-doo off the window with his special chamois leather,' to which he responded, 'Not *trying* to clean. Cleaning!' (When the film was shown in Switzerland after the flight, people failed to realize that the reference to bird doo-doo was a British joke and started speculating on how the stuff could have got there.)

Much as we enjoyed our time outside, we wanted to get on. Everything seemed to be going well and we felt in control, but we were both keenly aware that a tremendous effort had been made by dozens of people to create the balloon and send us on our way, and we felt almost guilty about playing around outside.

During the EVA the balloon slowly gained height as the sun heated it, and by the time we finished our various tasks we had climbed to 12,500 feet. Rather than descend to a really low level to trap the atmospheric pressure there, we opted to repressurize the gondola from our cryogenic tanks of liquid nitrogen and oxygen. Once again, we took particular care to clean the seal before closing the hatch. Then we inserted the ring-clamp and listened. There was perfect silence.

Our enjoyment of the excursion comes through in an ebullient fax which I sent Control at 11:13. After listing the tasks carried out, I ended:

Gave the Touareg tribesmen a gift of a lithium filter, several empty water bottles and a waste bag. Hope they can make good use of it. I suppose Alan will write it off on the books as a charity donation. Took several photos. Couldn't get the cat back in, so the damn thing will just have to stay out all night. Look forward to the next EVA. The desert is an amazing sight — saw the tanks hit the sand, so don't entertain any claim for personal injury.

Sue Tatford faxed back:

Good morning, boys. Sue here. Latest news on Andy: flight time 15 days 22 hrs 44 mins so far. Alt. 18,000 feet, 19.06 N 112.12, east of Hainan, over South China Sea.

Your ideal flight level for next 24 hours will be FL 220. The jet stream is around FL 260. Luc insists that at the moment its speed is too high and its trajectory too far north for the next two days, and would position you wrongly for later on. From now on our target is the triple point between Saudi Arabia, Yemen and Oman for Saturday evening.

Just received a letter, via the IOC, from Uday Saddam Hussein, son of the Iraqi leader. He says, 'It is with great pleasure that we can take part in the success of this peaceful flight.' He doesn't say you can't cross his country. But he adds, 'Sorry we can't ensure the safety of the balloonists.'

BERTRAND

People sometimes ask why we didn't start from North Africa, rather than spend the first three days of the flight slowly making our way southwards. The answer is that in most other countries there were too many difficulties. We would have had to transport the gondola on a big truck with a crane. People might have said at the last moment, 'I'm sorry, we're on strike,' or 'It's my sister's wedding – I can't come.' I wanted to take off from a country where we had everything under control. America would have been another possibility. There, everything is efficient and the jet streams are close overhead, especially in the south. But then we would have been faced with the Pacific for the last stage of our flight, and we thought that vast expanse of ocean was something to tackle early on. Also, an American launch would have made it extraordinarily difficult to aim for South China. All in all, we decided Château d'Oex was a good compromise. To launch from there was not, as some people thought, a marketing decision by Breitling. But the enthusiasm and friendship of the villagers helped us choose Château d'Oex in preference to any other Alpine valley.

Now at last we were heading due east. We didn't care much about Saddam Hussein, but we did want to make contact with Andy Elson and Colin Prescott in the Cable & Wireless balloon. The fact that they were over the South China Sea meant that they had somehow managed to get round the Chinese mainland. That seemed an amazing feat, and we were full of admiration, so, after repeated attempts to fax the balloon directly, we asked Control to pass on a joint message which we had written at dawn:

Dear Andy,
The sun is now rising on the desert of Mali, and it must soon be sunset for you. That's the disadvantage of being so far in front. It's strange to talk to you by fax during a round-the-world attempt, because I was used until now to be with you in the same balloon.

I hope your control centre sent you my congratulations when you got the duration record. Thank you for having brought Brian into the Breitling project – although I think he still doesn't realize he's now IN the balloon. Actually, I don't realize it either, after all this waiting. Please give my best regards to Colin. Take care. Best wishes, Bertrand.

Hi, guys, Brian here. Flew over your launch site two days ago. Seems I'm always having to clear up behind you. Hope you received my e-mails – otherwise I have to throw the insults all over again. Heard last night you were over Thailand. I can't believe that you're going to overfly all those lovely girls without stopping. After all the things I've done for you, surely you're going to slow down and wait for us?? Good luck, chaps – and stay safe. Don't go upsetting any farmers on the way. Remember we have to come after you.

I was also trying to make contact with *Mata Rangi,* the papyrus boat in which Kittin Munos was attempting to cross the Pacific from South America to Japan. The project was also sponsored by Breitling, and the aim was to check theories of migration, rather as Thor Heyerdahl had done with his raft, *Kon-Tiki,* in the 1940s. In 1997, when the first *Orbiter* ditched in the Mediterranean, Kittin was caught in a terrible storm off Easter Island. His boat was destroyed, and he survived only because he was wearing his Breitling watch, with its emergency beacon. He pulled up the antenna, attracted attention and was rescued. Now I felt a great sense of solidarity with him: we were exploring together, he on the sea, Brian and I in the air. When we tried to phone him that day we couldn't get through, but we did establish contact three days later and found he was doing as well as we were.

At 13:15 I reported that we were 'trying to stabilize our monster' at around 22,000 feet. Our track was perfect – 085 degrees, almost due east – and we were doing 40 knots. Twenty minutes later we were 600 feet lower and the wind had backed slightly to the north, to 078 degrees, but we were making 48 knots. From the control centre Sue Tatford reassured me, 'Your track is excellent, and from now on you can go up to FL 230 but no higher. Your speed will increase at around

18:00 to 50–60 knots. This is OK.'

At 15:19 Zulu we passed through the Greenwich meridian, which made us feel we were well and truly on our way. 'This time we really have the impression of having started the round-the-world flight,' I told Control. 'We have made the 180-degree turn according to our two angels' predictions and are finally flying east, with our full initial fuel reserve. Speed 55 knots. We are still eating the delicious meals prepared by the Hôtel de Ville. We'll go for the dehydrated Nestlé food in a few days, when the fresh food is finished.'

My last remark proved optimistic. That same day our menus took a downward turn because, even inside its vacuum wrapping, our remaining fresh meat had started to smell. After a careful inspection, we decided not to risk eating it, sealed it in double plastic bags and stowed it under the floor. The chicken lasted another couple of days, and after that we turned to vegetarian meat substitute with dried mashed potatoes, which proved to be excellent when reconstituted with hot water. To spice our food we had salt, pepper, tomato ketchup and mango chutney.

I made a note in my diary that it seemed extraordinary to be suspended *in* the air *by* air. The principle of having warm air and gas trapped in an envelope was absolutely simple, yet to make the balloon fly correctly was extremely complicated. As if to confound me, however, when Brian went for a nap that afternoon the balloon flew itself so perfectly and was so stable that I felt relaxed enough to listen to a CD for the first time. I chose a disc by a group called Era, who play a mythical kind of music – half religious, half mysterious – which had a marvellously soothing effect as I listened through headphones and gazed down at the desert.

In the evening our weathermen urged us to keep on the most southerly track we could find. Having swung round on the outside of the depression, the winds had begun to back north again, between 72 and 78 degrees. Our speed increased to 65 knots – the fastest so far – and Luc came on the phone in a state of some excitement. 'Bertrand,' he said, 'I'm so happy I have tears in my eyes. I really think this time you're going to hit the south of China, and that you'll make it.' Even though they weren't in the balloon, Luc and his colleague, like everyone in the control centre, were feeling just as emotional and excited as we were.

BRIAN

Day Four was also the day when Sean the bear came out into the open. I had forgotten all about him until I found him in my bag and put him on the pilots' desk. When we sent down a picture of him flying the balloon, John Albury was delighted and faxed, 'Hope he does not suffer from air sickness and likes your terrible jokes.' The people at Breitling, though, weren't very happy: they thought it a little unprofessional of us to be fooling around with a toy and didn't push for the photograph to be issued to the media. But this in no way dampened our own high spirits; at that stage of the flight we were in a state of euphoria, and everything seemed to be fun. With our good track, reasonable speed and low consumption of fuel, we even dared to start thinking that we had a unique chance of making a historic flight. Both of us were driven on by a colossal charge of hope, which sometimes became so strong that we had to take deep breaths and physically choke it down.

A lot of our pleasure derived from the fact that we were feeling more confident and were fairly sure we were not going to make idiots of ourselves. If, after all that build-up, we had landed only a few hours into the flight we'd have looked really stupid. The important thing now was to concentrate and not make any mistakes.

Sometimes we found that a layer of wind was thinner than the height of the balloon. Then it was essential for the pilot to work almost all the time just to keep the balloon stable. Also, if left to itself, it would usually start to sink gently, so even during the day it needed one push of propane every three or four minutes. We could never take our eye off the ball for long.

Another element in our enjoyment was the fact that we were getting quite good at flying our giant and were gaining confidence in our ability. Every balloon handles differently, and I'd never flown one with anything like *Orbiter 3*'s dimensions. In a hot-air balloon, a good pilot is at one with his craft: he flies it by feel, sensing what it is doing, and makes it react as he wants rather than letting it fly him. Now that was starting to happen on a big scale with Bertrand and me, giving us a sense of pride combined with one of relief at the realization that we were in control.

BERTRAND

Yet I was by no means complacent. I felt a special responsibility towards all the people on the ground who had backed me through three attempts: Breitling, the staff at Camerons who built the balloon, the IOC (godfather of the *Orbiters*), the control team, the air traffic controllers, the weathermen. They continued to give me their trust, and I could not let them down. I felt specially indebted to the Swiss Foreign Ministry and its diplomats in China, who had made such efforts to secure permission to fly over the southern part of the country. After all the work and worry I had given them, it would be horrible to have to land before we even reached the Chinese border.

The evening of Day Four brought another phenomenal sunset over the desert. After dark Luc sent a weather update and urged us to keep to 22,000 feet, predicting that during the night our track would turn south, from 080 to 115, and that our speed would vary between 55 and 68 knots. That all sounded ideal, so I went to bed happy.

BRIAN

So far our flight path had not been likely to cause any political difficulties. But now we were heading for Libya, and beyond it Egypt and other Middle Eastern countries, any of which could cause problems. We had asked them all for permission through the normal channels, and it had been granted immediately; but one had to remember that the last Allied aircraft to fly in Libyan air space were the F-111s that dropped bombs in a botched attempt to eliminate Gaddafi. The result was that American and British balloons were unpopular, to say the least, and Branson and Fossett had both been harassed. At least our balloon was Swiss — but there was a tinge of anxiety behind the joky fax I sent Control at 20:35:

Do you think the good Colonel is going to let us through without any hassle? We could save one of our special green bags in case we see his tent. Please ensure the Swiss are not about to declare war on any Arab state.

At that stage we were still over Algeria, about 120 miles north of the town of Tamanrasset. A message from our air traffic controllers told me to call the tower there, giving a telephone number and two radio frequencies. I tried the phone but got only a continuous tone, indicating that the number was invalid. The radios were no better. Not wanting to arrive in Libyan air space without warning, I relayed my position to a passing aircraft and asked the pilot to hand it on. John, on duty in Control, gave me the radio frequencies again, and at 23:37 I got through on one of them, but the reception was so bad that I didn't feel confident the Libyans knew we were coming.

For a few minutes the atmosphere was tense, and messages passed back and forth between balloon and Control in quick succession:

Control

Brian – Confirm receipt of met [report] from Pierre and Luc a few minutes ago. Air traffic control are happy with you, and Algiers will pass you on to Libya in the normal way on the usual frequency, which Greg [Moegli] will inform me of shortly. Be assured all is OK. John.

Control

Brian – Just had call from Greg. You will be passed when the time comes to Tripoli by Algiers. It apparently has to go via Tunis to Tripoli. Tripoli apparently are reluctant to give out the frequency to Algiers at this stage, but Greg does not see a problem. I have to fax ATC when you are twenty minutes from the Libyan border, so I will be watching you! John.

Balloon

John – Met received. Thanks. Now climbing to find more speed. Suspect track will back a bit and we will enter Libya at about 25.5 N around 02:10 Z. Now passing FL 191. 086M[agnetic]. 49 kts. Brian.

Control

Brian – Are you happy with my last message, ref. Tripoli via Algiers? Little Friend.

Balloon

John – Nag, nag, nag, nag, nag. Yes, I got your messages. Now FL 220. Have sacrificed about six degrees of easterly for the extra speed of 64 knots. Assume this is acceptable. Brian.

Our increased speed brought the balloon to the Libyan frontier earlier than I had forecast, and we flew over the border at 01:57. Algiers said they had handed me over to Tripoli on HF radio, but reception was still so bad that there seemed no chance of getting through. 'No contact with Tripoli Control on VHF either,' I reported, 'so go ahead and talk to Greg, please.' A few minutes later John faxed, 'Brian, Greg is trying Tripoli for us, so bear with me and I will let you know.'

On the ground, our control centre had woken Greg at 2.30 a.m. to seek his help. Tripoli had refused to give any radio frequencies – he never found out why – and somehow he had to clear our path. As he said, 'It was like a miracle. I called Algiers. They were very helpful. They gave me a phone number, and at three in the morning I rang Tripoli. That guy also was very helpful. He said, "The balloon's too far to the south. We cannot reach them. But there are some control towers down there, and here are the radio frequencies . . ." '

Radio communication remained difficult all night – but at least nobody was ordering us to land.

BERTRAND

I slept exceptionally well, and when Brian woke me with a cup of tea at 07:00 I felt thoroughly refreshed – except that, as usual, I had butterflies in my stomach. I was excited at the thought of going back to the cockpit and eager to hear what had happened during the night, as well as to read the messages.

We were still over the desert – 'Even more sand than on the previous days,' I noted – but soon I had reason to send Control a jubilant fax:

Hallo, Sue – I'm just back in the cockpit after a long sleep. FL 228, track 086 at 74 knots. Position N 26.29 E 16.43. If we admit the definition of the jet stream to be a wind over 70 knots, then you can announce to the press room that we have just entered into the jet for the first time.

Naturally I felt triumphant – and what was the reaction from the ground? Our weathermen immediately told us to slow down! 'Thank you for your message,' Control answered, 'but you were asked NOT to go faster than 70 knots. However, Luc says your present speed and altitude are probably OK. He is checking.'

The temptation to carry on as we were was very strong. I faxed at 08:36:

> The balloon is flying perfectly stable without burning or valving, but above speed advised: 75–76 knots. If Pierre and Luc want us to slow down, I can valve a little, but experience shows that it will then be hard to find a new equilibrium lower. And the track is closer to 80 than 86.

Luc and Pierre were resolute, and their strategy remained the same. We were still being carried along on the fringes of the big Mediterranean depression around which they had slung us at the outset. If we went too fast, we would get ahead of the weather system and be sent north. Our correct option was to move east at the same speed as the low pressure, keeping as far south as possible. So we had to go down – but only a few hundred feet. I opened the gas valves three times, for twenty seconds at a time, and lost 1,400 feet. I reported to Sue:

> Following your request I went lower and found 63 knots and 91 degrees at FL 214. It seems we can play with track and speed by changing little altitude, so please tell what would be the ideal track and speed, and I'll play to try to find it.

Alan replied that our present track was adequate, and we continued steadily on our way with the balloon stabilized at 21,400 feet. But its insulation was so good that we were flying far below its ceiling – the height to which expanding helium would lift it in the heat of the day before excess pressure started to force gas out through the appendices.

We discovered that by lying on our backs with our heads in the bulge of the rear hatch, one at a time, we could look right up and see the appendix tube on that side of the envelope. It was the same at the other end: we could squint up through one of the pilots' portholes and keep an eye on the other tube — so whenever we saw that the gas cell was very tight, we started monitoring the appendices. As the balloon approached its ceiling, we would watch as helium was forced down the tubes from the top: we could see them bulging as it was pushed progressively lower. As long as there were still five or six feet of floppy, uninflated tube at the bottom, we knew we were not losing any gas.

BRIAN

During the afternoon I'd become considerably irritated by the continued erratic behaviour of the Flytec variometer, and by the apparent failure of our control centre to get to the bottom of the problem. My faxes to Alan took on an edgy note: 'It's grouchy Brian here — Bertrand is setting up the Logitech camera for a video clip, if you're interested in having that before you return to the hotel and the comfort of a Teacher's.'

Alan bristled up suitably:

Dear Brian, I don't mind you getting grouchy, but you know the rules. There are people down here who want to know you are OK! Yes — I would like to download everything and anything in the next hour, so I can get back to my comfortable king-size bed with down-filled quilt and adjacent mini-bar. Flytec: between the two of you you couldn't accurately describe the difference between night and day.

Not to be put off, I persisted in trying to explain the problem and asked Alan to call Peter Joder, of Flytec, and get some advice 'before we go to Plan B and take it out. Plan C of course involves the fire axe.'

Alan did call Flytec, but while he was grappling with the problem on the ground, we had more urgent matters to attend to — not least, making contact with Cairo air control. We eventually managed this by means of a relay through an Egyptair aircraft. At 18:30 we gave a live interview on Sky Television.

BERTRAND

Later that day, still over southern Libya, I got a telephone call from the IOC, during which I asked them to send out the peace message signed by Brian and myself to all the national Olympic committees of the world, along with a note asking them to pass on the text to governments, the press and so on. We had hoped to transmit the message direct from the gondola, but it would have taken hours – and all our electricity – to send off 190-odd faxes, so we asked the headquarters to put them out on our behalf.

The message read:

> Our balloon has just taken off from Switzerland, location of the headquarters of the International Olympic Committee, which is sponsoring our attempt at a non-stop balloon journey round the world. Or rather our planet, as, seen from the sky, the forms and colours traced by plains, mountains, rivers and oceans inspire one's respect.
>
> We have no engine on board, and it is the breath of the wind alone which is pushing us towards your country. Perhaps we shall fly over it, or perhaps the air currents will carry us in another direction. Whatever happens, the wind allows our balloon to become, for a few days, a link among all the countries of the world as well as an ambassador of the Olympic ideal based on peace, mutual understanding and solidarity. But above all, we are motivated by the desire to enter into contact with the inhabitants of all countries to express to them what we see from the sky.
>
> When we contemplate the immensity of the firmament from which our balloon is suspended, we cannot but admire with humility and modesty this immeasurable whole to which mankind belongs. In a little corner of the universe, our planet is located, and we can look down affectionately on Nature, a kind of cradle in which human beings are born, grow up and die. We cannot help thinking of man's great good fortune in being able to live there, or rather the good fortune he would have if he could live there in harmony with his environment, his neighbours and himself.
>
> Seen from the sky, no two mountains are alike, no river draws

the same line as any other, and we well know that no human being resembles his neighbours. It is this diversity that constitutes the wondrous richness of our planet that, at the same time, sometimes gives rise to the most terrible conflicts. And yet, all men have their feet on the ground and their heads in the sky, just as every river has its source in the mountains. As it flows towards the sea, so human beings follow their destinies. They live their lives as best they can. They may do so in war and blood or in the wellbeing that arises from tolerance, sport or the innocent smile of a child. Everyone has the power to choose his way and to aspire to the height necessary to better understand the meaning of his or her life.

Today, our path has crossed yours and, tomorrow, the wind will push us towards another country. We shall continue our flight and you will continue your life, which is also a great adventure. In the final analysis, we are perhaps in search of something to guide our steps.

Already, we are saying goodbye. But above all, we ask you please to help us to spread this message of peace around our planet, which needs it so badly.

It was a great relief that we were crossing Libya without trouble. Ahead lay Egypt, but that seemed to present no difficulties, and at 19:00 I went to bed without any worries, little thinking that Brian was in for an exciting night.

BRIAN

More difficulties were looming: it looked as though our track was going to take us over the northeastern corner of Sudan, and we had been hoping to avoid the country altogether. Its rules stated that all pilots must give seventy-two hours' notice of any approach and, as far as we knew, nobody had done that on our behalf. Nevertheless, for the time being everything seemed to be going well, and at 21:00 I fired off a sparky fax:

My dear friends John and Debbie,
Hope I haven't made things awkward re Sudan. We have made it

our target to clip it, which shows that we have maintained the best southerly track, and it is another country to add to the list — Gosh, did you just see that flying pig go by? Bertrand tucked up in bed now. We had to fight over the teddy bear. FL 230, 114 degrees, 52 knots. I am determined to send just one nice letter to my friends which contains no insult at all — you may want to frame it. Lots of love, Brian.

Half an hour later things were looking less rosy. Belatedly, I saw from the map of Egypt that we were heading for a danger area. The wind was taking us just to the south of the High Dam at Aswan, around which was an exclusion zone that extended out to a thirty-five mile radius. One could understand the Egyptians' sensitivity, because if anyone managed to bomb the dam and breach it, they would probably release a flood big enough to destroy most of the country. But surely no one could imagine that our balloon posed a serious threat.

The air controller in Cairo began asking tiresome questions. What was our route? How long would we be in his zone?

At that moment the burners went out. The balloon began to lose height rapidly. I realized that our latest pair of tanks had run out and had to switch to a new pair. Then I found that a crucial valve had frozen solid and the pilot light would not ignite. Trying to deal with the radio and attend to the burners simultaneously was a nightmare because the radio headset had a lead only three feet long, and I had to pull it off every time I needed to stand up and move back to grapple with the burner control panel. So much unburnt propane was spurting up into the hot-air cone that, when it did finally light, there was a tremendous *whumph* of an explosion.

In the middle of all this Cairo came through demanding to know our exact position, and I couldn't give it because for the past ten minutes I had been struggling with the burners. When the Egyptian started ordering me to change course and avoid the restricted area, I grabbed the telephone, called up John and asked him to get our own air traffic controllers in Geneva to sort the fellow out.

Luckily for my peace of mind, it was only later that I found out how the exchanges went. Normally, in air traffic control work, everything is cut and dried. The controllers give headings and keep aircraft well apart, and the pilots do what they ask, without question, all in English, and all in standard air control jargon. But here, as Greg Moegli put it later, 'the mentality was improvisation. We had to adapt and be prepared to start arguing.'

Once again Greg was woken in the middle of the night. He immediately phoned Cairo and told them the balloon was on its way. The reaction was immediate and apparently final. 'You can NOT overfly the dam,' his counterpart told him. 'It's absolutely definite. You have to pass thirty-five miles north or south – otherwise we'll launch fighters.'

Greg took a deep breath and 'tried the honey', saying, 'Look – I understand your problem. We've got a problem, too, because they can't steer the balloon. You understand? It can only go with the wind. But by the way, I'm a controller, like you, and perhaps you can help us.'

That brought an instant response. 'Oh!' said the Egyptian. 'You're a controller too? Fantastic! Where are you working?'

'Geneva,' Greg told him. 'We have a lot of traffic here as well.'

'OK,' he cried, 'for you, I give twenty miles. I give fifteen miles!'

In the event, we passed twenty miles south of what John, by then, was calling 'the damn dam', and there was no further trouble on that score. In fact, Greg had made such a brilliant job of charming Cairo that the controller there kept trying to chat me up. 'Don't worry, don't worry,' he called over the radio. 'We've got you on radar now. You're OK.' But at 22:32 I sent off a fax to Brian Smith which showed how hectic things had been aloft:

Brian, hello! Welcome to Dante's inferno. Well – it was until the pilot lights went out. Why is it so damn typical that a pair of tanks that last in excess of thirty-six hours run out when Cairo control are telling me I have to change course to miss the damn dam? 650 feet per minute down, desperately trying to turn on the completely frozen valve, then the pilot light won't go. Then I have to switch to double burners, damn nearly blow the gas cell out through the top tent. Ah well – that's ballooning, as they say . . .

What's the good news? Well, the cameras weren't running, and Bertrand slept through it. Thanks for the assistance from down there. Headless chickens rule OK. What on earth do we do for fun when this is all over? FL now stable at 217, having recently visited several others.

We'd made a rule that the pilot on duty would never wake his partner except in a dire emergency, and I was glad I had stuck to it through that minor crisis. The balloon had never been in danger, but our temporary rate of descent had been very disconcerting because our clearance was for a protected flight level of 3,000 feet — and even if we'd been flying in the middle of that when the burners failed, we must have gone through the bottom of it and into illegal air space within a couple of minutes. In the event, we probably went a thousand feet lower than we should have, but there was no point in telling air traffic control; the only thing to do was to climb back out as fast as possible.

Next, Sudan. When I tried to contact Khartoum air traffic control on HF radio, there was no response. 'Can't we just sneak through Sudan?' I asked Control. Smiffy, who had recently come on duty, replied, 'Just sneak through? Not British, old chap. Go through all burners blazing.'

We followed his advice and never heard a word. Our transponder was continuously giving out our position and details, so the Sudanese must have known where we were, but they never so much as came on the air.

Just before midnight I got a pleasant surprise: a message from the Cable & Wireless balloon, typed in Andy Elson's inimitable style:

Hello brian and bertie
Congratulations on joining us in the air, We heard your inflation was a bit iffy? What do you expect if I'm not there?

Now we hear you are having trouble with ice. What's the problem not enough gin?

So you've decided to follow us and be second well done, lets all have a party at the end? I think cameron's should pay they have made most money from these adventures.

Sorry you missed your jet stream due to Iraq. What will you do now? We anticipate our flight lasting 26 to 28 days depending on how long we have to wait for the pacific and Atlantic weather systems. Currently waiting at Taiwan for 48 hours for the pacific route to open for us.

Very best wishes from both of us for a safe and enjoyable flight.

Colin and Andy

Sorry lost your number then been too knackered swimming the formosa straight towing a balloon is bloody hard nothing like training at Swindon pool loads of hugs andy.

That message made my spine tingle. Andy was stuck over Taiwan, forced to loiter for a couple of days for fear that the wind would sweep him south and dump him near Hawaii, as it had dumped Branson. In a couple of days we should reach China, and we might not be all that far behind. We were catching up fast . . .

The best feature of that night was the performance of our main-line fuel tanks. The first auxiliary pair had lasted thirty-six hours and the second thirty-three; but our first regular pair, designated Tank Pair 8, had held out for a record forty-one − a huge encouragement. By the time I turned in at 03:30 on 6 March, I'd had enough for one night, and told Smiffy, 'Oi, I'm off to bed now to dream of air traffic controllers falling off a dam because their engines won't fire.'

BERTRAND

When I took over from Brian before dawn on Day Six we were still over Sudan. I was at the controls when the sun rose − another beautiful dawn − and I wrote:

I will soon be a great expert on deserts, because this one, the Nubian desert, is different yet again. The mountains are very dark, with light grey sand in the valley-bottoms. It looks as though there is heavy rain at times, and all the sand is washed down. Nature is beautiful even when it is entirely mineral. This is how the whole earth must have been in the beginning. When I flew the Atlantic in 1992 we spent five days above water. This time on *Orbiter 3* we've had five days over sand. But this crossing of the desert gives much more motivation than the three last months, which were a cruel desert to cross.

One mountain stood much higher than all the rest, with cloud on the summit, and in an early fax I reported that I had just seen 'the local Fujiyama, except that the snow was replaced by a cap of cloud. He is alone in the Sudanese desert.' Then at 06:00 we passed over the coast of the Red Sea, and I could see that the desert ran right to the edge of the water – a wonderful sight. 'I'm so happy to see all these beautiful places on our planet,' I wrote. 'Brian and I are privileged indeed to have such impressive sights all round us.'.

By then we were rapidly approaching Saudi Arabia – or, if we were unlucky, Yemen. A telephone call from our control centre warned us not to go too far south, towards Eritrea and Ethiopia, because a small war was going on there. When I heard that, I felt that *any* war is horrible: it seemed impossible, inexplicable, that men could be killing each other down below while we floated by above them in a kind of paradise.

'People are fighting and dying without even knowing why,' I wrote, and I reflected on how ephemeral our own interest in war normally is. We read briefly in a newspaper that a war is going on and then turn the page. We see people dying on the television news and zap to another channel. But the people caught up in the conflict may be handicapped or suffer for the rest of their lives, especially if they have lost loved ones. We don't understand how terrible it is to be left with permanent scars. How few people, I thought, have the good fortune that Brian and I have had. Why were we so lucky? Why did we come from backgrounds so affluent that we could devote our energy to going round the globe in a balloon while other people were fighting to survive, to run faster than the enemies trying to kill them? I found no answers to these questions but started to feel more and more concerned for the life of our world.

In his first message of the morning Alan faxed:

Experience suggests that Saudi ATC will be more alert and helpful than Sudan. When you make contact with Jeddah please advise frequency and station in a routine message so we can keep Swiss Control happy.

> Have there been any further sightings of the flying insect Kieran says was in the gondola at launch? Did it escape when you did your EVA? The media are very interested.
>
> My wife said she heard Brian last night. She says she gets more information from the TV than from me. Was sorry to hear you had run out of fresh food. Of course, you could always eat the fly!

For once Alan had missed something. 'If you were a more attentive listener to *Suisse Romande* radio,' I told him, 'you would know that the little mosquito who tried to escape by going south with our balloon stopped living a few hours after take-off. I bit him before he bit me.'

As we approached the Saudi coast directly opposite Mecca the air was hazy, so we could not see the buildings. However, we were in contact with the air traffic controller at Jeddah, close to the holy city, and I wrote, 'This makes one respect God, whatever one's religion, and whatever name one gives Him.'

When Brian got up at midday he was full of indignation, and he lost no time in telling Control why:

> The blinking bed is wet. Bertrand and I have given each other some stern looks, and even Sean has been interrogated. Upon careful investigation, we found that the internal insulation only comes to the level of the top of the mattress, so there is a lot of condensation building on the gondola internal wall next to the mattress. The bedding is now hanging around in the gondola – it's like a Chinese laundry in here.

The temperature in the capsule was still comfortable, but I noticed that Brian seemed to need fewer clothes than I did. We both wore blue fleece-lined trousers, but whereas Brian was happy in a shirt, I usually wore a blue Breitling sweatshirt and maybe a fleece on top. It had been the same with Andy in *Orbiter 2*: I always had four or five layers on, while he was practically naked.

That afternoon was one of the most pleasant of the flight. We spent it together in the cockpit, and because there was little radio traffic our workload was light. We had time to watch big cumulus clouds float around the balloon, drink tea and talk about our lives. Brian told me about the places he had lived in and what had been important to him, and I spoke of my own experiences. Everything was extraordinarily peaceful and relaxed.

Sometimes, during a lull in the conversation, we would put in a burn to lift ourselves over a big cumulus ahead. The clouds weren't dangerous, but often we were travelling faster than they were, and if we had gone through one the balloon would have collected a lot of moisture or ice, so it was better to avoid them. We felt as if we were playing with the huge, fluffy white masses, hoisting ourselves smoothly over them, then coming down again.

As the sun was setting we spotted some small villages in the valleys – the first human habitations we had seen for five days. We were doing 46 knots at 18,000 feet, and anyone looking up would certainly have been able to make out that the silvery object high in the sky was a balloon. I remembered Per Lindstrand saying that when *he* was flying at around 40 knots, he felt sure it was far too slow to make it round the world. Now, our average speed since launch was exactly that – and still we reckoned we had enough fuel to keep going all the way. For us it was becoming clear that the right way to get round the world was not to fly fast at high level all the time but to play with different layers of wind, even if some were slow.

Yet fuel and the wind were not the only limiting factors: political constraints were threatening to play a part. Up came another message from Alan:

Warning. Your present track will take you across a large danger area in Yemen. We are calculating a new track that should miss most of Yemen. We want to reduce south track to a minimum until clear. So no lower than 220 and no higher than 240 for the moment. Further meteo in thirty minutes.

I answered, 'Warning received. Climbing to 220–230 and will give you the new track. I am a little worried because we are slower than the forecast received on 4 March. Is it a problem or an advantage?' Soon Alan was reassuring us – 'Luc says slow is good' – and giving details of the tracks and speeds we could expect at various heights. But ahead of us lay a prohibited zone over which, according to our aeronautical charts, intruders would be fired upon without warning.

CHAPTER SEVEN

TROUBLE AHEAD

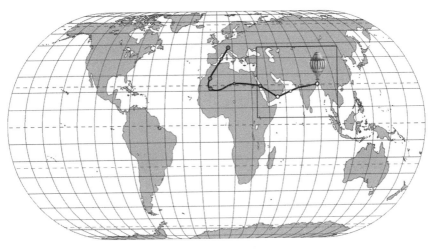

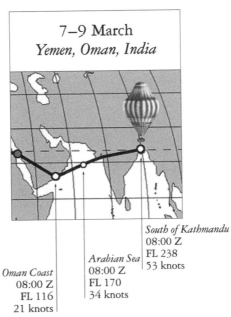

7–9 March
Yemen, Oman, India

South of Kathmandu
08:00 Z
FL 238
53 knots

Arabian Sea
08:00 Z
FL 170
34 knots

Oman Coast
08:00 Z
FL 116
21 knots

BRIAN

The danger zone – edged in red on the map – lay across our front in a broad band running from southwest to northeast, almost cutting Yemen in two. Our support team could see that we had little chance of circumnavigating it, and although Luc and Pierre did their best to steer us round the edge by telling us to fly higher and sending us more to the north, the wind would barely allow a big enough deviation.

None of us knew why the Yemenis had declared the area prohibited, and we could only suppose it was used for military training. But Bertrand was fairly cynical about the locals' ability to take out high-flying aircraft, reckoning that their heaviest armament would be a few shotguns normally used for riot control. So, as we were at 21,000 feet, we did not feel too vulnerable.

Nevertheless, even though we were going to pass over the red zone at night, anxiety ran high among our air traffic controllers in Geneva. As one of them – Patrick Schelling – said, you never knew what sort of fanatics might be loose in such wild country, and anyone might start firing at a strange target overhead. His mind went back to the dreadful incident over Belarus in 1995 during the Gordon Bennett balloon race, which started from Switzerland. The organizers had obtained clearance, but the local civilian authorities failed to inform the army, who scrambled a helicopter, forced one balloon to land and shot down another, killing the two pilots. Now he decided that if the Yemenis would not give us clearance, or at least reasonable assurance that we would not be fired on, he would have to bring us down.

He could see we were heading for trouble as soon as we came over the Red Sea, only 150 miles from the Yemeni coast, and he spent the whole of that Saturday afternoon battling with the problem. At least communications proved reasonably good, but the Yemenis' English was limited, and Patrick was never certain about the mentality or real intentions of the people with whom he was dealing. There was always the risk that they would agree to his request and then take hostile action anyway.

It had never been part of our plan to fly over Yemen, and so we had no diplomatic clearance. This meant that Patrick had to negotiate from scratch. His first call was to Sanaa Airport, but he had some difficulty getting through to the tower because the Yemenis rated it a secure area, and for a while refused to give him the number. In contact at last with the local controller, he launched into the first of many discussions. The man in charge asked him to send a fax to the Yemeni civil aviation authority requesting permission for an overflight. This he did immediately; but no answer came back, so he kept calling the Sanaa control tower, asking for clearance.

It took him some time to explain what was happening because the man on duty had only broken English and kept asking, 'What is the balloon's destination?' When Patrick said, 'It's going round the world,' he repeated '*What is its destination?* If you have flight plan, you must have departure point and destination.' The Yemeni insisted that he himself could not give clearance because he lacked the authority to do so. All Patrick could do was keep talking to him until he felt fairly sure that nobody was going to do the balloon any harm. All the while he was trying to gauge the man's mentality: was he really trying to help, or was he just giving worthless assurances and absolving himself of responsibility? Patrick realized that, although he was talking to a fellow controller whose job was to provide safe skies for aircraft, his opposite number belonged to a foreign culture and might take an entirely different view of round-the-world balloon flights. He might not give a damn about what happened to *Orbiter 3*.

In the end Patrick was reasonably sure that everything would be all right. He felt he had won a psychological victory by making direct contact with the person in charge of operations, rather than with some distant superior. But the controller never said, 'You're cleared.' He just talked round and round the subject. If the balloon had penetrated the closed zone by only fifty metres, it might have been enough for some idiot to make trouble. As Patrick drove home, having done his utmost, he was still haunted by memories of the Belarussian disaster. What went through the minds of people who could do something as barbaric as that?

If Patrick *had* decided to bring us down, we would have had to ditch in the Red Sea — but our own control centre never let on to us how close we came to being halted in full flight. One message from John Albury did give a hint that there was some difficulty on the ground: 'Ref Yemen. We have had no official reply but Patrick has spoken to Sanaa ATC and he gets the impression it will be no problem.' He also gave us a telephone number and radio frequency for the supervisor in charge, and said that if all else failed, he would call Alan in to speak to diplomats. We realized that Patrick must be negotiating on our behalf, but we had no idea how long and difficult his conversations were proving.

I reported my efforts to find a more northerly track and skirt the top edge of the danger zone:

John — Been up to 21,000 feet. Track between 099 and 104 all the way. Descending to FL 198, where I had 098 or 099. Best I can do, I'm afraid — My arithmetic says we will be at the area in 5.5 hours from now, so plenty of time for track to change maybe. Could you tell Nik, Patrick and Greg that we appreciate their efforts very much, and I will let them buy me another lunch when it's all over. Jeddah has us on radar and seems happy.

Bertrand and I were irritated by having to divert northwards after making such efforts to keep south over the past few days, but Luc, when pressed by Patrick, was implacable. Twice in one message he urged us to stay as close to track 090 as we could and then, after we had passed the restricted zone, to descend to around 13,000 feet to find a track of 100:

> We have confirmation of no problem with the zone in Yemen but it is suggested that you telephone the number given previously – I think this is really a courtesy call, but they have coordinated matters for your overflight. YOU may want to offer ME lunch, because I have been running around like a . . . on your behalf!

We never got through to the number John gave us, and at 19:15 I told him that although I'd 'been up and down like a whore's drawers' looking for 090, the best I could find was 093. 'So we go through the north end of the restricted zone, by the looks of things. My estimate is that we will fly out of the zone at 01:00 Z.'

In the control centre the atmosphere remained electric, but at 20:34, not realizing how difficult the Yemenis had been, I reported: 'Had powdered mash and veggie burger for supper. My, how the mighty have fallen.' John kept my mind off potential disaster by passing up the most important item of terrestrial news – that Dusty Springfield had died – and asked if I wanted to be informed of the result of tomorrow's Grand Prix. Later Jo chipped in with a message telling me that Andy and Colin, in the Cable & Wireless balloon, were now south of Osaka and expected to start crossing the Pacific in a couple of days. When Luc asked if we needed to go low, to shed ice, I replied, 'No, we do not need to go down. We are happy to keep our garbage on board if we can get to faster winds sooner. No ice that we are aware of.'

From 19,000 feet we were getting tremendous views of yet another type of desert. The small bumps all over it reminded Bertrand of chicken pox.

By 23:15 I reckoned we were over the northern edge of the prohibited zone and told Smiffy, 'It may be my imagination, but it appears that according to the topo chart we are in the area – What say you, Gunga Din?' Smiffy came back with, 'We reckon you're just in it, mate. Story of your life. Just skimming the top edge, but it depends on the thickness of your felt-tip pen.'

While Patrick fenced with the Yemenis, Luc and Pierre had been doing intricate calculations for the next leg of our flight, and just before I went to bed they came through with their master plan:

> Our computations for the next two days drive us to northern India between FL 180 and FL 240. The most northerly point of the trajectories is at around 90 E of longitude, and is a little bit too much in the north to avoid high ground over the Himalayas and to fulfil the Chinese requirements.
>
> Thus we have to gain a piece of south now! At the time which is best convenient to you, you should come down to between FL 100 and FL 130. Speeds have to stay between 20 and 25 knots. The goal is to reach a latitude of 17 N before crossing the Arabian Sea. This means you must stay at a lower altitude for about twelve hours.

Although we ourselves never spoke to Yemen, we knew from the orange light flashing on our transponder that we were interrogated by their radar as we went over — and we took the fact that they were watching us as a good sign.

BERTRAND

At 02:30 Zulu Brian went to bed, and after a couple of hours I was rewarded by the sight of a magnificent sunrise breaking over yet another desert. But before I had time to marvel at it, an astonishing message came in from Jo:

> I've just had a telephone call from Alan, who has been contacted by the Cable & Wireless Control Room to say that their balloon is landing seventy miles off the coast of Japan. The reason given is that the balloon is 'iced up'. They plan to land in the sea, and search-and-rescue are with them now. We are checking the web site and watching CNN on television, but as yet we have no further information. Will keep you posted.

My reply now seems rather flat — but perhaps I was in shock when I sent it:

> This is unbelievable news. I take no pleasure out of it, as it must

be very frustrating for them. But of course it gives us more chance to be the first around. It also brings fear that the same problem could happen to us.

I could hardly believe it. I was afraid for the two crew men – both good friends of ours – but at the same time I couldn't help thinking, 'If we do get round, we're not going to be second.' I felt immediately that the world's attention was focused on us because now we were the only ones left in the race. But I said to myself, 'If Andy's ditched, maybe we're also going to ditch if there's really bad weather ahead.' Altogether I went through a tremendous mixture of conflicting emotions.

Two hours later a fax from Smiffy confirmed that the Cable & Wireless balloon had come down in the sea and that the crew had been rescued. Of course I was desperate to pass on the news to Brian, but I kept to our agreement that neither of us would wake the other unnecessarily, and when eventually he stuck his head out of the bunk I said, 'Brian, I've got the most incredible news. What d'you think it is?'

Instantly he said, 'Andy's down.'

Maybe some telepathy was involved. Like me, Brian was surprised and shocked, but also hugely relieved. We had caught up a good deal on Andy, but when he went down we were still four days behind him, and we would have been inhuman if we hadn't felt excited by our new opportunity. We guessed that Alan, too, must be feeling pulled in all directions because the Cable & Wireless balloon had also been built by Camerons. Later that day he told us he had spoken with the Cable & Wireless Control:

> The official story is that the balloon flew into snow squalls, but this was not the only reason for landing. They say the main reason was lack of electrical power – some problems with solar panels – possibly lack of sunlight in poor weather conditions.

On the ground the news evidently had a wide impact. Alan told us the media would want to talk to us, and that we had better work out what we planned to say. He asked us to make a short video clip with a commentary in English: 'This would probably be used around the world if we receive it soon enough.' He also said that an aircraft would be coming up to film us the next day for an interview – 'they appear to be very interested in the icicles'.

Later, when we met Andy in Bristol, he gave a more detailed account. He said that, together with Siemens, he had devised some highly efficient solar panels, and he was so convinced by their performance that he took no back-up lithium batteries. When he found himself in cloud over the Sea of Japan, he had the choice of going up – which would have sent him in a dangerous direction, towards Hawaii, where big thunderstorms were raging – or of staying low and flying in the right direction, but under the clouds. Down there, the solar panels could not recharge his batteries, and after one day he ran out of electricity. Without power he could not pump kerosene from the tanks to the burners, and he could not talk to his control centre. The balloon just died and he was forced to ditch.

Meanwhile, we had to continue on our own track. Fax and telephone communication was becoming patchy because we had reached the very limit of the area covered by the East Atlantic satellite and were trying to switch to the Indian Ocean satellite, in geostationary orbit 23,500 miles out in space. The trouble was that, with the satellite almost directly overhead, our antennae were often in the radio shadow of the balloon. As always, Control was anxious that we should not go off the air for any length of time and, still early in the morning of 7 March, Alan urged us to maintain contact by any method we could, even if it was only by HF radio.

As we approached Oman, Smiffy tried to telephone Muscat air traffic control to update them on our progress, only to be told that the man in charge was out saying his prayers. When he called half an hour later and received the same reply, Smiffy, without thinking, responded jokingly, 'He must have been very naughty, then.' At 04:54 I reported, 'Somebody called me on 121.5, might have been Salalah Control, but he was unable to hear my answer.' It was nearly 07:00 when I at last made proper contact with the Salalah tower, and I told Smiffy, 'I guess he and I can't have had the same praying time up to now, but we finally managed to meet.'

Just after that I found that, by lying flat on the floor with my head in the dome of the rear hatch, I could get a contact through

Brian's cell phone phone using Oman's network; so I rang our control centre and found myself talking to Thedy Schneider. I knew that our flight had placed a huge weight of responsibility on him, and that if anything happened to us he would never forgive himself. So it was good to have a chat, and even though he was his usual gruff self, between the words I could feel how strongly he was wishing us well. I also spoke to Luc and Pierre, who confirmed that our position was perfect for entering China at the right point.

Stefano Albinati was also in the control room that morning, and he sent a long fax saying, 'Dear Pilots, Everything goes so well that I really feel useless . . .' But he gave us detailed results of the Australian Formula One Grand Prix, which had been won by the Ulsterman Eddie Irvine, and ended, 'The next Grand Prix is in only five weeks. You may have landed just before in Malaga! Big kisses, Stefano.' These were the only items of news we wanted to hear: we were happy to be protected from all the rest – wars, murders, catastrophes and political scandals.

Following the instructions of the weathermen, we had come down to relatively low levels – 10,000 or 11,000 feet – and with the heat reflected off the desert hitting us from below the gondola became uncomfortably hot, with a temperature of 28°C (82°F) and 76 per cent humidity. There was nothing we could do to improve matters, and Brian told John and Debbie, 'Every time I opened the window, blinking Bertrand closed it again. I'm fed up with that. When I grow up I'm going to be captain of a round-the-world balloon, and then I can have all the windows open.'

After a long spell over the pock-marked desert, we flew above the extraordinarily flat plateau of Oman until it plunged abruptly to the coast of the Arabian Sea.

My own thoughts often took a philosophical turn. I found the balloon an ideal place in which to think and write, and in my little green notebook I recorded:

This planet is beautiful. We have to make people aware of its beauty and its open spaces – not so that they believe it is paradise, but so that everyone can seek paradise together. I devoutly hope that it is not necessary to go through hell on earth to gain access to paradise. We can look for paradise also through harmony and wisdom.

BRIAN
My latest worry was that much of the Velcro round the outer skin at the base of the gas cell was hanging open. Peering up the sides of the envelope, we could see big gaps. The lower section of the outer skin could not separate from the top section because the two were held together by a large number of karabiners, but the failure of the Velcro seal looked alarming.

'Are we going to lose a lot of the heat we put into the hot-air cone straight up through the outside of the envelope?' I asked.

Alan's reply was reassuring:

It may in fact improve duration, as we want to ventilate the space between the two skins. If hot air gets between them at night, I think it will give up its heat to the gas cell before exiting at the top. Some loose Velcro was noted when the balloon was inflated. This was due to the rain that fell on the balloon when it was laid out. Velcro loses fifty per cent of its strength when wet.

I told him that we too had noticed that part of the Velcro sealing ring round the bottom of the waistcoat was open after take-off, but that much more of it had come undone since: 'It shows daylight in four segments, which amounts to approx fifty per cent of the equator.'

As soon as we were well out over the sea and had made sure there were no ships below us, we dropped three empty fuel tanks using the automatic release gear. This was operated by electricity: when we switched on the circuit, it heated an element which gradually melted through the nylon tape holding each cylinder in position. 'Some good news for you,' I told Control:

The tank disconnects worked perfectly. We have jettisoned tanks 7A and 7B, plus 8A. It was a bit disconcerting that the weight of Pair 7, before dropping, showed as 20 kilos, and that they took sixty-two and sixty seconds to release. Pair 8 showed a weight of 150, so we tried burning with them, and confirmed there was in fact no fuel left before releasing 8A, which took forty-four seconds to melt tape.

I was disappointed to find that the shedding of 200-odd pounds seemed to make little difference to the balloon's performance: our rate of climb remained practically the same. Fuel was so vital to us that Alan asked if the tanks we had dropped could have contained propane but no pressure, and, if the same thing happened again with an apparently empty pair, could we try pressurizing them with nitrogen? I replied, 'In answer to your questions, No, No, No, as Margaret Thatcher would say.' I pointed out that tank 8A had run out in the middle of the night, and that, together with its partner, it had given us 41 hours of burning. According to the computer at Control, each pair should give us 33 hours 15 minutes of heat, but so far we had averaged 35 hours 30 minutes – an important gain.

Now our target was India, and during the evening of 7 March John briefed me with details of how to contact Bombay air traffic control. 'Your first good move would be to address them as MUMBAI, as that is what the locals now like to call themselves,' he advised. Soon after that he confirmed that Greg Moegli had already spoken to the Indian controllers, and that they appeared to be 'helpful and friendly . . . Mumbai know you are coming and where you are now'.

At 17:32 John surprised me by sending up congratulations on passing the 10,000 kilometre mark. It was good to realize we'd beaten the record of 8,700 kilometres set by Bertrand in *Orbiter 2* – although in fact we had done it quite a few hours earlier – but galling to hear that champagne had been broken out in the press office. Bertrand was firmly asleep. We were making only 31 knots and seemed to be crawling towards the Indian subcontinent; at 10,000 kilometres a week it could take us a month to complete a circumnavigation. But Luc and Pierre insisted that we had to remain low and slow. In a met update at midnight they faxed:

We have to keep you at FL 180 for the next forty-eight hours in order to arrive over China at 26 N. Higher altitudes are faster, but lead more to the north . . . Overnight, look for a mean track of 070. Target on coast of India will be close to Porbandar [on the

Gujarat coast] early afternoon 8 March. The entry into China is expected the 10th at 00 Zulu. We can then climb to get higher speeds and stay below 26 N. The entry over the Pacific will need some adjustment in order to get the jet stream at the right moment. Early simulations show an arrival over Morocco the 19th.

Arrival over Morocco! What a thought! The precision of our weather wizards was inspirational — but we were going to need quite some patience to keep going for another ten or eleven days. Meanwhile, seeing that Jo had been doing several stints in the control room, I gave her the time of night:

> Hello the wife. Are you a glutton for punishment, or what? Another night shift? Not carrying on a secret liaison with Bertrand by Capsat, are you?
>
> Can't believe it's a week now. When I get back I'm going to give the travel agent what for. I have video pictures of tiny rooms, having to share bed with another holiday-maker, damp bedding, appalling breakfast buffet. Not even a minibar. I suppose the only good news is that there appears to be no building going on around. Of course I get to sit at the Captain's table every night. I'll be here till about midnight. Strange feeling the way the nights sneak up every day. Give a bob or two for a shower. Suspect Bertrand would pay more — for me to have one, that is. Found crooks and nannies that wet-wipes have never seen before.
>
> Celebrated Andy's landing by putting on clean underwear. If we fly too much longer, when I change my undies, it will be with Bertrand's. Have a nice evening — see if you can get a pay rise out of Alan. That should take at least all night. Lots of love — Brian at FL 156.

BERTRAND

When I awoke early on the morning of 8 March, I was thrilled to learn that we had beaten my own distance record. At least we had achieved *something*. Again I was bewitched by the beauty of the dawn. When the sun came up out of the ocean there was a lot of little cumulus below us, and for the first and only time in our circuit of the globe, I saw a ship – a tanker. An hour later, with Elton John on the CD player, I told Jo at Control that 'I would accept to change the *musique* for a good bottle of Bordeaux wine, but not the blue sky'. By constant experimentation I discovered that the layer of wind carrying us along on the 70 degree track we needed was only 300 feet from top to bottom.

In a telephone call Luc told me he reckoned we should be back over Morocco on 18 March – a day earlier than he had advised Brian. The news brought on a tremendous surge of hope and emotion. 'We haven't even reached India yet,' I thought, 'and yet he's confident we're going to succeed.' All the more reason to concentrate and make no mistakes. The distance ahead of us still seemed so colossal that the idea of finishing the course was almost impossible to grasp – but Luc was so calm and logical that he inspired me with enormous confidence.

During the next hour I composed a long fax, in French, and asked Control to pass it to Gérard Sermier, the Breitling press attaché in the press room. The dispatch included my outstanding memories from the first week of the flight, and I set them down (I wrote) because 'what interests me most is to retain the impressions, rather than just the facts, of this unimaginable experience'.

I rhapsodized about the variety of deserts we had flown over, 'the immense spaces without a single human trace', and recalled how Saint-Exupéry had sat writing beside his downed aeroplane 'facing the desert, facing himself'. Even inside our capsule I seemed to smell the odour of hot sand that burns in the pages of his book *Terre des Hommes* (Land of Men). I described how I had imagined that, like Saint-Exupéry, I was letting the sand run through my fingers, to gain closer physical contact with the earth, but decided that I preferred to stay far up in the sky for as long as God, the wind and chance allowed. I concluded with a brief sketch:

When the full moon had risen over the snowy peaks of the Atlas, the stars came out one after another above the Mauritanian desert, and a light, white mist enveloped the balloon. Now the regular snoring of the burners makes me think the balloon itself is breathing. Everything is calm. I'm still looking for the star of the little prince.

After the demise of Andy's balloon we had started getting numerous requests for media interviews. Every day messages were passed up by Control from journalists seeking appointments, and we did our best to fit them all in – but they all asked the same questions, making us wish that inquiries could be pooled.

My shift in the cockpit seemed to pass slowly, not least because our pace was so leisurely. 'Thirty-three knots is a lot of wind speed when you want to take off or land with a hot air balloon,' I faxed, 'but here I promise you it gives the impression not to move. Planes relaying our position to Mumbai every now and then.' The track I was holding averaged 70 degrees, and this obviously pleased Luc and Pierre because when they came into the control centre they were reported to be smiling, and they passed me a number of small adjustments to height and direction 'to make you arrive at exactly 26 N over China'.

Obviously they were excited that they had managed to line us up so that we would head straight for the magic point. After leaving the low pressure over the Mediterranean, we had been picked up by a high-pressure system centred over India. Because this was turning clock-wise, it would first take us a little to the north and then eject us to the east. It seemed a miracle that the high was in just the right place at just the right moment to push us out due east, at 90 degrees, precisely between the 25th and 26th parallels – exactly where we wanted to be.

BRIAN
At 22:00 on the night of 8 March I woke in high spirits. 'Hello and top of the morning to you. Who are you, anyway?' I blasted off at Control when I took over in the pilot's seat. 'Brian here well rested and out of the communal damp bed. Twice round the block, bit of Tai Chi, dropped Tank 8B (on purpose), and now feeling full of the joys of winter.' Smiffy and Cecilia hit back with, 'Glad you're feeling full of beans – good way to dry the bed, too. I have faxed your position and flight level to air traffic control.'

Alas for our jokes! Little did we realize that in Geneva our people had suddenly seen a major obstacle looming ahead. Nik Gerber was on duty at Swiss Control at 11 a.m. local time when he got a call from our team, who told him they had a problem with India. He was surprised, because flight plans had already been forwarded to the Indian stations on our route, and no query had come back. Now Bombay was claiming that we did not have diplomatic clearance. Because no papers could be found, they said, the balloon could not fly over India.

At first Nik did not take the threat too seriously, thinking it could be easily sorted out. He told Control he would come in soon after 1 p.m. and help untie the knot. But when he arrived he found everyone in a panic. Sue Tatford was uttering curses as she searched furiously through a file of documents. After a desperate hunt, she had to admit that no permission existed. Alan had applied for diplomatic clearance back in August and asked for it again by fax and teleprinter, but it seemed that no document had ever arrived, and in the rush to get the balloon ready the matter had been overlooked.

Now what? There was no way the balloon could fly round India — and no time to obtain clearance through the normal channels. Disaster threatened. At 14:54 a message came from Bombay saying, 'No authority available with DECA [the aviation authority]. Advise Hotel Bravo — Bravo Romeo Alpha to avoid Indian territory.'

That was a totally unrealistic request. To us approaching in the balloon India offered a front 2,000 miles wide, and we were heading right for the middle of it.

Nik rang the air traffic controller in Bombay and urgently tried to make him see reason, but all the man would say was, 'Listen, we have no secondary radar, so we can't pick them up. There is great danger. They're about 400 kilometres off the coast. It is a waypoint for airliners. We can't see them, and we have no radio contact. It's impossible for us to get them through the Bombay approach area.'

When Nik continued to reason, the controller asked, 'What *is* this balloon, anyway? How does it steer? How many engines has it got?'

'No engines,' Nik told him. 'It can't steer except a little bit by going up and down.'

'All right,' said the Indian. 'I give you the phone number of Mr Saran, Deputy Director General of Civil Aviation.'

In Delhi it was already 6.30 p.m. but, with everyone in the control room on edge, Nik put in a call, reached the Deputy Director, and spent the next fifty minutes on the phone. Mr Saran, hull-down in his bureaucratic bunker, could not understand why the balloon had no clearance. Nik explained that repeated applications had gone unanswered. The Deputy Director then demanded an exact route and precise estimates for the overflight. He insisted that the balloon maintain an altitude between 20,000 and 22,000 feet. Pierre immediately said that would be possible from the met point of view. After nearly an hour of discussion and argument, Mr Saran at last gave permission, and issued instructions to his controllers to let the balloon through. But, he said, Nik must telephone Mr Wasir, his Number Two, and explain everything to him because he did not have time to do it himself.

Fortunately, hardly any of this reached me in the balloon. One message from John did say, 'Chaos here ref India, but Nik is doing a great job sorting it out.' He told me I would need to give him a position report with flight level 'at least every hour without fail' – but we never realized that our flight was threatened with sudden, premature termination, and only when we were half way across the subcontinent did Control let on that the Indian authorities had demanded that we ditch in the Arabian Sea.

BERTRAND
When later on I heard about all that fuss, I couldn't help thinking of Jules Verne's novel *Around the World in Eighty Days*, first published in 1873. The central character, Phileas Fogg, is confident that he can cross India swiftly on the new railway, but when he reaches a hamlet called Kholby the train stops and he finds that the line goes no farther, leaving him with a gap of fifty miles to cover to Allahabad. His response is to buy an elephant and cross the gap on that. Latter-day bureaucracy had almost proved our own undoing, but skilful advocacy by Nik – the modern equivalent of the elephant – had kept us going.

We came over the coast in the dark, so all we saw were the lights of Porbandar, 250 miles northwest of Bombay. That night our fuel consumption was the lowest ever: one second of burning every twenty-eight seconds – an insignificant amount. Part of the gain seemed to come from being at relatively low level – we were at 15,000 feet – although nobody could explain why altitude made so much difference. Later in the night, to find the track of 73 degrees that the met men wanted, we went up to 25,000 feet, and our speed picked up from 35 to 50 knots.

At sunrise we were between Porbandar and Bhopal, and to celebrate the fact that we were back over inhabited territory I changed into clean clothes. I was happy to be flying over India again: a year ago we had glided over the subcontinent at low level in *Orbiter 2*, sitting on top of the gondola as though on a magic carpet, and now, as we passed on a far higher trajectory, I enjoyed remembering how the smells of cooking and incense had wafted up to us, along with children's voices.

That day, our ninth in the air, was a crucial one because it was the last on which we could adjust our approach to China. As I concentrated on holding the course dictated by Luc and Pierre, I suddenly heard an aeroplane calling me. 'Hotel Bravo – Bravo Romeo Alpha,' said the pilot, 'I have a surprise for you.'

'I love surprises,' I replied. 'What is it?'

'Just a second,' – and then in my headphones, speaking French, I heard the voice of a good friend, Charles-André Ramseyer, one of a delegation from the Swiss Tourist Office, flying out for a conference. He told me that another of the passengers had seen us and started to shout: 'Look! There's the Breitling balloon!'

It was Charles-André who first introduced me to the world of ballooning: in 1978, when he was director of the tourist office in Château d'Oex, he phoned to say that he was organizing the first ballooning week in the village and that he would like me to go up with one of the balloons, be dropped and give a hang-gliding demonstration. I accepted immediately – and that was how I entered the world of ballooning. So now it was fantastic to have this man suddenly come past in a plane over India, and to hear his voice. He told me he had tears pouring from his eyes, and that the whole of the Swiss delegation was crammed into the cockpit, all crying, such was the emotional shock of seeing our beautiful balloon, alone in the sky, riding the winds of heaven 10,000 kilometres from home.

That encounter was one of the little signs of fate that seemed to mark our enterprise. As I said, *Orbiter 2* took off on my grandfather's birthday, and *Orbiter 3* on my own. Luc Trullemans came from the very institute of

Flying over the Alps was the moment of truth. In complete silence, Bertrand and Brian were able to observe the perfect functioning of their new balloon (*Edipresse – S. Féval*).

As they were carried south by slow winds, they got a great view of the Matterhorn through the left porthole (*Bertrand Piccard and Brian Jones*).

Meanwhile, in the Geneva control centre, there was plenty for all the team to do: (Above left) Luc Trullemans explains to the press the forecasted trajectories (*Keystone*). (Above right) Greg Moegli and Niklaus Gerber cleared the way for the balloon through all the air traffic during its long journey (*Edipresse – Di Nolfi*). (Below left) Pierre Eckert calculated the trajectories of the wind from the computer. (Below right) Patrick Schelling, the third air traffic controller at Swiss Control (both *Patrick Schelling*).

During the first EVA, Brian concentrates on dropping one of the empty auxiliary fuel tanks. Bertrand washes the outside of the portholes with a sponge tied to an HF radio antenna and a boat hook (*Bertrand Piccard and Brian Jones*).

Flying for a week above the North African desert created a lasting memory of its different shapes and colours. Observing the desert and its emptiness shows how miraculous and fragile life is on this planet (*Bertrand Piccard and Brian Jones*).

Brian installed in the cockpit in front of the instrument panels. Under his left hand is the laptop computer used to send and receive the faxes. Inside the main corridor of the gondola, Bertrand mops the floor of all the water and ice chipped from the fuel control unit on the ceiling (*Bertrand Piccard and Brian Jones*).

Bertrand showing that, even when Mum and Dad are not there, you have to brush your teeth! (*Bertrand Piccard and Brian Jones*).

Brian and Bertrand celebrate their successful crossing of China by making Chinese hats out of their navigation maps (*Bertrand Piccard and Brian Jones*).

Trying to keep the right altitude in order to maintain a good trajectory, the balloon was sometimes only a few hundred feet above the top of the clouds (*Bertrand Piccard and Brian Jones*).

As the sun rose over China, the entire country was covered by clouds (*Bertrand Piccard and Brian Jones*).

Travelling for five days at slow speed and low altitude above the Pacific, with thunderstorm clouds in the distance that could tear the balloon apart, the ocean became a mirror in which Bertrand and Brian confronted their emotions, doubts and anxiety (*Bertrand Piccard and Brian Jones*).

On the sixth day of the Pacific crossing, the balloon finally entered the jet stream south of Hawaii and was surrounded by typical cirrus clouds coloured by the sunset (*Bertrand Piccard and Brian Jones*).

The crossing of the Gulf of Mexico was the worst period of the flight. The balloon began to head for Venezuela instead of Africa at low speed, consuming far too much propane. Inside the gondola, Brian and Bertrand were out of breath with suspected pulmonary pre-oedema. When Brian woke up, both of them realized they needed to wear oxygen masks to get their breath back (*Bertrand Piccard and Brian Jones*).

meteorology that had guided my grandfather to the stratosphere in 1931. Later, over the Pacific, we flew close to the Mariana Trench, where my father made his dive to the deepest part of the ocean.

Also over India, the film producer Garfield Kennedy sent up a chase plane to film the balloon in flight. After several delays, including one caused by an intake of the wrong fuel, the turbo-prop aircraft flew past us three or four hundred metres away and took some reasonable footage. Unfortunately, all it showed was the balloon flying in the sky, and we could have been anywhere in the world. Another problem was that the microwave link between our cameras and theirs did not work, and the film crew had to wait until after we landed to get shots inside the gondola.

That afternoon brought one of the most memorable moments of the flight: Brian and I were together in the cockpit, and we suddenly realized we could see the peaks of the Himalayas, poking up through the clouds away to our left. They were probably 300 miles off, but we were so high that they made a stunning array along the northern horizon. One mountain stood out taller than all the rest, so we thought it must be Everest. I had always been envious of Branson because he had phenomenal views of Everest when he crossed the prohibited part of China: the shots taken from a chase plane of the *ICO Global Challenger* among the 8,000-metre peaks are the most fabulous pictures I have ever seen of a balloon in the air. Now, even though the Himalayas were far away, seeing them for ourselves we felt we had to some extent caught up with him.

I had already begun faxing ahead, once a day, to the Chinese to say that we were on our way and were going to be able to fulfil the conditions they had imposed. I also gave them our estimated time of arrival over the southwestern border. They never answered, but because I had had some experience of dealing with them I didn't really expect to hear much and took no news to be good news.

I felt more and more grateful to the three stalwart air controllers in Geneva who were smoothing our path around the world with such efficiency and good humour. At 11:34 on the morning of 9 March I faxed our own people:

Hello. Would you please pass on this fax to Swiss Control. We specially want to thank Patrick, Greg and Nik for all the work they do for our expedition, and all the help they bring us. It is so comfortable and safe to know that local air traffic controllers are also informed by Swiss Control. Many thanks and best regards to all of you. Brian and Bertrand.

BRIAN

India went to our heads. The jokes passing between capsule and Control became more and more ridiculous. Because I had mis-typed my name on a previous fax, I continued with variations and took to signing faxes 'Banir', 'Bnria' and 'Biriani'. Brian Smith signed himself 'Nairb'. All this was brought on by the inefficiency of Indian communications, which drove us nearly demented. Radio contact was almost always difficult, and we relied a lot on relays via passing aircraft. Pilots were helpful about passing on messages, but it was annoying that local air controllers kept demanding to know our position – often every ten minutes.

On the night of 8–9 March our burners had started faltering again, and at midday on the 9th I faxed down:

> Having thought we had fixed the burner autopilot trip-out last night, Captain B took control and the thing tripped again. One really does have to talk to it in English, and especially if one gets serious then it is *très important* that it is a genuine English lump hammer . . . Calcutta handed us on (or is it off?) to Dacca. 'Radar service terminated' – he could have fooled me. Bertrand going to bed soon, so hopefully the burners will settle down too.

Soon we were over Bangladesh, and the controllers there proved thoroughly hospitable, the tone being set by the first message we got from Dacca:

> Hotel Bravo – Bravo Romeo Alpha. This is Dacca Control. On behalf of the authorities and the people of my country, I wish you the best of luck and a very good flight around the world.

Our passage over that friendly country was brief. Soon we were over Indian territory again and heading for Burma, now known as Myanmar.

Although we were heading almost due east, we were gradually edging to the north, creeping up towards the critical 26th parallel – and this kept us on tenterhooks. Back in Geneva our weathermen were absolutely steadfast, telling us we had to go right up, almost to the limit, where the wind would take us dead east at 090 degrees. Our air controllers were also working with their usual tenacity. 'ATC in Myanmar are aware of your position and are happy,' John Albury told me on the evening of 9 March:

> Greg is looking after Myanmar and Patrick is on the case with China. There is no traffic in the area, so that is one thing less to worry about. Be sure that you have the mountain heights absolutely correct. I have the highest peak at 14,000 feet at a place called DALI, by a large lake approx 30 km from the large town XIAGUAN. Peak is at 25.42 N 100.04 E. If you miss that, you are OK. Please confirm receipt for sure.

The Myanmar air controllers obviously knew about us, but they had trouble grasping the idea of a round-the-world flight, and we had a splendid exchange:

> *Air traffic control:* Hotel Bravo – Bravo Romeo Alpha, what is your departure point and destination?

> *Myself:* Departure point, Château d'Oex, Switzerland. Destination, somewhere in northern Africa.

> *Air traffic control, after several seconds' silence:* If you're going from Switzerland to northern Africa, what in *hell* are you doing in Myanmar?

In Geneva Greg was having similar conversations. His contacts were quite helpful but intensely bureaucratic. 'We need a clearance number,' one of them insisted. 'We cannot give you permission without.' As lengthy discussions proceeded, the balloon was speeding across the northern part of the country, and when, after about four hours, the controller phoned Geneva with the great news that he had finally obtained a clearance number, Greg was able to tell him, 'Thank you very much. The balloon's already over China!'

We seemed to flash across Myanmar. We were making nearly 80 knots, and in any case we went over a narrow part of the country. For the first time we encountered the particular kind of turbulence – in the form of waves – that is caused among mountains by wind hitting steep faces and becoming unstable. As I watched my instruments I suddenly noticed the variometer shooting downwards. The balloon was dropping at the rate of 600 feet a minute. For a few moments I thought there was something wrong and that we were falling out of the sky. The movement was nothing like as sudden and violent as when an airliner hits turbulence, but it was alarming to see from the variometer that we were changing height so rapidly. Instinctively I started burning, but found I couldn't stop the descent – and then I realized what was happening. When I took my hands off everything we started climbing again, just as fast. I reported to Control:

> I think we must be in mountain waves. Balloon going up 600 feet per minute and the same down, track varying widely. Think I'll just let it do its own thing for a while and see what happens. No point in fighting it. Flight level varying between 240 and 255.

Keeping to our normal schedule, Bertrand had gone to bed. Before he did, we had held a discussion about how we should enter China. Should we both be in the cockpit when we crossed the border? After all, it was going to be a momentous occasion – one towards which we had worked all out for more than two years. In the end we decided that it wasn't worth breaking the sleep patterns which we had established so successfully: we would both be tired the next day, and nothing much would be gained. So Bertrand went to sleep, feeling slightly sad to miss what he felt would be a 'fabulous moment'.

The Chinese had seen us coming, and their first reaction was entirely characteristic. They called Control and said, 'Your balloon's heading for the prohibited zone. It must land.' Luc and Pierre told them not to worry, assuring them that the wind would keep us south of the 26th parallel and that we would not break the magic barrier. Control faxed us:

When you get a minute it might be prudent to try to raise the Chinese on HF. They have requested we contact them by radio. Please try Kunming Control . . . just so they know you are kunming.

The day before, using a special number which he had obtained from the Swiss Embassy, Bertrand had tried to call the head of the air traffic control at Beijing. He got through all right but found that nobody there spoke English. When he said, 'This is the Breitling Orbiter balloon', only Chinese came back, and when he asked for an English speaker there was no further reply. After a baffled silence, the man had hung up on him.

A few minutes later I reported:

John — Thanks for the concern. I have spoken to Yangon [formerly Rangoon] on HF with difficulty but OK. I have tried Kunming Control, without success so far. Re 'No traffic to worry about': there was an aircraft at similar level, probably no more than five miles away, crossed in front. I put out a call on 121.5 to draw his attention to me, but no response. I think I can choose a track now. Do you want 090 or 085? I know I want to stay south of 25.5 N.

John confirmed that our best track was 090, 'so stay with that if you can'. He said he would bring the other air traffic to Greg's attention, and suggested that we were probably still too far from Kunming to make radio contact, as well as being shielded by mountains. When I did eventually get through to a Chinese controller, his immediate response was none too welcoming. 'You are not allowed to cross 26 degrees north,' he said. To which I replied, 'Yes, we're aware of that.' John — about to go off duty in the control centre — sent a fax saying, 'Nice doing business with you. By the way, we reckon it is now 5 a.m. where you are, so you should see the sunrise soon on the horizon.'

Shortly before dawn on the morning of 10 March we were speeding towards the Chinese border at 84 knots and a height of 26,000 feet, within half a degree, or thirty miles, of our permitted limit. I faxed exultantly:

Step right up for the main attraction, boys and girls. Ninety degrees you have. China here we come.

CHAPTER EIGHT

CHINESE PUZZLES

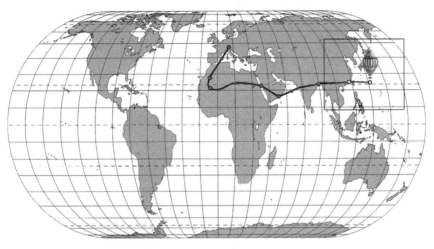

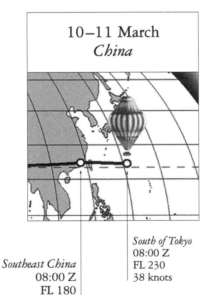

10–11 March
China

South of Tokyo
08:00 Z
FL 230
38 knots

Southeast China
08:00 Z
FL 180
70 knots

BERTRAND

I don't think Brian would ever have been in a position to utter those words had it not been for the intensive diplomatic manoeuvring that took place in the months leading up to our launch. Before the flight of *Orbiter 2* the Swiss Embassy in Beijing had been extremely active on my behalf, working to negotiate permission for an overflight. Arthur Mattli, the *Chargé d'Affaires*, and his wife Florence had even spent hours standing in the snow in front of the closed door of the Ministry of Foreign Affairs trying to deliver a diplomatic note. After our attempt had ended in Burma, they told me they were prepared to try again, but this time they reckoned there would be no chance of success unless I myself came out to China. The Chinese, they said, always preferred to meet the people they were negotiating with to make sure they were serious.

So it was that in August 1998 we went out. The party consisted of Alan Noble, Tony Brown, myself and Michèle, and Pierre Blanchoud, the team's aeronautical adviser. We flew Swissair from Zurich to Beijing, where we were delighted to meet our diplomats. Although we had talked to them for hours on the telephone and exchanged innumerable faxes, we had never met them in person. They arranged for us to visit the National Sports Commission, the Ministry of Foreign Affairs and the Civil Aviation Authority, where we met the deputy director of all the country's air controllers. Discussions were conducted through an interpreter, though the Swiss ambassador, Dominique Dreyer, spoke excellent Chinese and was often able to clarify important points.

At the Ministry of Foreign Affairs we had a formal meeting, sitting in big armchairs ranged round the sides of the room, with nothing in the middle. The first words of our hosts, translated by interpreters, were:

> We are grateful to you for coming to see us, because we think we can solve the problems together. But you have to realize that by heading straight for China last year in your other balloon, and asking for permission to enter only the day before, you caused us enormous difficulties. We worked very hard to arrange clearance, and you had it two days later. But unfortunately, due to other problems, by then you had had to land in Burma.

This was not correct. We had applied for clearance more than a year before that take-off, and the Chinese knew it perfectly well. But all I said was, 'I'm really sorry we caused so much trouble last year, and that's why we've come now, with an important part of our team, so that the same problem doesn't happen again.' So our discussions got off to a good start, and after we left the meeting I asked the Swiss ambassador, 'Was I right to answer like that?'

'Absolutely,' he said quietly.

'Well!' I said indignantly, 'I really wanted to tell him that what he was saying was wrong.'

'He knows!' the ambassador exclaimed with a smile. 'He knows perfectly well. There's no need to tell him. By being polite you saved the situation. Now we're talking about the future, so don't worry about anything said about the past.'

On our way out, the man from the Ministry of Foreign Affairs said quietly, 'I hope you win this race round the world. You're a good team, and we thank you for building good relations with China.'

At another meeting our hosts assured us that they were sympathetic to our project, not least because ours was the only team that had taken the trouble to travel out and meet them. Nevertheless, they explained that to have balloons flying over China would cause them serious problems. One difficulty was that in most places they had no radar, and civilian traffic was controlled by telephone. When a pilot wanted to fly from A to B, he had to call air traffic control and ask for clearance. He might easily be told to wait for ten or twenty minutes because another aircraft was already using that route. If a balloon came across the country, the authorities would have to cancel all flights for the duration of its passage. There would be no difficulty if, two months in advance, we could send precise details of where, when, at what height and speed and on what heading the balloon would cross the border.

That was impossible, of course, and we said so.

Then, through the interpreter, the deputy director said, 'I have an idea. Could you fly above the traffic?'

'We *could*,' I told him, 'but at that altitude there would probably be hardly any wind, so it might take us a month to cross the country.'

He laughed and said, 'We don't want that. So you'd better stay at 30,000.' He emphasized that he did *not* want us flying over northern areas, and least of all over Tibet. He was afraid that we might be forced down in some place so remote or mountainous that the Chinese would not be able to rescue us. They would then lose face by appearing to be incompetent.

The best I could promise was that we would let the Chinese know three days before take-off that we were about to start, and we would warn them when we were twenty-four hours away from the border. We could then tell them our entry and exit points, and once we were in their air space we would send a satellite fax every ten minutes giving our exact position to within twenty metres.

This satisfied them. On those conditions, they said, they would allow us to fly, but only along a precisely defined corridor, which would be specified three days before we arrived. If the wind brought us to the border at a different point, they would move the corridor to accommodate us.

At the end of the week we went home happy, with the feeling that the Chinese liked and trusted us. Three months later we received our permission. So did all the other teams – although in their case they were required to keep their flight path either below the 26th parallel or above the 43rd. As I mentioned earlier, when Richard Branson made his flight in December 1998, we passed up one favourable weather window because we could see that the wind would probably push us over the areas that we knew were out of bounds. Sure enough, as Branson flew southwards over Nepal, the wind changed suddenly and sent him far to the north, across the prohibited parts of China.

The reaction was predictable: through their embassies the Chinese immediately sent faxes to all the other balloon teams saying that permissions were cancelled until the situation had been re-evaluated. I quickly responded with a message saying, 'I accept your decision. We're not at all happy, but we will not take off until new permission is forthcoming.'

We then began intensive discussions, pointing out that we had taken the trouble to visit China and had promised to respect whatever conditions were imposed on us. In reply, the Chinese said they had supposed a pilot would have better control of his balloon. According to the letter we received from them, Branson had been unable to steer accurately and had not spoken to any air traffic controllers; nobody knew where he was (they wrote) and the authorities had had to cancel ten commercial flights.

Now, they said, we must give an absolute guarantee that if we wanted to overfly China we would keep south of 26 degrees latitude or north of 43. As far as we were concerned, north of 43 was impossible because it lay along the border with Russia and was the most danger-ous air space imaginable: any aircraft passing through it was liable to be shot at by both the Russians and the Chinese. The southern alternative was possible, and the Chinese favoured it because in those areas – the main commercial air corridors – they did have radar, and all the air traffic controllers spoke English.

But what had happened to the earlier promise of a special corridor? The answer was that the military authorities, infuriated by Branson's flight, had clamped down and refused to allow it. After a while we began to feel that we were dealing with two different groups – one that wanted to help us, the other opposed to all balloons – and it seemed that there was a good deal of argument between the two.

Our exchanges were conducted partly through the Swiss Embassy in Beijing and partly through the Chinese Embassy in Bern, and with the latter I had a stroke of luck. One of the diplomats in Switzerland had translated some of the *Tin-Tin* stories – Hergé's wonderful cartoon series about a boy adventurer – into Chinese, and when he realized that Hergé's model for Professeur Tournesol (better known to English readers as Professor Calculus) had been my grandfather, he was thrilled. Although he had no power to influence decisions, he was immensely helpful, preparing all transmissions and forwarding them promptly. He also came to see our balloon in Château d'Oex, where he was able to test the quality of our communications equipment for himself by calling Beijing from the gondola.

Even with his help, the process of negotiation was extremely wearing, mainly because of the time difference: 8 a.m. Chinese time, when the working day began in Beijing, was 1 a.m. our time, and often we would get a telephone call between two and four in the morning saying that our latest fax had been received but that extra documents were needed. At our home in Lausanne Michèle would often be up half the night, typing, printing and faxing the documents which I was dictating from the Hôtel de Ville in Château d'Oex.

We tried every possible channel: people who had contacts in the Chinese press, people who knew the Chinese President, people who knew the air traffic controllers, people with friends working for Chinese commercial airlines. Other balloon teams were badgering away as well, all of which must have produced an incredible amount of work for the Chinese.

Many factors swayed things in our favour. Chief among them was the deep involvement of the Swiss Ministry of Foreign Affairs and the Ministry of Defence and Sport, whose representatives put our project at a level of national interest in their discussions with China. Then there was the fact that we had a Swiss-registered balloon, and the Chinese were angry with British balloonists. In the past I had taken the trouble to obtain a certificate of airworthiness from the Swiss Federal Organisation of Civil Aviation, and this appeared to be helpful. Finally, there was our behaviour: we never criticized any Chinese reaction.

For two months, every time we saw a good weather slot coming up, I faxed the Chinese to say that we had a chance to launch but that we were not going to take it because we respected their decision. Finally, I think, we won their confidence, and they granted us permission on three conditions. First, we had to guarantee that we would fly below 26 degrees north; second, that if we strayed north of the limit, we would land; and third, that if we found ourselves approaching China on a trajectory that would bring us to the border at an inappropriate point, we would come down in India, Pakistan or Iran.

Brian and I went to the Chinese Embassy to give the necessary guarantees. The papers were in both languages, and when the First Secretary asked me, 'Are you willing to sign?' I said, 'Do you think I have any choice?' That made him laugh, and he replied, 'Well – it's the only way you can do it.'

In one way we had achieved an important victory, but at the same time we had signed what might turn out to be an official death warrant for our flight, for we had put our names to an agreement that would force us down if the wind sent us only slightly off course. Our target was minute, amounting to only about five per cent of the country and offering a very narrow front to anyone approaching from the west.

At one stage the Chinese attempted to add one more condition: the Swiss government had to guarantee that I would keep my promises. Naturally the government said it could not give guarantees on behalf of one of its citizens – to do so would be illegal. I phoned the Chinese Embassy.

'Can *your* government give a guarantee that none of your diplomats will exceed the speed limit on Swiss highways?' I asked.

'Of course not,' came the answer, 'but we don't care. Just get a guarantee from your government and we'll give permission.'

The exchanges went on and on. It was terrible – a real dialogue of the deaf. But at last we managed to find a formula which the Chinese could accept: our side guaranteed that M. Bertrand Piccard and Mr

Brian Jones committed themselves to land if they were pushed out of the correct approach corridor.

All this made me realize that if we wanted to go round the world, we also had to make a tour of all the countries, mentalities and personalities involved. We would not just be dealing with wind and weather: we would have to accommodate the whims of a huge number of human beings.

When I woke up at 23:00 Zulu on 10 March 1999, the first light of dawn was breaking. I stuck my head through the curtain and asked, 'Where are we?'

'We're in CHINA!' Brian replied.

That was an incredible moment – *so* nice! We could feel that everyone at Control was tremendously excited. Our weathermen had sent us on a swirling trajectory of 13,000 kilometres and threaded us through the eye of a needle. Their feat was a masterpiece of planning, and quite rightly they were proud of it.

Excitement was also running high at the Swiss Embassy in Beijing. The diplomats there had become real friends, and when at last they heard my voice emanating from Chinese air space they came through on the satellite telephone, describing how they too had burst into tears of sheer delight. Florence and Arthur Mattli faxed to Geneva a cartoon of a decidedly Chinese-looking balloon bearing the hand-written message, '*Chers Bertrand et Brian, Bienvenue en Chine!*' and embellished with the signatures of all their colleagues, including the ambassador, Dominique Dreyer. Control described the cartoon to us as they had no means of faxing pictures.

Cecilia Smith was on duty and told us that everybody at the control centre was thrilled by our progress. 'Sometimes we feel as if we are living in a dream,' she faxed:

Jo is writing her diary, and has just mentioned that while she slept today you left India, flew over Bangladesh, over Burma and approached the Chinese border. And she wasn't asleep that long! Well, these are extraordinary times.

Feeling very emotional, I replied:

Hallo, my friends. Thank you very much for your nice fax. I think one of our greatest strokes of luck is to have such a wonderful team. It's fabulous here to feel how much you are behind us and with us. Warmest regards, Bertrand. PS FL between 240 and 250, with constant track 88 at 79 knots.

The weather did not match the occasion. Rain was falling on China. Almost the entire country was covered by bad weather, and the only hole we found in the clouds was over Kunming. There we saw the airport runways and planes on the tarmac. I called the air traffic controller and said, 'If you look up now, you'll see our balloon. We're exactly overhead.' He replied, 'I have no window. I cannot look outside.' Then another voice broke in, saying, '*I* can see you. It's beautiful!' The speaker never identified himself, but we thought he must have been a pilot, sitting in his cockpit on the runway. Then and later we found the Chinese air traffic controllers extremely professional. Their English was adequate provided that we stuck to the limited vocabulary of international air-control jargon. Talking to each other in Chinese, they passed on our position from one controller to the next.

We had about 1,500 miles to go to cross China, but already our met men had almost put that huge country from their minds. They knew we were going to skim across it, straight as an arrow, on our 90-degree heading, with the 26th parallel no more than thirty miles to our left, and their minds were already ranging far ahead:

We are very happy that we could drive you into China within half a degree latitude of the target. This is the result of eight days of sweating for you and us. From now on it is important to stay on a northerly track in order to attack the Pacific. If we stay at the present altitude we risk to drift towards the equator in the medium range.

So we propose that you come down to FL 180 after 04:00 Zulu . . . The track should evolve to 095 magnetic during the next twenty-four hours. It should not exceed 100. The speed should evolve to 60 knots first, below 50 knots later. The weather will become cloudy, but the top will not exceed FL 120.

We will leave China at around 15:00 Zulu. The track should then slowly bend northwards. We will stay at this altitude for forty-eight to sixty hours. We can then catch a good jet stream at higher levels, leading into the middle of the Atlantic in nine days. Best regards, Luc and Pierre.

There we were, sweeping on at 80 knots, and they were telling us to slow down! That was a really difficult moment for me because I loved the feeling of going fast on that easterly track – and now, without really understanding why, we had to vent helium, lose height and slow down. The clouds were starting to build, and some were right beside the balloon, with their tops above us. They did not look really dangerous, but they could have created serious turbulence. Also, we didn't want the envelope to get soaked by their condensation. I felt very tense. The balloon was moving like a porpoise, dropping 900 feet, climbing 900 feet, and the clouds were boiling all round us – a fascinating but most unnerving combination.

As always, our air controllers were smoothing a path ahead of us. For Patrick Schelling, Taiwan was 'an easy one', because he had personal contacts in the tower there and had arranged everything in advance. Also, our steady track and speed enabled him to predict exactly when we would enter Taiwanese air space. As we approached, a peculiar fax reached Swiss Control from Vietnam, addressed to British Airways:

Vould you plese lett us hev the balon campton present position and ETA over Ho Chi Minh FIR.

Greg replied that he was at Swiss Control, not British Airways, and that the balloon had already passed Vietnam – whereupon a second fax arrived:

We are received message of you. Your reply is highly appreciated.

BRIAN
When I joined Bertrand in the cockpit he craftily turned on the video camera and caught me preparing my breakfast. As I started spreading

butter he said, 'That's wonderful *panettone*. I'll zoom in on it – it will give everyone an appetite.'

'This is breakfast on 11 March at 8 a.m. Zulu,' I commentated.

'If you're already making your *panettone* for tomorrow,' Bertrand told me, 'it may be a little dry, because today's the tenth. I have to check with your beard. Yes – it's a beard of ten days, not eleven!'

After that burst of high spirits he became preoccupied because we had lost our track and he was having to burn repeatedly in an effort to jump over clouds. He phoned the weathermen and said that conditions were lousy. 'Why do we have to fly so low?' he demanded. 'Well,' they said, 'we've done a re-evaluation, and you can go back to your original flight level of 270.' Back we went, with the impression that in the past three or four hours we'd lost helium, burnt propane and wasted time – all for nothing.

After such a build-up, China was a bit of a non-event. We could hardly believe that we would keep going fast and straight across the entire country – but that was what happened. With minimal steering by us, the balloon held its 90-degree track with an almost uncanny accuracy. As somebody remarked, it was like walking a 1,500-mile tightrope. Because of the bad weather, we saw nothing until we approached the east coast. There the clouds began to break up, but the air was hazy and the visibility still poor. My main feeling was one of relief that we had gone through the eye of the needle with no difficulty. Until that moment China had been the great bogey looming ahead – the one place where our flight might be brought to a sudden halt by sheer human obstinacy. Now that the danger was past, we both felt buoyant.

Just before we left Chinese air space at 12:04 I faxed, 'Got the next map out – it's all blue.' For the second time in the flight we were at a point of no return. The first had been at take-off, and now the biggest obstacle of all lay ahead of us: the Pacific. Just to raise Bertrand's morale, I said, 'D'you realize that the Pacific is wider than the distance we've done from Château d'Oex to here?'

As if to show that he knew what we were feeling at that moment, Stefano Albinati, a very straight guy not given to displays of emotion, sent us this fax:

I just wanted to tell you that although I'm comfortably seated in the Control Centre, my heart is beating at 200 knots per second. The Pacific in front of you is big, but not as big as my admiration for what you are doing. I wish you all the best for the crossing.

CHAPTER NINE

PACIFIC BLUES

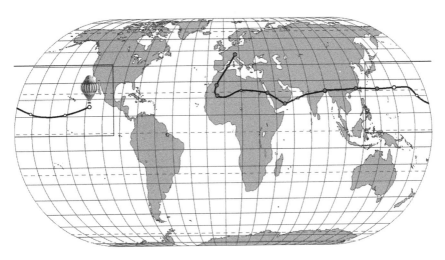

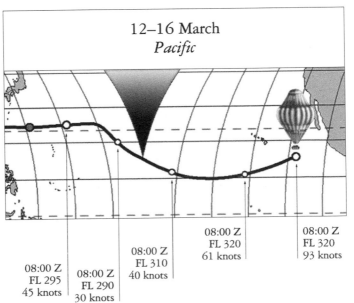

12–16 March
Pacific

08:00 Z
FL 295
45 knots

08:00 Z
FL 290
30 knots

08:00 Z
FL 310
40 knots

08:00 Z
FL 320
61 knots

08:00 Z
FL 320
93 knots

BERTRAND
Faced by 8,000 miles of water, I picked up my pen and wrote:

> This is exactly my definition of adventure. Adventure is some-
> thing out of the usual pattern, a point at which you cannot avoid
> confronting the unknown, so that you have to dig inside yourself
> to find the courage and resources to deal with what may lie
> ahead, and to succeed.

Many major human achievements are not real adventures because
although they may be very dangerous, the people involved know
exactly what is going to happen. For us, the ocean ahead was a
complete unknown: facing it was a difficult moment – but a fabulous
one. I love dealing with that kind of situation, because I find that having
to tackle the unknown helps me to deal with life when I come back.
Life itself is a big unknown and a big adventure. But many people never
realize how interesting the adventure of life can be. So when we were
confronted by the Pacific, I found it a beautiful metaphor of life itself.

Yet if I was excited, I was also frightened. As the sun went down,
while we were between China and Taiwan, the electrically operated

valves on one side of the burner array jammed open. Huge flames roared up into the hot-air cone, and to stop them burning a hole in the envelope we hastily shut off the fuel. Switching to the three burners on the other side, we had to reset the timers on the instrument panel and stabilize the balloon. We wondered if dirt had got into the system, but technicians on the ground thought that the cause of the trouble was probably cold, and that the valves were becoming iced up. We could well have done without such problems at this point: now that we were approaching the colossal expanse of the Pacific, the possibility of total burner failure was infinitely more alarming than when we had been over land. I had only to think of Richard Branson and Andy Elson, both of whom had gone down in the ocean.

To make matters worse, our heading had swung down to 101 degrees and the wind seemed to be taking us much too far south. At that stage our plan was to cross the Pacific in a straight line – but already were losing the track we wanted. It was a southward deviation that had ended Branson's latest attempt.

For the first time I wondered if our valiant met men were fully confident about the next move. They had worked incredibly hard to steer us safely to China and across it, and perhaps because all their energy had been focused on the mainland, they seemed unsure what strategy to adopt for the Pacific. Certainly they were hampered by a shortage of information – there was very little weather information coming from those vast wastes – and while one of their models showed that we should take a northern route, the other showed the opposite – that a southern route was our best bet. All they could suggest for the moment was that we dawdle while they calculated new trajectories.

'These problems shatter the fragile confidence that we've built up,' I wrote. All our high technology had been working so well that the sudden malfunction of the burners gave us quite a shock. When I went to bed I felt really scared, and to get to sleep I resorted to self-hypnosis.

To disconnect from the concentration of flying the balloon, and to stop doing fuel calculations in my head or worrying about the noise of the burners, I employed a favourite technique. Lying on my back, I closed my right fist and squeezed hard, with my curled-up forefinger and thumb facing me, imagining that I was crushing all the stress and tension inside my hand. Then I inhaled deeply and held my breath, exerting as much force as I could in blocking my breathing and clenching my fist while gazing hard at a point on my hand. When I could not hold out any more, I breathed out and let my fist open of its own accord. Already I could feel the tension transforming into relaxation, and in my head I recited a slow account of how the lassitude was spreading to my wrist, to my forearm, to my upper arm, to my shoulder, to the other arm, to my head, to the back, the abdomen, the stomach and the feet – until I felt completely relaxed.

Then I told myself a story about how I had gone outside the gondola and was lying on a very warm and comfortable cloud, looking at the balloon, which was drifting gently away from me and being flown by Brian, so that I didn't have to take care of it.

Relaxing on my cloud, I visualized the balloon flying through a gigantic rainbow and passing through all its colours. First came red, the colour of excitement and stress; next, orange (a bit softer); then yellow (like a wonderful field of oilseed rape, very restful to the eyes and spirit); then green (like the prairies of the American Mid-West, with a gentle breeze moving the grass in soft waves). Then came blue (even more relaxing, because it is the sky and the sea together, with no horizon between). Finally the balloon went into indigo, the deep shade of the night, with practically no colour any more, everything almost black. When I could scarcely make out the balloon any longer, I turned on my side and fell into a deep sleep.

BRIAN

Like Bertrand, I was thoroughly on edge. We never became the slightest bit irritated with each other, but as the night wore on I did get more and more ratty with the control centre. We had signed a written agreement with Oakland Oceanic Control, the organization near San Francisco responsible for air traffic in the area ahead of us, and just before 09:00 Zulu I faxed our own team saying:

Well, it looks like the decision has been made to have a go at this large puddle in front of us. Please confirm that you have a copy of the Oceanic airspace reporting contract available for all teams to read. We assume you will take care of initial notification. Good morning from Brian. FL 180, climbing to FL 260 with permission.

I followed that a few minutes later with, 'Lock Luc's skis in the cupboard until this flight is over. By order. Captains Piccard and Jones.' The message continued:

> These problems have put Bertrand completely off his dinner. I find it very hard to believe the trouble with the valves is a temperature problem. We had a lower ambient temperature over Burma last night and they worked perfectly. Anyway, it's only minus 23 degrees. What will happen if it goes to minus 56?

Minutes later, up came another message, this time from Alan. Evidently he felt we weren't doing enough to let other people know where we were, and his patronising tone did nothing to soothe my feelings:

> The Pacific Ocean is a large and reasonably empty place. And I don't want to alarm you, but . . . the air lanes between Taiwan and Honolulu, and Japan and the Americas, are quite busy. There is no radar control and possibly nobody looking out of the front windows of passing jet airliners. Aircraft will be flying assigned flight levels, and it is important that you advise the controlling authority on HF, and the Control Centre by Inmarsat, before – that is BEFORE – commencing any altitude excursions. Technically, I think you should have permission before executing any change.
>
> If you change flight level by mistake, or in an emergency, you should broadcast on 121.5 your position and details of your old/present flight level and intended new flight level. Then advise ATC and Control . . . suggest you leave a transponder squawking, as some modern aircraft have anti-collision radars that will pick up your signal.
>
> Some new video/digital pics would be welcome celebrating your passage across China. Tomorrow it won't be news.

It seemed to me that almost everything Alan said was perfectly obvious. Talk about teaching grandmothers to suck eggs! My answer, partly ironic, showed distinct signs of irritation:

> Thank you for that confidence booster. I read the Oceanic agreement a couple of hours ago. Three hundred feet margin is very difficult to keep to, but I'm sure we'll do our best. Transponder has been permanently on for fixed-wing collision-avoidance systems. Bertrand Spielberg is in bed now, so no piccys for a while. We were too busy over China to play with the cameras.

By midday I had more to worry about than the erratic valves. 'Track seems to be veering slowly but steadily,' I reported. 'On this track we will be a long, long way south. Would like some reassurance please that all is OK, and an idea of what is likely to happen track and speed wise.' For the first time in the flight I felt that the people on the ground weren't really responding to our needs.

On top of worries about our heading, I saw that dead ahead of us on the map lay two danger areas, designated W 172 and W 184, about which we had no information. Perhaps it was just as well that I did not know that, at Swiss Control, Patrick Schelling was already grappling with a sudden and potentially explosive problem. The first time he heard the name Naha, he was unaware that any such place existed; it turned out to be the main city on the island of Okinawa, and above it was an air-training area. When Patrick called the Naha control tower, the supervisor, who had only limited English, kept saying in a high voice, 'Danger area! Very hot! Very hot!' The man seemed extremely nervous, crying, 'Circumnavigate!' But our air controllers could see that if we kept going we were going to penetrate area W 184, and once more their only option was to negotiate. As on previous occasions, they were dealing with people from another culture and had to be extremely careful not to give offence.

Patrick tried every conceivable way of getting his opposite number to give us clearance: he soft-soaped him with his spiel about all being brothers in air traffic control, but he never succeeded in making him utter the magic word. The supervisor told him that Japanese aircraft were flying and that he could not ground them. Several times he repeated his warning cry, 'Very hot! Very hot!' Eventually, after protracted discussion, Patrick confronted him with a radical question: 'Can you ensure the safety of the balloon?' The sudden answer was, 'Yes, yes' – and that was the end of the argument.

Up in the gondola I was unaware of these exchanges, but I was nervous about the danger zone and agitated by the lack of information coming from Geneva. My deteriorating temper showed clearly in successive messages:

John – Looks like the Breitling bus is going to blunder on through the danger area W 172. Has anybody said anything about it in Swiss Control? FL 250, track 097, 84 knots. So fast in fact that my hair (what little I have – lots compared to some, though) is blown back. We have built-in showers here. One can stand under the top dome or the fuel control unit most of the day and get lots of cold water falling. Course it's all frozen at the moment, saving itself for when Bertrand steps out of the bunk right below it.

John – I don't mean to get a strop on, but . . . Have you stopped putting our questions on a board? Last few messages have asked if all the teams are *au fait* with the procedures over the Pacific as per the contract we signed with the Americans, HF frequencies, reassurance from Luc/Pierre that we are going the right way, any progress on setting up the satellite phone for Pacific on rod antenna, and comments on the danger area coming up . . .

This last brought a sharp retort from Alan:

Listen, Testy Face. We thought you were joking. Have you read the contract? It doesn't affect you for several days crossing the Pacific, until you come under the control of Oakland, California . . . At the moment you are under the control of the Japanese, with whom we do not have a contract . . . Luc says track 094 is the perfect track, but your last reported 092 will be OK if you can't do better . . .

Danger Area W 172 is permanent and unlimited. ATC will

normally tell you if you can't go through, in which case you must turn round and go back. Seriously, you've been through quite a few danger and restricted areas — you can't balloon around the world without doing this — and if any are active, it would be normal for Swiss Control to be notified when the flight plan is filed, and then advise the aircraft before penetration. We are checking W 172 and W 184 with the Japanese by phone and will get back to you.

Danger area W 184: coordinated with the supervisor at Naha for clearance, but they have a big air-warfare exercise there tonight at 22:00 Z, with fighters, bombers, missiles, submarines, so better get a move on and don't worry if the bangs and flashes rock the gondola a bit. The Japanese self-defence force is aware that you are in the region and that you will probably cross the area. So don't worry . . . too much.

I thought this must be at least partly a joke, but it didn't strike me as very funny. 'OK, Buggery Bollocks,' I exploded. 'You said you were going to look in the book re Satphone. We know you of old — you probably have the procedures in your head and in your Burgundy bag, neither of which the team can get to.' Presently I realized that the exchanges were getting overheated: after receiving a hesitant and sweet note from Debbie asking for our flight level I felt a little guilty and calmed down:

I'm not really miffed at anybody down there. It's just that our dearly beloved Flight Director is more efficient at winding up than the chain on a cuckoo clock.

John replied:

You upset us so much that everyone has gone back to the hotel for nosh and wine, and I have been given the duty of turning the lights off before I join them! Joking really. No — we still all love you dearly . . . I thought you would have enough entertainment watching the forthcoming air display around you. Can you let me know if the Japanese air force are using F-16Js or the older version of F-16Gs with the earlier radio antennae and extra wing stores and older leading-edge flaps (serial nos would be appreciated).

Tense as things were in the capsule, we heard later that the atmosphere in the control centre had become far from comfortable. I was so preoccupied with my own difficulties that it did not occur to me that our teams in Geneva were also working under considerable stress. Their hotel accommodation was comfortable enough, and they were getting good meals whenever they wanted them, but at work the pressure was steadily building. Paradoxically, the farther we flew and the greater our chance of success, the higher the tension mounted. My own close friends – John and Debbie, Smiffy and C – made my and Bertrand's safety their paramount concern, and they were on tenterhooks for every minute of every shift, fearing that something could go wrong. As Smiffy remarked when the flight was over, 'It was like holding our breath for three weeks on end'.

After those barbed exchanges, he took Alan aside and asked him to ease off. Then Jo – who, according to the others, had been exhibiting heroic self-control for days on end – had a fit of hysterics, screamed at Alan that he was going to wreck our chances by being so unsympathetic, burst into tears, ran out of the room and locked herself in the loo.

The remarks about a major military exercise, which we thought were jokes, turned out to be absolutely true. We passed straight through danger area W 184 without seeing a thing – but we might have given ourselves a fright if we had had our noses glued to the portholes because a good many aircraft were flying that night.

Bad radio communications were yet another annoyance. 'No contact with Naha on this awful HF set,' I told John. 'Have had two aircraft call me on 121.5 to tell me to call Naha, but I can't hear a damned thing.' Just as I handed over to Bertrand, with the sun coming up, we got some reassurance in the form of a friendly fax from Oceanic Control at Oakland, California, promising us every assistance – but by then I'd had enough for one night.

BERTRAND

'Hello to all of you,' I faxed when I took over. 'I'm letting the balloon stabilize with no burning. It stays around FL 271 at track 092 and 74 knots. No HF contact with anybody except VHF on 121.5 with planes relaying to Naha or Tokyo. Time for my morning cup of Earl Grey tea.'

Later that morning we went over the island of Iwo Jima, which American forces captured from the Japanese after desperate battles in February 1945. A hat of cloud sat on top of its single volcanic peak, and on another little island nearby I could see an airfield, so I called the controller and said we were passing. He wasn't the slightest bit interested, but an American pilot picked up our conversation and came so close that I heard his engines.

'Who's flying near the balloon?' I called.

'US Navy Gulfstream 4,' he answered cheerfully, and asked a lot of questions about what we were doing. I reported to Control:

> Flew overhead Iwo Jima. They didn't even bother looking up to see the balloon. Probably the last time something strange appeared in their sky it was some US Air Force bombers, fifty years ago. Maybe this time they were all in the shelters, but I promise you, I didn't use the toilet at that moment . . .

A reassuring message came from Control, settling the points that Brian had raised earlier: our teams in Geneva were all briefed on Pacific and Atlantic procedures, Luc and Pierre were confident we were going the right way, and the satellite telephone was now working. That same day – a big moment for me – we flew past the Mariana Trench. I was delighted to find that the line of my horizontal adventure was crossing the site of my father's great vertical endeavour, and I phoned him there and then to tell him.

At the end of the 1950s deep-sea diving had developed into a race rather like ours. On one side was the bathyscaphe *Trieste*, invented and built by my grandfather and father; on the other was a copy of their submersible built by the French Navy. I had read newspaper articles describing how keen the competition had become to reach the deepest point of the ocean, and I was very proud that my father had won the race. Now, overflying the Mariana Trench, I was taking part in another international contest of the same kind, against very rich and well-equipped competitors. Could I add one more victory to my family's tally? At some moments I was confident it would be my fate to succeed, but at others I began to think it impossible that my generation could continue this success story. As in the preparation of the project and the flight, I was oscillating between hope and anxiety. To have lived in that state for five years had been a most exhausting experience – but at least I was now close to the moment of truth.

BRIAN

People were now watching our progress from all over the world, and excited e-mail messages of encouragement had started to pour into the Breitling website. We learnt later from Alan Kirby – a retired British nuclear physicist who cheerfully described himself as 'a balloonatic' – that he downloaded nearly 5,000 e-mails from well-wishers, and altogether, during our flight, between 8,000 and 9,000 flooded in. They came from every corner of the earth – from Australia, New Zealand, Dubai, Malaysia and Brazil, as well as from Europe – but the majority were from North America, and it was clear that thousands of enthusiasts there were hoping we would overfly their country.

'Good evening, Bertrand and Brian,' wrote Ralph R. Davis of Walnut Creek, California. 'You may not be Americans, but you sure have some fans here in the States.' Jane Matheson, a former classmate of Bertrand's at North Palm Beach in Florida, sent fond remembrances and asked if he still had scars on his knees where she kicked him. A man who styled himself 'Montgolfier' was planning to put up 'a small armada of balloons' to meet us as we hit the West Coast. 'Would like if possible for you to drop altitude, to meet us,' he wrote. 'Will let you know well in advance if armada is in position or has been aborted.'

All at once, however, our circumstances changed, and our chances of a flight across North America vanished. At Control Luc announced a drastic change of plan. Rather than keeping us to the north, he and Pierre had decided to send us southwards, far down over the Pacific, to pick up a jet stream that was forecast to form there in three days' time. The proposal was so startling that Brian Smith took Luc aside and asked to see this new jet stream on his laptop. When Luc said, 'Oh – you don't understand: it doesn't exist yet. It'll be born three days from now,' Smiffy turned pale.

The decision to go south threw all our air controllers' forward planning into chaos. They had expected the balloon to fly over North

America, but now they had to file a plan for a flight via Mexico and Cuba, and the communications centre at Geneva Airport hastily had to look up the relevant new addresses: Miami Oceanic, New York Oceanic, Honolulu, Oakland Oceanic, Havana, Kingston (Jamaica), Curaçao, Santo Domingo – all had to be alerted.

Evidently realizing that their new plan would alarm us, Luc and Pierre broke the news by sending us a detailed analysis of the latest weather situation:

Dear Brian and Bertrand,
After a lot of discussion with Alan, we decide to take the southerly route over the ocean. Luc will phone to explain. The required flight level will be between 260 and 280, with tracks between 093 and 098, and speed around 35 knots until 00:00 Z. Afterwards you may climb to the ceiling. I think it is 295 for this period. Track will go from 095 to 150 in twenty-four hours, with speeds between 25 and 30 knots. The day after, you will descend in latitudes between 13 and 15 north, with speeds between 20 and 25 knots.

This very special manoeuvre is necessary to catch the very fast sub-tropical jet stream that we observe now, starting southwest of Hawaii through Central America going to North West Africa.

This major departure from earlier strategy made us all the more anxious because we had the impression that the weathermen themselves were confused. In fact, after trying the northern route for twenty-four hours, they had seen that it would give a bad result. After re-running all their calculations, they had discovered that if we went north the distance would of course be shorter and our speed would be greater, but – fatal flaw – bad weather coming along behind would catch up with us, and we would risk being brought down in the sea by thunderstorms, as Steve Fossett had been. The southern route, towards the equator, would mean three or four days at low level and low speed – a depressing trajectory, but one that would bring us to a jet stream which would start to build south of Hawaii in a few days' time. So far, the jet stream they were talking about existed only on their computer models, three days in the future.

The prospect of going south was horrific – not least because Richard Branson had come to grief doing that very thing. After setting out on the northern route he had diverted southwards, and disaster followed. Now our own team was telling us to follow the same course. Instead of heading straight east across the Pacific and hitting the coast of North America somewhere in California between Los Angeles and San Francisco, we were going even farther south than he had – a thousand miles south of Hawaii, passing at one stage closer to Australia than to any point in the northern hemisphere, and adding a couple of thousand miles to our journey.

BERTRAND

Brian and I both formed the impression that our met men, with no really good weather pattern available, were choosing the worse of two poor options. I had serious doubts, and felt so depressed that I telephoned Michèle and told her I thought we were going to fail because we didn't have enough fuel to fly so far and so slowly.

'Bertrand,' she said, 'I don't understand. An hour ago Luc and Pierre were completely confident. You only have to do three or four days at low speed, and then you'll get the jet stream. What are you afraid of?'

'Well,' I told her, 'I don't see how we can rely on a jet stream that doesn't exist yet.'

She called the met men again, told them how apprehensive we were, and asked what they really thought. 'They've no reason to be depressed!' Luc cried. Immediately he phoned me back and we talked in French. When I asked if he was truly confident about sending us south, he said, 'Bertrand, do you trust me? Yes or No?'

In that situation I felt it was better to say yes.

'Yes,' I said.

'OK – so just do it! The situation's under control.'

That was the defining moment of the flight. If we'd kept to the northern route we would have failed because it was leading to violent thunderstorms that could have torn the balloon apart and sent us hurtling to the sea. In any case, it would not have brought us to the jet stream. At the time, though, we could not tell what lay ahead, and I said to Brian, 'I have to admit, I feel a little afraid.'

'Thank God!' he replied. 'I've been wanting to tell you – I'm shit scared too!'

That was a wonderful moment. The confession that we were both so frightened brought us closer together than ever, and gave us strength to face whatever lay ahead.

BRIAN

I'd always had this fear of the unknown – and it was certainly a comfort to know that Bertrand was scared as well. But just admitting it didn't make me feel better for long. I continued to feel really frightened, not least because I kept remembering Steve Fossett's terrifying crash – the worst thing for me was thinking about what would happen if we ditched.

Before the flight of *Orbiter 2* Camerons had tested the gondola, and we knew it floated very well because the kerosene tanks were relatively light and the capsule had keels that were designed to fill with water and stabilize it. *Orbiter 3*'s gondola was far more top-heavy. What with the weight of the load-frame and outriggers round the top of the capsule, plus the titanium propane tanks, I thought it would almost certainly turn over if we came down in the sea, and we might never be able to escape from the capsule through either of the hatches.

If we found ourselves upside-down in the ocean, our only chance would be to pile all loose equipment at the front and hope that the gondola would tilt nose-down at a steep enough angle to bring the rear hatch clear of the water. Even then, we might easily drown trying to escape: with a hatch open, the gondola could fill with water and sink, taking us to the bottom with it. If we had to parachute from a height – forget it. We were six, seven, eight days away from rescue: the chances of anyone finding us in time to save our lives were extremely remote, and even if an aircraft managed to locate us and drop a large life raft, there was no guarantee we would survive until a ship arrived.

At sunset I looked out of the porthole and saw these whacking great cumulo-nimbus clouds (known in the trade as CBs), any of which might contain wind-shear and hail violent enough to destroy our envelope by ripping it to shreds. It was vast clouds of exactly this kind – bigger than any that form over land – that had nearly killed Steve

Fossett the previous summer. As dark came down I wondered, 'Am I going to fly into one of them during the night?' There was no way of telling if one lay in our path.

The only sure way to avoid the clouds was to fly above them, but at dusk they might easily be two or three hundred miles away, sitting on the horizon, and it was impossible to tell how high they reached or where they might move to during the night. It was the prospect of feeling the balloon suddenly start to shake about in the dark that haunted me most. I became a little paranoid, and every few minutes I would dim the lights in the cabin and peer out to see if the stars were in view. If they were, I knew we couldn't be in cloud.

BERTRAND

Generally the clouds would form in the morning from moisture rising off the warm sea and condensing in the cooler air above; in the middle of the day they grew huge, and by evening some would start to dissolve.

We were trying to hold a track of 123 degrees, but we were surrounded by these CBs, whose tops reached to 28,000 feet. Our ceiling was 30,000 feet, so we generally had 2,000 feet of clearance above them. But luckily, whenever we came close to one of the really enormous clouds, our track diverged a little from the direction of the wind which was moving it. As we wove in and out of the threatening monsters, we had the feeling that the balloon was being guided from above by a benevolent, unseen hand. The sky was full of dangerous clouds, yet in some miraculous way we never ran into one.

Often we found that the lower part of a cloud was travelling in the same direction as us, but more slowly. Far above, one saw that the wind had sliced off its top and thrown it hundreds of miles away, turning it into cirrus clouds – masses of tiny ice crystals, shining in the sun. In some places we would see a whole flotilla of smaller clouds clustered in a circle round a single big one, and we thought such formations must be caused by local depressions.

'Over the Pacific the clouds are alive,' I wrote in my journal. 'They grow as much horizontally as they do vertically, and by good luck all the tallest ones – the dangerous cumulo-nimbus thunder clouds – are to the south of our track.' In one of his faxes Luc told us there were gigantic storms to the south, and said, 'Maybe you can see them?' We could, and very menacing they were – tremendous masses of cloud on the horizon.

Communications became extremely difficult. Our fax and telephone both went dead because we were right beneath the Pacific satellite: with the shadow of the balloon blocking the antennae, we floated on for two days out of direct contact with Geneva. At one point Jo noted in her diary, 'We've been out of communication with them for almost twenty-four hours, and everybody in the Control Room is quiet.'

The fact that the telephone and fax were dead inevitably increased our sense of isolation. It was an extraordinary feeling, to be drifting in silence over the middle of an ocean 8,000 miles wide. The Pacific became like a vast mirror in which Brian and I could see our emotions nakedly reflected. It was impossible to cheat or fool ourselves: we really were afraid. Brian quoted lines from *The Rime of the Ancient Mariner*:

> *Alone, alone, all, all alone,*
> *Alone on a wide wide sea!*

Our only contact was with the air traffic controllers at Oakland, outside San Francisco, whom we could reach on HF radio. As we drifted on in the middle of nowhere, I smiled to myself when I remembered how, when we were planning the gondola, I had told Alan I didn't want any HF radio on board: I said it was too expensive and heavy, and didn't work anyway. Satellite devices, I assured him, were much better. Fortunately the HF was still a legal requirement for this kind of flight.

Now we were entirely dependent on HF – and when I asked San Francisco if they could patch me through to Luc on their telephone line, a minor miracle occurred. The man in Oakland said, 'Of course – just tell us who we have to charge,' and put me through. At that very moment Luc was hurrying into the control centre saying, 'They're only 130 miles away from storms. I *have* to get a message to them somehow.' The words were hardly out of his mouth when the phone rang, and there was San Francisco with: 'We have a radio relay call for you.' Luc stared at our people and said, 'That's incredible! He's here! God's here!' Over the link he warned me of the CBs ahead, and told us to climb as high as we could to avoid them. So for the first time in ages I was able to talk to Luc, and I vowed that I would never make bad jokes about HF radio again. Once more, some outside force seemed to be directing events on our behalf.

BRIAN

Inside the gondola it was so cold, and so many things were going wrong, that it only needed a little spark to put me in a bad temper. Control didn't seem to understand what we were going through: they obviously didn't appreciate how tired we were or how demoralizing it was to be so cold. Angered by their failure to put themselves in our place, I really snapped back at upcoming messages from Alan. It was mainly my fault that the atmosphere became antagonistic – but at the time I did feel there was a certain lack of sensitivity on the ground.

When the weather guys changed their minds, for the first time I was tempted to think, 'Well – it's easy enough for *them*. They're not thousands of miles away from the nearest land.' After what they had already achieved I could not doubt their ability – but what they were now proposing seemed crazy. Did they know what they were doing? Doubt made it impossible to keep my own fears at bay.

It so happened that, in the moments of worst anxiety, technical problems multiplied. For the first time in the flight we were struggling to get as high as possible to keep above the clouds, and the higher we went, the lower the temperature fell. The cabin heaters, which ran on propane, were hardly working; and the pilot lights were failing because they were getting clogged with ice, so at night the gondola became miserably cold – only a degree or two above freezing. I had taken to wearing three pairs of survival-type, fleece-lined trousers, as many layers as I could manage on top, and a huge blue duvet jacket which had been supplied for Wim Verstraeten, with my feet wrapped in the detachable hood. Bertrand and I shared the jacket, because it was always warm and comforting to the pilot coming on duty. The difference was Bertrand wore the hood on his head.

We could live with it – but cold definitely saps the spirit. In the first fax of my stint on 11 March I complained that it had taken me half an hour to de-ice the fuel control unit in the ceiling of the central passage. Before, we had been able to clear it by scraping with a credit card, but now I had to nip away with pliers at the great chunks of ice which had built up on the burner valves. No. 3 electric valve was still jammed in the full open position, and No. 4 was jammed slightly open, so that the whole right side of that burner system had to be shut down. No. 1, on the left side, had jammed open twice in the previous two hours. I was scared that all the burners would soon be out of action and that our flight would come to an abrupt end. 'It would be really nice to know what is happening,' I faxed:

> The learning curve for juggling is quite steep up here. We will now make a video clip, assuming we can force a smile.

Alan's reply was by no means sympathetic:

> Brian: I go off duty at night to the sound of your moans. I come back on . . . to be faced by yet another bleating fax complaining that some bit of kit isn't working . . . Reading your messages has become so depressing that we have had to start a Real Message file and a Message No One Can Read Without Worrying file. We prefer the nice cheery messages that Bertie sends.

For all his sarcasm, he had to admit that nobody could yet explain what was wrong with the fuel system, and I became still more apprehensive when tank pair No. 6 ran out after only twenty-four hours and fifty minutes of use — which showed how much we had been having to burn. Then Alan made things still worse by telling me that Luc expected our speed to decay even further, from our present 45 knots to 35 or even 30. This, he assured me, was 'part of his game plan', and he was still estimating our total round-the-world time at twenty days. 'At your present rate of use,' he said, 'you should have enough propane to keep going past the necessary line of longitude in Morocco as far as Egypt.'

Was that estimate realistic? Or was he just saying this to cheer us up? It was all too easy to feel cynical.

To raise my own morale, I began composing limericks and faxing them down. By no means all were printable, or even very good, but one or two caught the prevailing atmosphere:

> *Of a hairy-faced pilot called Jones*
> *'Twas said that he frequently moans*
> *Of the burners all night,*
> *With no pilot light.*
> *The boss — he just sits there and groans.*

Alan hit back with:

> *One of those chaps flying Breitling*
> *Was dyslexic when it came to his pilotling.*
> *He went on to say*
> *That flying this way*
> *Over the Pacific was really quite frightening.*

The exchange of verse lifted my spirits. By then we had swung on to a heading of 155 — steeply southeast — and our speed was down to 35 knots. Even so, my next message to control was much more cheerful. 'Hello John, Old Bean,' it began:

> The moon appears in my porthole about every five minutes. Are you sure we are not flying in circles? The bed's wet again. So the sheet is hanging up to dry. Doesn't help much when it falls in the puddle on the floor. Come on, then — who wrote the ditty for Alan? It was far too clever for a Cameron executive.

Another boost came in the form of a fax from the indomitable Steve Fossett, who wrote, 'Dear Bertrand and Brian, Your flight is truly impressive. Your patience with the launch and slow trajectory are paying off. I hope you will enjoy a safe flight to Mexico.' Typical Steve, we thought — implying we would get no farther than Mexico. Our reaction was to phone Control immediately and say, '*We're* not stopping in Mexico!' Alan laughed and said, 'It's precisely because of faxes like this that you have to succeed.'

Our team on the ground had been consulting the makers of the valves for clues about how to get them functioning properly, and Kieran Sturrock suggested several ingenious possible methods for making the burners work better. In the end, however, he agreed that they must be frozen up, and the only way of sorting them out properly was for us to go down to low level, where the ice would melt, and make another EVA, during which we could thaw the valves out with hot water if necessary. 'When you EVA,' Alan wrote, 'throw out everything you don't need. Height will mean speed within the next few days.'

BERTRAND

The EVA was an extraordinary experience. We brought the balloon down to 6,000 feet, and below us the Pacific lay totally calm – absolutely no waves of any kind. Once again we were in the middle of nowhere. We looked at each other, and I said, 'Well, the last time we went outside, we were over a desert of sand. This time it's a desert of water – but this one's really frightening.'

It was early on a glorious sunny morning when we climbed out through the top hatch, and for a few moments we sat there awestruck by the utter silence – no cry of a bird, not the slightest sound of wind or sea. This time there were no icicles round the skirt of the balloon, but water soon started to pour down on us as sheet-ice melted from the inner surface of the envelope. As we had no hammer, Brian took the T-piece junction from the pipes of the auxiliary tanks and hit the ice coating from the solenoid switches on the defective burners. In our survival packs we had some chemical hand-warmers, so we squashed the gel contents around to start the reaction and tied the packs around the electronic valves.

We then discovered that the valve for the No. 9 tank pair was leaking and decided to bypass it by changing the hoses round, substituting the ones which had originally been on the auxiliary tanks – and which we had almost jettisoned during our first EVA, over North Africa. We must have been quite severely stressed, because we both had difficulty trying to think through the fuel system. We'd had so many confusing problems that we had to talk everything through, and we spent some time sitting out in the sun, saying, 'If we close this valve, how will the fuel transfer? If we've got a leak here, how can we bypass it?' We made no mistakes in effecting the repairs, but we erred on the side of caution.

We also threw overboard everything we didn't need, including used scrubbers (the lithium hydroxide filters for the cabin air system) and any unused ones we knew we could do without. Over went all the remaining sand ballast, the fresh food that had gone off – the meat in an advanced state of decomposition – and accumulated garbage. Altogether we shed 128 kilos of weight. Once again I cleaned the portholes with my improvised apparatus, and we moved one of the external video cameras so that it would film the front of the capsule and the bottom of the envelope. The whole exercise cost us about six hours.

Inside the gondola again, Brian sent down a report on what we had done, and ended:

> Laying along the outriggers to get to tank valve 14 A from the outboard side, because of the antenna tray, with Bertrand holding my foot, was not much fun. Anyway, we are very pleased with ourselves, and the gondola smells much nicer after some ten days or whatever inside. Now you are going to lock us up for another eleven days – bloody sadists.
>
> Totally alone and very surreal, sitting on top of the gondola 6,000 feet above blue, blue and more blue.

By now time and date had become thoroughly confusing. In the gondola we were still at 18:00 Zulu on 11 March, but dawn was already breaking, and if there had been anyone below, it would have been the morning of 12 March. In the centre of the instrument panel was a Breitling clock – a collector's item, borrowed from the company museum and at least fifty years old – with hands, showing only twelve hours. To keep us straight on Zulu time, behind the clock I fixed a long, slim piece of paper, with 'AM' on one side and 'PM' on the other, which we could slide back and forth to show whether it was morning or evening.

After the EVA Brian went to bed, leaving me in charge. Soon we were heading southeast at the highest flight level we had achieved so far

— 30,500 feet. I had expected the balloon to go higher, but that seemed to be its ceiling for the time being. In three days' time, our met men told us, we would need to go to 33,000 feet. On our maps the expanse of the Pacific looked terrifying. The first map showed one tiny strip of land on the left, and the rest was blue. The next map was blue from edge to edge. The third map was blue except for a small strip on the right — and as we were making only 35 knots it seemed we would take for ever to cross that vast expanse.

Our control team, obviously realizing we were not happy about our new track, sent reassuring messages, saying that they had spoken again to Oakland and Tokyo, and that Tokyo air traffic control had wished us good luck. Smiffy and C faxed:

> Just to let you know — we know how you feel about the change of the met plan, but we are getting very good vibes from Luc and Pierre. Have every confidence in their forecast. The fast winds will be worth waiting for.

When I spoke to Smiffy and told him how daunting our surroundings seemed, he passed on a fascinating e-mail message from Jan Abbott, an astrologer in Devon, who said that for the past two years she had been charting the attempts at round-the-world flights:

> Over the last six days I have been following your flight progress against the astrological chart cast for your take-off on 1 March. As the relevant planets on that day align with your own birth charts and the chart of the first-ever manned balloon flight, in 1783, the possibility of your success is great, and may be destined. I send my very best wishes. Safe journey, and hope your landing by the pyramids in Egypt brings you back to earth gently.

'Isn't that incredible?' Cecilia faxed. 'And to receive it just at this point in time!' Incredible indeed it was to get such a message at the moment of greatest doubt. Then came a fax to say that we had passed the 20,000 kilometre mark, and for a while my spirits went up again.

Not for long. Soon Alan was telling me that, although we had just completed one EVA, he might want us to do another almost immediately:

> It seems that you are still carrying some pieces of equipment that are of doubtful use. We may need to plan another EVA to get rid of those and absolutely everything you don't need – spare water, dirty clothes, excess filters. We have to get you to 36,000 feet if you want to be in North Africa on 22–23 March. Suggest you start planning now what you will be able to drop at next EVA . . . Sorry to nag, but it's a priority to get your weight reduced.

He also repeated that the Americans needed to be told our flight level every hour, but after I had told him that I could not get through to anyone on the radio, and that it was difficult to write faxes because I had no pilot light and had to keep standing up every few seconds to re-ignite the burners by hand, his tone softened:

> Bertrand: I am sorry you have to deal with some technical problems, and that the Pacific is so wide and the winds slow, but Dr Noble – the well-known psychiatrist who will shortly be opening an office in Lausanne – warns against allowing depression and tiredness to set in.
>
> I know we are sitting in comfort, and well fed, but the feeling here is very positive. Luc is close to betting a year's salary that he will get you to North Africa, but we will have these slow winds while we move you towards the tropical jet. I have seen the forecasts from the US computer, and they are brilliant – and you know I wouldn't lie to you.

After six years of collaboration, I knew I could trust Alan completely and was confident he would never hide the truth from me. We had gone through so many experiences together – and this adventure, if it came off, would be an extraordinary victory for him as well.

In spite of our uncertainties, I was able to enjoy the beauty of our surroundings. We had a wonderful, radiant sunset, and with the repositioned camera I was able to film it igniting the bottom of the envelope with fiery light. We noticed that when the burners lit, the air went up in one side of the hot-air cone, and we could see vapour from the burnt propane escaping from the mouth of the balloon on the other side.

That night I slept very well — despite dreaming that I was in a commercial airliner which had to ditch in the ocean. I remember the plane going down, and when I woke up I just hoped that the dream hadn't been a premonition.

Alan urged us to get the HF radio working, and suggested we try contacting the airfield on Wake Island, 600 nautical miles to the south-southeast, or any aircraft that might be flying from it. 'Don't worry about the press office or anything that is non-essential,' he wrote — and twice more he emphasized, 'Please remember to include flight levels with every message.'

BRIAN

The twelfth of March was one of my worst days. After the EVA I developed a ferocious headache, and in my diary I scribbled, 'Was completely useless and had to go to bed. Fitful sleep and had to get up to take Ponstan.' My first message to Control said, 'Alan — Just up from feeling absolutely terrible — much better now. Give me twenty minutes or so to get my head round the situation, and I'll come back to you.'

When I did fax again it was with a dire list of deficiencies. We couldn't raise anybody on the HF radio, I told him; the satphone wasn't working on either antenna; it was taking an age to stabilize the burners; our track was all over the place, and too much to the north. Nor, I wrote, was there much future in trying to shed more weight:

> The only significant weight left is the fuel — before we get to desperation stakes like getting rid of the high-pressure nitrogen tank. By my calcs, our ceiling should be in the order of FL 320, but obviously I'm about 3,000 feet out. In order to get to 360 we would need to lose another 1,500 kg — almost ten full tanks.
>
> Whilst you may seem confident down there, up here things are quite different. We are having to give ourselves a good talking-to in order to keep it all together. The positive thing is

that we definitely complement and support each other – so 100
per cent for CRM [crew resource management].

Then Alan sent a fax which really got my goat:

> You have been in the Oakland FIR since 155 degrees east. Aren't
> you reading your Aerad chart FEP 3? This FIR covers ten per cent of
> the surface of the globe. Don't you remember our exchange of
> messages about the Memorandum of Understanding? You wanted
> our assurance that we had read it. We had. Had you? The MOU
> refers to Oakland. So you're in the hands of the Yanks. Regards Alan.

That was too much. The atmosphere was getting nasty, and I hit back:

> Alan, my sense of humour failure warning light is flashing. I don't
> need lectures or criticism – just advice. OK? There are so many
> confusing things going on up here, and I'm freezing cold. I have
> good comms with Tokyo. Can't get Oakland. So I'm staying put.
> FL 263, 100 degrees magnetic, 31 knots. Brian.

Alan's reply was uncompromising:

> Brian – when I criticise you, you will be in no doubt. I pointed
> out – quite humorously, I thought – that you are strolling
> through air space that belongs to one air traffic unit, and have
> been doing so for many hours, and are not aware of it. You could
> have endangered your safety, and the safety of others. Not
> something to keep quiet about to preserve your sense of humour
> – unless you want to die laughing.
>   Better keep yourself warm and check the oxygen levels. Could
> you be hypoxic?

He went on to a detailed discussion of what could be wrong with the
valves, the autopilots and the linkage of the tanks. His message ended,
'Friends again?' But I was in no mood to be conciliatory:

> Alan – let me summarize things for you. I came on duty from a

fitful sleep with a headache. Bertrand was in a bit of a state, rather like me the day before yesterday. We were unable to relax and rationally discuss the problems at that time – mainly due to tiredness and stress over quite a few days. It was important for him to go to bed.

The phone doesn't work. The HF wasn't working. The pilot lights don't work. The fuel control unit is just one big lump of ice. We can't run the kettle and the HF together, so we are keeping warm the best we can. I have to leave the desk every two minutes or so to relight the burners and try to stabilize them, whilst trying to keep the balloon level.

I'm sure when the sun is up our spirits will rise, and hopefully our efficiency along with them. Until then we need all the help and advice you can give.

Never not friends. You just piss me off sometimes . . . Brian

Alan, realizing what a state we were in, came back with a much gentler message addressed to 'Brian, my old mucker, my old friend,' and saying: 'Sorry to have given you a hard time earlier. I wasn't fully *au fait* with the health problems.' He ran through various possible solutions for our burner problems, said he was consulting Pete Johnson and Kieran Sturrock, and suggested that we should go for another EVA to reconnect tank pairs 2 and 9 in their original coupling.

BERTRAND

Before the flight we had held many discussions with Alan about how relations between air crew and ground control tend to deteriorate after a few days' flight. The balloonists start to think that the control centre is not pulling on the same rope as they are, and both sides become angry with each other. We knew this had happened before, and within a few hours Brian and I realized that we were falling into a similar pattern. Alan, too, saw that the tension was the product of normal stress and nervousness, and tried to smooth things down.

I said to Brian, 'You know, it's good that Alan is able to play the role of the bastard, because he's got broad enough shoulders to take what we throw at him – and that's fine.' Brian laughed, and recovered his sense of humour – but in the preceding hours, for the first time during the flight, he really had lost it. We realized that his aggressive exchanges with Alan were a good way of discharging some of the anxiety that we had on board – a method of transferring some pressure from ourselves to him on the ground.

I wrote in my journal:

March 13 is an important day. The news is good. We still have to do forty-eight hours at low speed before picking up the jet which should bring us to Mauritania on the morning of the 19th – forty-eight hours crawling across the biggest desert in the world, the Pacific. I have to suppress every desire except to follow the path of the winds. But hope is coming back. Brian and I are making plans and dreams again. Maybe the most difficult thing is to control our impatience, and our tremendous desire to succeed.

Thinking of the immense distance of sea that we had to cross, and the two coasts so far apart, I felt highly emotional, and I remembered the Chinese ideograms used in the ancient *I-Ching* book which I had studied in February, before we took off. My teacher had explained to me one special paragraph about how one can learn to go through fear, to jump over the abyss. The Samurai, for instance, are taught to go beyond fear in order to become stronger and better connected to themselves; the hexagram of the Samurai shows a baby bird being pushed out of the nest, so that it has to learn to fly before it hits the ground. That hexagram is a very difficult one to master, but it is the one that produces the best results if you manage to go with it. Now, over the ocean, I had to go through my own fear and learn to fly: I had to dominate my own feeling of vertigo as I walked on the edge of the abyss.

Usually, in normal life, it is possible to avoid fear. Man does this by changing his activities or by taking medication or drugs. But here in mid-Pacific there was no escape, and this new experience was full of rich lessons. If you accept fear or anxiety instead of fighting it, you can learn to go through it and connect yourself to inner resources that will bring you a new confidence in life.

BRIAN

Added to everything else, I had always had a great fear of water. When I was a kid, I was a complete wimp when it came to water, and that was why I took to flying so well. I felt an affinity with the air, and from the start loved flying.

Still the e-mails were piling into the Breitling website:

Looking up to the sky, I wish you a good journey. And a safe return towards the earth, but not too soon. (Jonathan Adriaens, Belgium)

Hold on. The world is not too big. Just wind must be your friend. FLY FLY FLY FLY FLY FLY FLY FLY FLY FLY to finish. (Pavol Kvackay, Slovakia)

Congratulations gentlemen on your continuing success and good fortune as Zephyrus's sweet breath carries you gently around our beautiful earth – May a huge bottle of champagne and a hot shower await you – God bless. (Greg Eastlund, Minnesota, USA)

I am curious what are the toilet arrangement on board? (Dodo, t.a.)

Congratulations, you are now in one row with the Wright bros, Amelia Earhart etc. Maybe you can go non-stop to the moon by a balloon next time. See ya. (Hooly, Rotterdam)

One of the most stirring messages came from Neil Armstrong, who wished us good luck, and another memorable one, published on the Internet, reached us on 13 March:

Dear Bertrand and Brian, All of us at Virgin take our hats off to you for an incredibly bold flight. It really does look like you could do it this time. Look forward to greeting you back in Europe. Have a safe and very uneventful journey across the Pacific. May the winds be kind to you. Kind regards, Richard Branson.

BERTRAND

The message set me thinking about Branson. He is someone I admire, because he puts a lot of energy into everything he does, and he has done very well. Of course, when it comes to flying, he is more interested in breaking records than we are because we fly more for the fun of it. During the race to be first round the world, we were in an interesting relationship, each of us saying nice things about the other. Every time Richard was asked about me during interviews, he described me as a friend, said how much he liked me, and remarked on what a pity it was that he had not got to know me earlier as he would have asked me to fly with him.

In my own interviews I spoke of my admiration for him and said how friendly I found him. In winter 1997–8, when his envelope flew off on its own and the gondola of *Orbiter 2* fell from the crane, I got him on the phone and said, 'We should really fly together. You bring your gondola, I'll bring my envelope, and we'll make a balloon.' Only a joke perhaps, but it gives an idea of the good atmosphere that existed between us.

Hope came in the form of yet another forecast from Luc and Pierre. On Saturday 13 March they said our track would continue to be southeasterly and that we would see no improvement in speed above our miserable 35 knots. But then on Sunday, as the track backed from 145 degrees to 105, our speed would begin to pick up. By Monday we would be travelling due east at 100 knots, and on Tuesday our speed would increase to 120. At that rate it would be 'Saturday into Mauritania for dawn landing at 0 knots'.

'The other good news,' Pierre told us, 'is that in these equatorial latitudes the air is less dense, and you are higher than you think you are with an altimeter setting of 1013. Luc says that in real terms you have to add 3,000 feet to the height shown on the altimeter.'

Yet again Alan reminded us to 'REMEMBER FLIGHT LEVELS', and sought to encourage us by writing, 'Luc wants me to tell you that the met is getting better and better. He now predicts North Africa 19 March.'

In my journal, on 14 March, I wrote:

I believe that by surviving these days above the Pacific, surrounded by doubt, veering from hope to anxiety, we will be able to do a lot when we get back to normal life. At least we have discovered that inside ourselves we have resources to cope with many difficulties.

I was thinking of Peter Bird, a man of superhuman endurance, who rowed across the Pacific. His first two attempts failed, but on the third he rowed from San Francisco to Australia in four months, making an amazing film of himself on the way, talking to his camera. Then he tried to cross in the opposite direction, and disappeared in the ocean. After his death a friend of his in Dijon commissioned a trophy, in the form of a flight of titanium steps, to commemorate his extraordinary perseverance, and began awarding it annually to people who had made exceptional efforts. The first four recipients – Peter and three friends – all died trying to row the Pacific. Next Peter's friend gave it to someone who successfully crossed Antarctica on foot – and then, after the flight of *Orbiter 2*, he awarded it to me. I was really impressed by the knowledge that at some point we would cross Peter's track. I felt humble when I reflected that he had performed such incredible feats not with an agreeable companion, but alone. I wrote:

I want to remember what I am feeling right now for the rest of my life. We are crossing a desert of water, but I would not like to stay in it for forty days. In any case, it would take me more than forty days to learn to have more inner freedom, to let go more, to be less tense, to trust life, and trust the winds.

BRIAN

Early on 14 March Bertrand woke me so that we could make our third and final EVA. Kieran agreed with our theory that the link-up of fuel pipes which we had improvised during our second excursion had actually made things worse: as the balloon rotated slowly, the sun would strike the tanks on one side, warming them up, so that fuel automatically transferred itself from that side straight across to its cold partners opposite, and the burners would not work properly because they kept getting vapour instead of propane liquid. Our mission, now, was to re-establish the original connections and deal with the leak in another way.

We knew we would lose communications as we went down to low level, so before we started we told San Francisco what we were doing. Then, to save time and fuel, we descended only to 15,000 feet, and put on oxygen masks, connected by long tubes to our tank, before opening the top hatch. It took just a few minutes to rearrange the hose connections and jettison as much weight as we could. We kept only the food that we needed for five more days of flight and dropped everything else, including a lot of water and even most of our spare filters. Alan wanted us to throw out spare clothes as well, but that would have improved our ceiling by only five or ten feet. Because a great deal of water was falling from the envelope, we stayed at low level for a while to get rid of most of the ice.

What we could not know was that Oakland had become so worried by our silence that they had declared an air–sea rescue alert. Strict international rules govern such situations. Normally, if any aircraft is thirty minutes overdue, air controllers automatically progress to what they call the Distress Phase, and launch a rescue sortie. Especially in the Pacific, every minute is critical because the distances are so great. Oakland, telephoning Geneva, said that because they had lost all contact with the balloon they were preparing to move into the Distress Phase. Alan asked them to wait, explaining that we had merely gone down to do the EVA and that he felt sure we were not in trouble. But, to his dismay, when he asked if Oakland had any aircraft flying that might be able to get in touch with us, the controller answered, 'We have no plane in that region, sir. Nobody ever goes there.' Alan was horrified. 'Nobody ever goes there?' he echoed. Not the least of his anxieties was the colossal bill which would land on Breitling if rescue aircraft did take off from the Marshall or Midway Islands: he knew it would run into hundreds of thousands of dollars.

Luckily, before that happened we re-established contact. At 19:52 Zulu, as we were climbing again, I faxed Control to say 'EVA successfully completed' and gave a few details of what we had done. A message from Jo warned us that Alan was 'heading for some supper with steam coming out of his ears, so he might slap your wrists later'. I replied:

Reference Alan's smoking ears – we're not monkeys up here. We told San Francisco exactly what we were doing. We spoke to them during the descent, and then called them all the way up on the climb. Eventually got them at around flight level 200. We had also agreed with the Control Centre that during communications loss, as long as our EPIRB [emergency beacon] was not transmitting, we were OK.

I was annoyed that our professionalism had been criticized when the loss of communication was really not our fault. Later I reported to John:

Threw out most of our food this morning, so not much choice now. Bertrand won't open the *pâté truffé* until we're over USA – I told him I'm not going round again. So it's pasta with cheese sauce once more. Burners are huffing and puffing a bit, have to keep getting out of the seat to re-light them. Kieran should know there's a design flaw here: we should either have sparkers on the front panel, or an electric chair-lift to get me to the burner control panel – but a sports model, because it doesn't half go *whumph* when a couple of shots of unburned propane go up there.

In an attempt to solve that problem, during one of his shifts on duty Bertrand built an ingenious connection made of wire and string that allowed us to open the manual valve from our seats. I, too, made a small innovation designed to ease our life. I took a mirror and lashed it in position on the instrument panel, angled up so that I could see through the top hatch whether or not the burners were working without turning round. This was particularly useful at night – and during the day, by repositioning the mirror, I could keep an eye on the bottom of one appendix, also without getting up.

BERTRAND

While our telephone and fax were out of action, I suddenly heard an Air France pilot talking on the radio to Tahiti in French. So I put in a call, got Tahiti first, then the pilot, and we spoke in French. I asked if he would call a friend of mine, Gérard Feldzer, President of the French Aero Club and a captain on Airbus. 'Oh,' said the pilot, 'I know him very well. I'll give him a message.' As soon as he got to Tahiti he sent off an e-mail, so that Gérard received greetings from the middle of the Pacific.

After the EVA the wind swung us to the east and our speed increased to 60 knots. A form of countdown had begun, because on the GPS the degrees of longitude – which had been increasing steadily with our easterly progress until we reached the international date line – were now decreasing, from 180 west towards the distant and magical figure of 9 west, which marked the finishing line over Mauritania.

By 02:00 Zulu on 15 March we were doing 70 knots, and our speed kept creeping up: 73, 74, 76. We were finally entering the jet stream, and all round us were gorgeous colours. The balloon was flying so high, at 32,000 feet, that we seemed to be enveloped in pink veils of cirrus. My notebook records that we were surrounded by cirrus clouds and residual CB heads, cut off from the main clouds by the wind. Up there, at our ceiling, the balloon formed a cloud of its own consisting of very small crystals; and as this kept direct sunlight off the envelope, I had to burn repeatedly. With every push of propane moisture condensed outside the envelope, so that a dark cloud, like smoke, formed around the balloon and came along with us. It was rather unpleasant, and to get rid of it I went down slightly.

Worries about fuel grew ever more insistent. In my journal I wrote, 'I feel the kind of tension I would if I were spending money borrowed from the bank, without any hope of being able to pay it back. Every push of propane is something we're losing for ever.' Our reserves seemed perilously small – we were down to six pairs of full tanks – and we had thousands of miles to go. We had burnt two-thirds of our propane in covering only half our course. And the higher we flew, the shorter the time each pair lasted: from the record duration of 41 hours, we were down in the twenties. Everything now depended on the weathermen: if they were right, we still had a chance; if they were wrong, we were doomed to fail. We just had to believe them and their computerized models.

BRIAN

The fifteenth of March, our fifteenth day in the air, was a more cheerful day altogether – partly because Bertrand chose to believe that one of the air controllers at Oakland was in love with him. As a joke, Bertrand had more or less made it a rule that we would never talk about women because, cooped up as we were in the gondola, it would be too cruel. But suddenly we were in touch with this woman, who had an incredibly sweet voice. When she kept calling, hour after hour, to ask our position, I reported to Control: 'Good comms with San Francisco. One of the controllers is a lady, and Bertrand is sure she fancies him.' Her presence certainly stimulated us to put in positional reports more often, in the hope that we would hear her voice again.

The downside of the day was that, from some inexplicable source, I caught a cold and a sore throat, and also got a mysterious soft swelling on the back of one hand. At least the minor ailments gave us another chance to open Bertrand's expensive medical kit, which had scarcely been touched. A dose of paracetamol reduced the cold symptoms, but the swelling presented more of a problem. Fearing that it might have been caused by an infection, Bertrand said that if it didn't go down in a couple of days, he would prescribe antibiotics. But I – thinking of all the champagne that would be flowing if we got round – resisted the idea, as being on antibiotics would deny me my share. Instead, I rubbed emu oil on the swelling and waited to see what would happen.

On the ground, our controllers were on a bit of a high. 'Things really ARE looking up,' faxed Smiffy and C. 'Pierre has told us it's such a good jet track he's making plans for you to continue round again. What a scoop!' Limericks came back into fashion and flew in both directions. I was pleased with one I sent down:

> Wiv Smiffy and C in control
> My mate said, 'They're out on parole
> From the Betty Ford clinic.'
> I fink it's a gimmick:
> Next week they'll be back on the dole.

The Smiths lost no time in returning the ball:

> There was a young girl from Madras
> Who had the most beautiful ass –
> Not round and pink,
> As you might think:
> It was grey, had long ears and ate grass.

For as long as everything was going well, our messages remained on a high level of facetiousness and ribaldry. At that moment my only real problem was the temperature. 'I'm at flight level 310,' I told John at 06:50:

> It's jolly dark and jolly cold. I've got three pairs of trousers on, a pair of Jo's knickers (so she's probably not wearing any), and a rather large jacket that Wim had last year. I'm just considering whether to eat or put my balaclava on. Can't do both, of course. Wondering whether I can put the hand-warmers in my boots, or should I keep them in case the burner valves freeze again?

Lucky for me that I did not know what was happening in Geneva. At Swiss Control Greg Moegli was on duty and trying to make contact with his opposite numbers in Mexico. As he said afterwards, 'The guy didn't speak English well, and when he couldn't understand what I was saying, he started to sound aggressive. So I said, "Stand by. I'll call you back in twenty minutes." '

Greg rushed home and woke up his wife, Claudia, who is from Colombia. 'Speak to this guy,' he said, and she talked to him in Spanish. The Mexicans then became very helpful, but they pointed out that the balloon had no clearance to cross their country; so at 3 a.m. Claudia had to sit down and type a letter in Spanish, which Greg immediately faxed to Mexico City and Cuba. Greg feared that Cuba might present a big problem, but Claudia managed to charm the Commandant General of the civil aviation authority and, four hours later, clearances came through from both places.

BERTRAND

By the end of Sunday, 15 March, we were heading for Mexico at 73 knots, exactly as Luc and Pierre had predicted we would. Our confidence in them was fully justified, and hope ran high again. 'We are very happy to be here,' I faxed Control, 'even if it is sometimes difficult.' I had been listening to a CD of the Eagles, and the words of the song 'Hotel California' – 'We're prisoners here of our own devices' – seemed to apply perfectly to Brian and myself.

Then Luc advised us to gain one more degree southwards to pick up speed by positioning ourselves in the centre of the jet. We did move south, but, as it turned out, slightly too much: the jet was probably spreading, and we strayed towards the outside of it. When we were above the clouds, we had the impression we were being pushed northeast, but below the clouds we went the opposite way — illustrating again that a jet stream is not a single, unified mass of wind, but probably includes a variety of air currents that wind round its core in a spiral.

None of us could know it at the time, but that was the only mistake Luc or Pierre ever made, and it was the beginning of our worst problem.

CHAPTER TEN

CAST ADRIFT

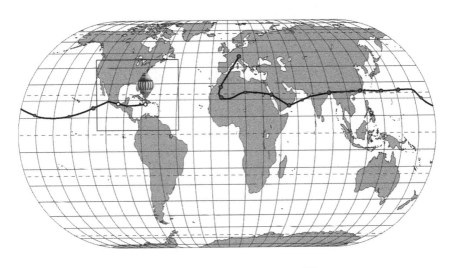

17–18 March
Mexico, Caribbean

Southern Mexico
08:00 Z
FL 340
54 knots

Jamaica
08:00 Z
FL 350
56 knots

BERTRAND

On 16 March I went to bed just after sunset, but I was cold in the bunk, and it seemed to take me hours to get to sleep. Then I had a very strange dream: Brian and I had got round the world but were the only people who knew we had done it. We had to avoid everybody until the official ceremony – I wasn't even been able to say hello to anyone.

As usual, Brian woke me a few hours before dawn. He was holding a flashlight to his mouth, as if it were a microphone, and said, 'Hello, Dr Piccard. How do you feel about being the long-distance record holder for ballooning?' I played my part, as if in an interview, and said, 'Well – the distance record will only be a consolation prize if we don't make the whole circuit. So I really hope we'll get round.' Then I added, 'Wasn't that a good answer for someone who has just got out of bed?' 'Yes,' he said, 'it was a brilliant answer – and this is Brian Jones, speaking in *Breitling Orbiter 3* for Radio X.' What I didn't realize was that he had set up the video camera and was filming the whole performance.

During the night we had beaten Steve Fossett's distance record of 14,236 miles, made before he came down in the Coral Sea in August 1998 – although in a balloon you don't really *beat* anything or anybody.

Your passage is too gentle for such a term. Rather, I think of every record as a gift of the wind. Anyway, a lot depends on how the calculation is done. In terms of sheer distance we had outstripped the record long before, but the FAI (Fédération Aéronautique Internationale) had decreed that, in determining total distance, flights must be broken up into segments and that a segment only counted if its length was at least half the earth's radius – that is, 3,000 kilometres (or 2,000 miles). Our initial passage down to Morocco was too short to count as a segment, so our distance was measured directly from Château d'Oex to Egypt, losing us 6,000 kilometres.

During the night the balloon had exceeded 100 knots for the first time, and in the middle of the day I reported a 'personal speed record in a balloon' of 102 knots. Luc and Pierre were in ecstasies: they had brought off their incredible gamble of sending us so far south and were confident we would remain in the jet all the way to Africa. Brian and I really thought we were going to make it, and in all media interviews everyone sounded euphoric. Everything suggested that we would come hurtling home, and the press started to say that we were on our way to success as we 'just had the Atlantic left'. In fact we still had 8,000 miles to go.

BRIAN
The faxes show how spirits picked up all round, and Sue caught the general tone with her umpteenth limerick:

> There were two balloon pilots over the Pacific
> Who said, 'Now we must be specific.
> With a record to break,
> We could do with a cake –
> And a glass of champagne would be t'riffic.

I'd never dreamt that we would get all the way round, but I had been praying inwardly that we would at least reach the USA. If we conquered the Pacific, we would automatically have the distance record – and probably the duration record – which in itself would be a triumph. Already we had accomplished an unbelievable flight, and even if it ended west of the Atlantic we would still be fêted. Realizing that we couldn't now fail altogether was a tremendous relief to me.

One result of crossing the Pacific was that the Atlantic suddenly seemed far less daunting. In fact, ridiculous as it sounds, it seemed such a small challenge as to be almost insignificant.

BERTRAND

All through 16 March we continued eastwards at high speed, flying at our ceiling of 34,000 feet. But one major disadvantage of travelling in the jet stream is that cirrus clouds come with you, shading out direct sunlight. And because we were in cirrus and the balloon was forming its own cloud around the envelope, we had to keep burning a lot to maintain altitude even in daylight. The result was that we were getting through an awful amount of fuel, and for the first time we had to start using our lithium batteries at night because the sun wasn't charging the main batteries enough during the day. To save power, we sent messages to Geneva by fax (which uses very little current) and asked them to inform Oceanic Control in Oakland about our position. So I lost contact with the amazingly beautiful woman – as I'm sure she was – who had been fancying me.

Geneva was getting position reports automatically every hour from our Capsat system, and once we had established the relay procedure, all we had to do was to fax them on the half hour with our flight level and a confirmation of our position. They would then pass on details to Oakland, telling them precisely where we were. The system was a great boon to us because it meant we didn't have to monitor the HF radio continuously and could listen to music on CD. To be constantly tied to the radio was frustrating because whenever one of us was asleep, the other had to switch off the loudspeaker and listen through headphones, and the leads were so short that we couldn't reach either the kettle or the burner controls with the headset on.

Then came the first hint of trouble. Having pushed us farther to the south to stay in the centre of the jet, Luc and Pierre suddenly told us we were going *too* far south: we needed to pull our heading back from 84 to 80 degrees.

In the afternoon Oakland Oceanic Control handed us over to the Mexican control centre at Mazatlán. 'Mexican ATC is happy,' Alan told us. 'So are the Cubans. And New York is orgasmic at the thought of having you in their airspace over the Atlantic.' The media were behaving as if we had already completed our mission. 'Garfield Kennedy, ITN and NBC are planning to put chase planes in the air over Mexico,' Alan faxed. He continued:

> Unfortunately, you will arrive over Mexico at dusk and be out over the Caribbean before daylight. Garfield will want to attempt to download the good video footage again. Last time they got no pictures, only sound. Could you please follow the wiring round and make sure that all connections are good. They can't say what is wrong – only that we should check everything and make certain the green light is on on the transmitter under the desk. Many thanks.

Later that day I encountered another problem. Luc wanted us to climb still higher, so I tried to shed weight by dropping two empty tanks – 10A and 10B. I saw 10A fall away all right, but I never saw 10B go, though it made the normal noise of a tank being released, and in some alarm I reported to Control that it might be stuck.

Our method of ditching the tanks was to pass an electrical current through the bit of a soldering iron. The nylon tape holding the tank in place was wound round the bit of the iron and held fast by a spring. When the bit became hot it melted through the tape, releasing the tank. But when this one failed to drop off, I couldn't tell what had happened. Through the dome of the top hatch I could see that the retaining strap was still tight, but not why.

When Alan heard about the situation, he too became worried. 'Maybe when Brian is awake you should both jump up and down to shake the gondola,' he advised, and went on:

> I am serious about this suggestion, because it would be terrible if the tank was to drop over Mexico. Also suggest when you talk with Garfield in the chase plane that you ask him to count the number of tanks on each side – but don't tell him why! If the tank is stuck, you will need to go down and outside to see if you can release it manually while still over water.

BRIAN

We didn't have long to deal with the problem because we were only a few hours from the Mexican coast. The idea of another EVA seemed outrageous. We were flying at 34,000 feet and 105 knots: if we went down, we would lose the jet stream – and probably our whole flight. At the very least, a four- or five-hour delay would cost us 500 or 600 miles and a big expenditure of fuel. But we were prepared to make the sacrifice, and fail in our mission, to avoid injuring or killing anybody on the ground. The dilemma was torture for us.

We talked to the technicians at the control centre, but nobody could throw much light on what the cause of the problem might be. Because there had been so much ice around the cylinders, we first thought that the rogue tank must be frozen into place. If so, there should be no problem because we were going to pass over Mexico at night, when the temperature would be well below zero, and there would be no chance of the ice melting and the tank falling away.

All the same, following Alan's instructions, we tried to dislodge the tank by jumping from side to side in unison, one of us at the front of the capsule, the other at the back. We certainly got the gondola rocking, and we could hear the full cylinders clanking against its sides – which suggested that they were loose, and not iced up. But nothing fell. Through the outrigger bars we could see that the strap that held 10B in place was still under tension, so we assumed the tank was well secured. Concluding that the straps must have been routed wrongly and that there was no chance of the cylinder falling on its own, we felt very relieved that we didn't have to go out again and could carry on safely. In fact (as we discovered just before landing) heat had welded the burnt edge of tape into a hard lump, which was too thick to pull through the eye of the weighing mechanism, making it jam.

But Alan was still not satisfied. He advised us to try various other moves, suspecting that the cylinder had become wedged between its neighbours. If that was so, he faxed, we might have to consider an early EVA, possibly on oxygen at high level. 'Warning:' he added, 'very soon you will have an island below, or almost below. Check the position carefully on your charts before any drop.' After all our efforts, the strap still appeared to be tight.

In spite of the problem, and the major anxiety it was causing us, there was great excitement in the control centre. 'Hi, guys,' Cecilia faxed. 'Enthusiasm and spirits are running high throughout the world in support of your flight! Thought I'd share a few of the messages that have come through on the Internet:

Go on! Do it! (Karl, Bulach, Switzerland)

You guys are a great source of encouragement for people with dreams. PLEASE LAND IN EGYPT, by the Giza Pyramids. You can make it! God bless all your excellent team. (Nabil Mikhail, Cairo, Egypt)

Beware, free-range chicken farm by the Pyramids. (Tom Holt Wilson)

Hello, this is Apron Control Crew from Zurich airport. All the best. You will make it!'

The mention of the chicken farm was a reference to the occasion when, during a festival at Northampton, with eighty-odd balloons taking part, I inadvertently flew over a chicken house and was banned for the rest of the event — no mean humiliation for the chief flying instructor. The incident has pursued me ever since.

That night, after seven days over water, we at last made landfall by crossing the coast of Mexico. From 34,500 feet I could see nothing below us, but I was elated and sent down my latest offering:

> *The girls in Mexico City*
> *I'm told are incredibly pretty.*
> *But we're just passing by*
> *In the Mexican sky.*
> *Dammit — it seems such a pity.*

In the early hours of 17 March I reported:

Contact with Mexico City on VHF. Huh — so that little puddle was what they call the Pacific. Thanks for the Internet messages. It's really nice to know that so many folks are following our little jaunt.

Soon, however, trouble set in. To maintain our extreme altitude I was having to burn constantly, and our latest pair of tanks were about to go dry after only sixteen and a half hours. If the remaining four pairs did no better, clearly we were not going to make the Atlantic. 'Could be ice, or just the burners at this altitude,' I faxed. 'We need to ask Luc if there is any chance of achieving this speed at a lower level, otherwise we could be in the dwang.'

Then came the worst shock. We were already well inland when I felt the gondola twitch and heard a faint noise. 'I'm pretty sure we just lost the tank that was hung up,' I reported – and I gave our precise position in case someone should later find the tank, or, worse, the damage it had caused. Bertrand – in bed at the time – also heard the noise, felt a flush of adrenaline course through his entire body and pulled the pillow over his head. Later he told me he could not go back to sleep because of the terrible visions racing through his mind.

It was a dreadful moment. If we'd killed somebody, the whole flight would be ruined and our dream destroyed. After that, the night was full of worries – about the tank, our fuel, our speed, our heading. At 05:10 I reported:

At FL 335 track is 095 – too far to the south, I fear. This is a really tricky one. Tank pair 3 is still going, but I'm sure it's running on vapour. With the size of these tanks there seems to be an enormous amount of vapour. Therefore difficult to assess fuel usage until I go on to a new pair. I am already south of Luc's target for 06:00 Zulu by about half a degree, so I assume too far south is bad.

I think I'm most concerned about the fuel situation, though, if the Atlantic crossing needs to be high. Will let you know what transpires. Hope we don't get our collar felt by Mexican police-man for hostile acts from the air with regard to that tank. It looks as if it fell over the lower part of the mountains, according to the map. Fingers crossed.

Messages flashed up and down as I urgently sought advice on what compromise to make between height, speed and direction. At 06:10 I sent down my latest assessment:

> Pair 3 lasted nineteen hours to absolutely empty. They started in the middle of last night at 10:30 Zulu. Sunrise was at 14:00 Zulu. They have lasted until 05:30 Zulu. We did quite a lot of burning during the day. It seems that when we are in the jet there is often stratus/cirro stratus above us. There is no doubt, I think, that we do have to burn more fuel above, say, 30,000 feet. So if the last four pairs give similar performance, they will last until 12:00 Zulu on Saturday – that is, completely out of fuel, with no landing reserve, of course.
>
> I think we would use less fuel if we managed to stay clear of cloud, and/or could fly at around FL 300. I don't know how much, so the trade-off between speed and altitude is a difficult one . . . Down to Luc's and Pierre's calculations now, I suppose. But the gut says we have to go for it.

Along with all the other irritations, the alarm on the burner control monitor had started going off every minute even though nothing was wrong, and I faxed for immediate instructions from Kieran on how to disable it without damaging anything else. In due course he faxed back, and I managed to quell the noise by delving into the mass of wires in the burner control panel – though not before it had started going off every twenty seconds. In spite of the difficulties, I was enjoying things and told John and Debbie, 'Never a dull moment, is there? We're certainly having to fight for it.' I was becoming more and more preoccupied with the question of whether or not we had the resources to tackle the Atlantic, but still I felt fairly buoyant. At 09:34 I told Alan, who had just returned to the control centre:

> Tank Pair 9 [which we had reckoned to be empty] still going after four hours. Every little helps. Assuming we are going for the Atlantic, would like to be kept abreast of current thinking and be part of the decision-making process, please. Unfortunately we can't see the tank which was hanging on. The dome is just not tall

enough, even trying to use a mirror. I'm pretty sure I felt it go, though . . . One of the webbing straps is gone, whereas before we could see it . . . Hope to God we didn't hit anything.

Alan, trying to analyse why we were using so much fuel, reckoned that at some time during the past twenty-four hours we must have accidentally pushed the balloon through its ceiling and caused it to vent helium, thus reducing its lift and forcing us to burn more often. Ice on the envelope would not make much difference, he assured us – but he was very concerned about fuel. Advising us to come down from 34,000 to 33,000 feet, he added:

> It is VITAL that you do not push the ceiling. You need to squeeze every last gasp of propane from each tank, and monitor fuel use constantly. Our [computer] programme still says you can complete the circumnavigation with a little to spare, but we need good wind speeds and no further increase in fuel consumption.

By 10:00 Zulu I was exhausted, and faxed, 'Bertrand up now, so both active for a while. I think I'm going to let him put me under a spell tonight. If I don't sleep soon, my skin is going to be terrible for the homecoming.' Then, as an ominous last thought, I added, 'FL 335, but we've lost 10 knots and gained five degrees right.'

BERTRAND
It was so cold in the bunk that even with two sleeping bags together, one inside the other, I was still shivering and only dozed lightly. When Brian woke me, he told me the balloon had burnt a tremendous amount of propane and that our chances of reaching Africa seemed poor. Soon he went to bed and left me alone in the cockpit, with my stomach full of butterflies.

I think I had been undermined by the cold. Whatever the cause, my morale hit rock bottom that morning and I saw no beauty in the dawn as the sun rose over the wooded mountains of Mexico. Our speed dropped dramatically and our track veered from due east to nearly 110 degrees: we were no longer heading for Africa but for Venezuela, and final disaster threatened. Even when Luc came on the phone and said,

'Don't worry – your trajectory will swing to the left, and in eighteen hours you'll pick up the jet stream again', I found it very hard to believe him.

A temporary lift arrived in the form of a message from Buckingham Palace, relayed by Alan, who added 'I'm not joking' at the end of it:

> His Royal Highness the Duke of Edinburgh requests the company of Dr Bertrand Piccard and Mr Brian Jones when he visits Cameron Balloons in Bristol on 1 April 1999.
>
> If Dr Piccard and Mr Jones are successful in completing their round-the-world balloon flight, the Duke will be accompanied by Her Majesty the Queen.

'Wonderful to see the Queen if we succeed,' I replied, 'but even more wonderful to succeed.' Not being in a good mood, I added over the phone, 'I like people who believe in us whether we succeed or not. So if the Queen is waiting to see what happens before she decides whether or not to visit us, she'd better not come!' Alan laughed and said, 'Bertrand, generally speaking, you're right, but the Queen is an exception.'

By then I was direly worried by our speed, which had fallen to 42 knots, and by our track of 100 degrees, which had swung back a little but was still too much south. 'When is the jet going to help us again?' I wanted to know. To take my mind off our present anxieties, I asked about the new duration record claimed by Andy Elson before he came down in the Sea of Japan, and whether we stood to beat it. John answered:

> Andy's record claim is seventeen days, eighteen hours and thirty-five minutes. Per Lindstrand has claimed an altitude record of 11,095 metres (we think you have probably exceeded that!). Dick Rutan's round-the-world flight [in the powered *Voyager* aircraft] was 41,000 kilometres.
>
> Luc is happy with your track, but has warned that speed will not pick up for twenty-four hours. However, this has been accounted for in his plan, and he is still expecting the round-the-world to be OK for Saturday.

At that very moment, a ceremony to celebrate Colin and Andy's flight was being held at Camerons in Bristol. When Don Cameron congratulated the crew on their new absolute duration record, Andy responded with a wry smile, 'Until bloody tomorrow!'

In spite of these various encouragements my spirits remained low, not least because I had begun to feel very strange. For some reason I couldn't explain I was completely out of breath, panting even when I had made no physical effort. As time went on I became more and more uncomfortable – and then, well before his rest period was up, Brian emerged from the bunk looking white and unsteady.

'I can't breathe,' he said.

'I can't either,' I told him. We were both shaken by our sudden disability. Soon I felt so ill that I called Control on the satellite phone and, hearing that Michèle was there, asked to speak to her. That was probably a mistake, for at the sound of her voice I broke down and burst into tears.

'Can you imagine,' I sobbed, 'it looks as though we're going to fail *now*, so close to our goal. After all this effort . . . We're going more and more to the south and we're running out of fuel. We can't see any way out of this problem. We're never going to make it.'

Michèle was very sympathetic, but she remained perfectly calm. 'I don't understand,' she said. 'The weathermen are confident you're going to get back to the jet.' She was certain everything would work out all right. Her good sense steadied me a little, but still I felt very ill.

That was also my first chance in ten days of speaking to Swiss Radio, which had been broadcasting my father live from the studio every afternoon. So I phoned them and gave a short commentary: 'I am in the cockpit. Brian is trying to sleep. We're both out of breath and it's really not the best of days.' When they heard me gasping and hardly able to talk, everyone on the ground became extremely anxious and started to call doctors and specialists for advice. It was all too easy for them to visualize horrific scenarios: the two pilots falling unconscious and silent as the balloon drifted away southwards, out of control, to vanish for ever in the wastes of the ocean.

Brian and I, though uncomfortable, were quite clear-headed. We knew where we were and what we were doing. We could calculate perfectly well. But Control, not being sure of that, started asking obvious questions to test us. At first Brian didn't realize what they were doing and became angry. When Alan asked him, 'When's your birthday?' he burst out with, 'For Christ's sake! We've got enough fucking trouble up here without you worrying about when my birthday is!' Alan persisted, and Brian said, 'Well, it's the twenty-seventh of March.'

'OK. What's your phone number?'

'For fuck's sake, Alan . . . ' And then he suddenly realized that they were trying to check whether we were hypoxic – short of oxygen – whereupon he laughed and calmed down.

Our symptoms were not those of hypoxia. Nor did it seem we were suffering from another possible problem – a build-up of carbon dioxide in the atmosphere of the gondola. The digital read-outs of the CO_2 monitors had not moved at all, and neither of us had a headache. One sensor, on top of the bunk, had been covered with clothes and so may not have been working; but the other was right at the front of the capsule, behind the instrument panel, and was probably functioning properly. In spite of the reassuring readings, we felt we were slowly being asphyxiated.

BRIAN

While in bed I had been finding it hard to breathe, but it wasn't until I got up that I realized something was seriously wrong. As I looked out through the curtain I saw Bertrand sitting in the right-hand pilot's seat, slumped against the bulkhead, gasping like a fish.

When he started talking to Michèle in French, I couldn't follow what they were saying, but clearly he was distraught and in a hell of a state. I realized we were both suffering from accumulated stress, though luckily I had slept reasonably well and wasn't feeling too bad at that moment. 'Look,' I said, 'it's all right. You're knackered, so get yourself into bed.'

Off he went, burying himself in three sleeping bags, with all his clothes on and wearing an oxygen mask connected by tube to our central supply. Every five or ten minutes, wearing my own oxygen mask, I went to look at him to make sure he hadn't died in the bunk.

On the ground, people were telephoning doctors and specialists in a frantic search for clues as to what could be wrong. Alan faxed:

> Brian, I am talking with the top professor in Switzerland. He wants to know if you have the drug Nifedipine on board. This is used to help prevent something called pre-oedema. He is concerned that your symptoms may be those of early pulmonary oedema [an accumulation of fluid in the lungs], which could be serious.
>
> We recommend you descend to FL 250, or less, until we have further medical discussions. You should also increase oxygen content of atmosphere – but be careful not to make it explosive. Can also use bottled oxygen for direct delivery. Please report results. Back soon, Alan.

As I sat at the pilot's desk, I kept thinking, 'I *don't* feel at all well, but it's hardly surprising after what we've been through,' and I tried to accept the breathlessness as just another discomfort. Then, with the benefit of the oxygen, I gradually began to feel better.

As my head cleared, I thought, 'Well – screw the instruments. They may not be working. I'm going to change the filters and see what happens. So I changed both the CO_2 and the carbon filters, and in a few minutes things started to improve.

Through all this I was still having to fly. We had been at 34,400 feet, but I kept finding that the balloon wanted to go down and was having to burn every twenty seconds to maintain altitude. So I settled at 32,000 feet and, after consulting Alan about other possible flight levels, I added:

> If Michèle is there, please tell her Bertrand is OK. He is still in bed and is on oxygen. He was a little emotional on the phone.
>
> Got your message re oedema. I'll ask Bertrand when he wakes. But we have both been on constant-flow oxygen for half an hour, and I feel much better. Cabin oxygen level now 18.9 per cent – equivalent to 26.9 per cent at sea level. I will be careful, but we don't want to jeopardize the flight unnecessarily.

The balloon has stabilized reasonably well around FL 320. I am certainly using a lot less fuel at this level, and have 100 degrees, 38 knots.

Alan replied:

Luc is happy with your float altitude of around 320. If we lose a little speed but save a lot of fuel, it's a good strategy. Track is also OK.

We are considering whether you might be suffering from long exposure to styrene [in the glue used to bind the shell of the gondola]. To clear that, you could de-pressurize at altitude, and re-pressurize using nitrogen and lox. However, this might be a wild goose chase.

Please ask Bertrand to stop calling radio and TV stations. His breathing problem is now the talk of Switzerland, and we are telling the media that you are both too busy and tired to talk to them.

To re-pressurize, we would have released oxygen for one second and nitrogen for four seconds, and repeated the process until correct pressure was obtained, creating a mixture of 20 per cent oxygen and 80 per cent nitrogen. In the end, though, we had no need to do this.

The one positive result of our discomfort was that everyone on the ground at last realized we were not having a picnic but were engaged in a difficult and dangerous endeavour. To the public, everything had perhaps seemed too easy until that moment.

Control had phoned the manufacturers and discovered that styrene can in certain unusual situations act as a depressant and can also cause difficulty in breathing. For a few moments this seemed to fit the bill. Although not exactly depressed, we were tired, frightened and saddened by forebodings of failure – and we were certainly having trouble with our respiration. But when we looked back on our mysterious affliction, we decided that the Swiss professor's diagnosis had probably been correct and that we were suffering from a pre-oedema of the lungs brought on by breathing exceptionally dry air for days on end. It was so cold inside the gondola that all moisture was condensing on the hatches, and the moisture content of the air was very low – only about

29 per cent. Breathing air like that when we were tired and cold could have caused the condition. When we put on masks, the oxygen helped, obviously, but the masks also trapped moisture, which gave further relief. Bertrand had included drugs for oedema in his medicine chest, but we didn't take anything because we were so uncertain.

After checking Bertrand again and finding that he was still comfortable, I called Michèle myself. I didn't know what had passed between them, but I wanted to reassure her. 'Don't worry,' I told her. 'Bertrand's OK. He's gone to bed, he's on oxygen, and whatever this crisis is, we'll get through it.'

'Thank you, Brian,' she said. 'You're a very nice man.'

I also spoke to Jo, who came up with a wonderfully moving remark: 'If love and best wishes could be your fuel, you'd now be on your second lap.'

I asked Jo to contact the head of the RAF Aeromedical Centre at Boscombe Down, who had put us through our hypoxia drills in training. He thought our symptoms pointed to carbon dioxide poisoning – except that neither of us had a headache, normally the first sign of excessive CO_2 in the atmosphere.

BERTRAND

In spite of the cold and the bulky mask, I fell into a deep sleep and woke two hours later much refreshed. Physically, things were better, but we were in a dilemma. I still wasn't sure what was for the best. Should we fly high to achieve a better speed and track? Or should we fly low in order to use less fuel and have more time to think? The weathermen wanted us to go high, but Alan was insistent that we burn less fuel.

While I was asleep Brian had brought the balloon lower, but our speed had fallen drastically. He had done exactly what Control had instructed, yet we felt powerless as we headed more and more to the south, being pushed further away from the jet.

A friend of mine, Pierre Steiner, a doctor who practises hypnosis, had heard me panting during the radio interview and had an intuition that he must help me; so at 10 p.m. local time in Geneva he went to the control room and asked to see Pierre Eckert. The met man was a bit surprised, as were the controllers, who thought this stranger might be some sort of freak. But Pierre Eckert came through on the satellite phone and asked, 'Do you want to speak to him?'

'Of course!' I exclaimed. 'Immediately!'

So the second Pierre came through and gave me a hypnosis session over the phone. He knew me very well because we had conducted some workshops and training sessions together, and he knew my 'safe places' – a technical term that means the thought, feeling, image or memory in which you feel safe and comfortable. Once a hypnotist establishes what a person's particular refuges are, he can always lead him or her back to a state of calm.

Pierre said, 'Let your safe places come back into your memory' – and at once I started to feel better. Then he went on, always speaking when he heard me breathe out:

> You know, you and Brian are doing the most difficult thing in the world. It's absolutely normal that you're anxious. Before every great success, there's bound to be a phase of anxiety. Without that, there's no big achievement. If you felt comfortable above the Gulf of Mexico, it would probably mean that twenty people had gone round the world before you. In fact, the more anxious you are, the better it is, because it means you're that much closer to success. You and Brian have already flown farther than anyone in history. Don't give a damn about being anxious! It's great to be anxious! Enjoy it! When you land in Africa, you'll look back on your anxiety as the first sign of your triumph.

In professional terms, he had 'reframed' our situation: he had described what was happening but had put a completely different interpretation on the facts. The result was wonderful: I felt infinitely better. When Pierre Eckert came back on the line, I thanked him for putting the other Pierre through; I said I felt much better and would like to try something new. What should we go for in terms of heading and altitude?

'Go as high as the balloon can fly,' he told me. 'Go to the extreme limit. I think you'll find the wind a little more to the left, and you'll escape from Venezuela. As high as you can – that's the last chance of saving the flight.'

So I switched on the burners and went up and up, regardless of fuel consumption. Then I phoned Michèle again. I told her I'd had two hours of good sleep, and that after the hypnosis session with Pierre I felt a new man. 'Brian's now in bed,' I said, 'and I'm trying the last possible manoeuvre to save the flight.'

Being in contact with her made me feel better still; but as we talked I was burning, burning propane like there was no tomorrow – and still we were heading disastrously for Venezuela. Then suddenly I said, 'Michèle! Something's happening. Wait . . . Yes! The wind's changing. The GPS is showing one degree more to the north. Now it's two degrees! Now it's three! This is *fabulous*.'

I was so excited that I kept up a running commentary. 'I've only a hundred metres left before we hit the ceiling . . . But look! Incredible! Now we're really turning . . . We've gone round *ten* degrees! Can you believe it, Michèle? Twelve degrees!'

'No!' she exclaimed. 'How strange we should be talking at this very moment!'

'Even better,' I told her. 'From a hundred, the track's gone to eighty-five. Amazing! Now, really, I think we're going to do it!'

It did seem extraordinary that Michèle was live on the phone when the miracle occurred, and that she was able to share my excitement. By the time she rang off we were at 35,000 feet, and all at once we were no longer heading for Venezuela but for Jamaica. Our speed was still only 41 knots, but our track was 82 degrees and exactly what we wanted. In a few minutes our prospects had been transformed.

When Brian took over again after a two-hour rest, I was thrilled to tell him about the momentous change in our fortunes. I then went back to bed and, keeping Pierre's words in mind, used self-hypnosis to bring on sleep. The safe place I chose was a scene from my childhood. Every evening when I went to bed as a boy, a turboprop plane used to come droning over Lausanne on some regular flight, and I would always listen for the comforting sound of its engines coming through my window as I was falling asleep. Now, imagining that the roar of the burners was the sound of the plane, I quickly fell into a deep sleep.

BRIAN

Back in the cockpit, with hope rising, I found that our drift to the north kept increasing. I faxed the Smiths, on duty in the control centre:

It's been quite a day – as if we hadn't had enough of those already. Need to ask a question at this critical stage. We've been given a set of targets, but already we're tracking to the north of them. Is this OK? Is it an advantage to encourage more north?

Cecilia replied:

In answer to your questions, I wish you could see the map we have here that shows the jet stream lying just to the north of you. It extends right across the Atlantic. Luc is not here now, but before he left I asked him if your track is good, and he said it was. Luccing at the map, the jet lies just northeast of Cuba, and it shows a steady increase in speed as you progress east . . . Jamaica know you're coming: 124.0 or 128.1 [MHz] when you get in range.

I realized our people on the ground were doing everything they could to keep our spirits up – and we were both heartened by a message from Bertrand's father, passed on by the press centre at Geneva:

Mes chers Bertrand et Brian,

Vous avez presque la victoire. Vous êtes fatigués, tendus, impatients d'atteindre le but. Qui ne le serait pas dans ces conditions? Tout le monde vous soutient de toutes les forces possibles.

Tout en étant prudents, ayez encore le courage d'aider, en réussissant, tous ceux qui vous aident ici de toutes leurs forces, de tout leur cœur, et de toute leur capacité. Il ne vous reste guère à faire que le millième de ce que vous avez fait en comptant les années que vous avez passées sur ce projet. Moins de trois jours pour arriver à 'votre Méridien' – avec un vent qui va encore accélérer pendant ce temps.

Courage. Tout le monde vous aime et vous embrasse.

Papa, Mercredi soir, 17 Mars.

PS. Peut-être qu'un peu d'exercise physique vous ferait du bien? (Je juge de loin.) Pourrait-on envisager une descente à 2,500 m et une bonne aération de quelques heures au hublot avant la traversée de l'Atlantique? (De nouveau, je parle de loin!) Pardon pour les conseils. C'est seulement pour vous dire combien on pense à vous.

My dear Bertrand and Brian,

You have victory in your grasp. You are tired, stressed out, impatient to reach the end. Who wouldn't be in these conditions? The whole world is backing you with every possible kind of support.

While remaining prudent, in the midst of your success, have the courage to help all those who are helping you here with all their strength, with all their heart, and with all their might. If you take into account the years you have devoted to this project, you only have to accomplish a thousandth of what you have achieved already.

Less than three days to go before you arrive at your meridian – with a wind that's going to keep accelerating all the way.

Courage. Everyone loves you and embraces you.

Papa, Wednesday evening, 17 March.

PS. Maybe a little physical exercise would do you good? (I'm judging from afar.) What about a descent to 2,500 metres and a good airing for a few hours with the hatch open, before the Atlantic crossing? (Again, I'm speaking from a distance!) Forgive me for offering advice. It's just to tell you how much everyone is thinking of you.

Bertrand was much moved by his father's solicitous good wishes, but there was no realistic chance of another low-level EVA, pleasant though that would have been. Our only option was to stay high. And just when we needed it, another psychological boost arrived from the air controller on duty at Kingston, Jamaica. When I came on the air with 'Hotel Bravo – Bravo Romeo Alpha: flight level three-five-zero, tracking zero-eight-one,' a delicious woman's voice answered.

'OK,' she said. 'What you doin', man?'

'We took off from Switzerland,' I answered. 'We're hoping to get round the world and aiming for Africa.'

'Hoowhee!' she cried. 'You guys sure am takin de chance!' Then she asked, 'Where are you anyway?'

'Overhead Kingston.'

'Stand by.'

Everything went quiet for a couple of minutes. Then she was

back, sounding a little disappointed. 'Bin outside,' she reported, 'but I can't see ya!'

Afterwards Bertrand claimed that I'd fallen in love with her – just as he had with the lady from Oakland, California – and when I'd gone off duty he called her up to say goodbye on my behalf. But even if the romance was short-lived, it came at just the right moment to raise morale.

As our speed wound up to 60 knots, everyone started piling on the jokes, saying they would see us in the bar at the weekend, and so on. But our people on the ground knew as well as we did that our fuel was critically short, and nobody was sure whether we had enough to cross the Atlantic. 'Most important,' Debbie faxed me at 10:30 Zulu, 'can you please give us exact status of fuel situation, tanks in use now, and for how long, and tanks remaining full. Alan suggests we take the yes/no-go decision for the Atlantic over Puerto Rico.'

There were too many unknown variables for anyone to make an exact computation of how long our propane would last. One was the temperature at high altitude over the Atlantic: how often, and for how long, would we need to burn in order to stay above 35,000 feet? But the most important factor was the speed of the jet stream. If it picked up to 100 knots or more, as we hoped, we would be home and dry.

BERTRAND

When I got up and came into the cockpit, I asked Brian where we were. He swivelled round in his chair and said, with a huge smile on his face, 'Bertrand – we're already past Jamaica and on our way to Haiti.' By then our speed was 65 knots – a fifty per cent increase over the 45 knots which had been predicted – and the miracle had begun. From that moment we were always faster than the forecast.

Flying over the Gulf of Mexico we had seen beautiful islands, and when we passed along the north coast of Honduras, many different countries were in sight: Mexico, Guatemala, Belize. But we had ceased to care about the scenery. The important thing was to have islands beneath us, and if we decided we had to ditch rather than tackle the Atlantic, it was here – before we passed Puerto Rico – that we would have to do it.

By the time dawn broke on 18 March, we had overflown Haiti and were overhead Santo Domingo. Our team at Swiss Control could not get through to Haiti, but the Puerto Rican air controller was a ball of fire. 'Don't worry,' he said, 'I'll tell them what you want.' Obviously he enjoyed acting as a relay. His counterpart in Santo Domingo was just as lively, and after talking to me exclusively in specialist jargon for a few minutes, he asked eagerly, 'What's it like up there?' When I tried to explain, he said, 'That sounds great! If you do it again, please give me a call, and I'll come with you.'

In the control centre eyes were starting to focus on Africa, and Alan reported:

> Everything is looking good at this end, but we should talk in around three hours when you are over Puerto Rico, just to check numbers and confirm the Atlantic crossing is feasible.

The balloon was at its ceiling. Heading and speed were perfect. Then suddenly we started drifting south again. When I called Luc and Pierre, they said, 'Don't vent any more helium than you have to, but your heading *is* bad: you have to lose height.'

What had happened was that we'd again been flying in cirrus cloud but, strangely enough, this time it had the effect of keeping solar heat trapped around the balloon so that the envelope became hotter and hotter and started to shed surplus helium through the appendices. I could see the tubes bulging full, right down to their lower ends.

It was a horrible dilemma. What was I to do? Every instinct told me to stay high. If we descended, we would have to burn more to gain height again later. In a game of poker it would have been a case of double or bust. But there was no point in having a bad track and enough fuel; we would be better off with a good track and dwindling propane. So I chose to double and took the terrible decision to open the valve at the top of the envelope and vent precious helium to make us descend.

Swivelling my seat round, I turned on the nitrogen tank and twisted the knob. *Psssshh* went the gas, forcing its way up the tube. Red lights came up on the instrument panel, showing that the valve was open. I vented five times, for twenty seconds each time, keeping my finger on the button. (We had made this a rule so that the valve wouldn't be left open by mistake.) After a while we started to lose altitude, and the descent seemed to do the trick, putting us back on the right heading; but for the whole of the rest of the day I had to compensate for the lost gas by burning precious propane.

Our remaining stock of fuel was pathetically small. We had one pair of tanks still full and one half-full – at most, forty hours of burning time. But as we headed towards Puerto Rico there was another favourable omen. We were shaping up to take the critical go/no-go decision when I noticed that the transponder code which Puerto Rico had given Brian to punch in was 5555. My lucky number, my favourite number, has always been five because for all the luckiest, happiest parts of my childhood, before my mother died, we were always five in the family. Fives had already appeared at particularly important moments in my life, and when I saw them again now, I couldn't believe they had come purely by chance. When I noticed the figures on the screen I stared at Brian and said, 'This is incredible! I don't know where this comes from, but surely it's a sign that we have to go, and that we'll do it.'

On the ground the media were becoming frantic. After the high drama of our falling ill, which went out live on radio and TV, everyone was hanging on one big question: were we going for the Atlantic or not? So many journalists were converging on the press room, which was separated from the control centre only by a partition, that the place was becoming seriously overcrowded. Some of the horde were forced to squat in the restaurant, and every time one of our team moved anywhere a dozen reporters pounced. 'It's just like a zoo here with journalists,' Alan told us. 'Pierre even gave an interview while he was having a piss! But I guess it's what Breitling invested in, so we're doing our best to keep everybody happy.'

It was during the afternoon of 18 March – already evening at the control centre – that we had to take the official go/no-go decision. Alan was proposing that we should do it live, in the middle of a staged press conference, so he faxed some instructions:

The conversation will be short and in English, because most of the crews here at the moment are British or from America –

every big network. I will ask you about fuel tanks, number left; check life support; will advise brief met; ask how you feel about continuing on across; say it's OK by me, but final decision is yours.

Please do not prolong the call by asking to talk to Luc. We want to clear the Control Centre as quickly as possible, and then we can get Luc/Pierre to call you for any further briefing you need.

At the appointed hour, with television cameras from all over the world focused on him, Alan came on the phone and asked formally for our speed, our heading, our height and our fuel state. In the cockpit, with the loudspeaker switched on so that we could both hear, I held the receiver while Brian sat beside me with the necessary papers.

When we had run through the agreed formalities, Alan said, 'I think you can go for it.'

'Bertrand!' cried Brian. 'Tell him we're going anyway!'

Into my head came a marvellous remark made by Dick Rutan in a message which he sent me before the launch of the first *Orbiter*. Describing his own flight round the world in the *Voyager* aircraft, he told me how, for the last two days, he was convinced he had too little fuel to make it and how, when he landed, there was just half a gallon left. In conclusion he said, 'Bertrand, you always have to remember, the only way to fail is to quit.'

At that critical moment of our own flight, I quoted Dick's words. 'The only way to fail is to quit,' I said, '*and we're not going to quit*. Even if we have to ditch in mid-Atlantic, we go for it.'

Brian was one hundred per cent with me. We both had the feeling we could do it, that this was our last chance, that we had to go. To ditch in the big waves of the Atlantic would be dangerous and unpleasant, but not nearly as bad as going down in the Pacific. The odds were that rescue aircraft or ships would reach us fairly quickly. Yet our decision to carry on was not made in a fit of madness or despair: there was humour in it too. With our camera running, I consulted Sean the bear, who was sitting on the pilots' desk as usual. 'Sean,' I said, 'if you *don't* want us to do it, make a sign.'

Of course he did not move – but just in case, Brian addressed him sternly: 'Sean,' he said, 'before you answer, remember something. If you don't want to face the Atlantic, we have to ditch off Puerto Rico. And in Puerto Rico they *eat* bears.'

When the little fellow still made no move, we thanked him formally for being so helpful and said, 'Let's go!'

Emotion welled up again when a fax arrived from our three faithful colleagues at Swiss Control:

Cher Bertrand, Dear Brian,

Just to tell you how we three controllers, along with all our colleagues at Swiss Control, are gripped by your voyage round the world. All of us are living through highly charged moments. We're being constantly interrogated at meals, and people are trooping around the big display board with its map of the world to check up on your progress.

We all wish you good health and the form, both physical and psychological, to attack this grand finale. And even if you decide to stop, you can be assured that you have given us the chance to take part in a huge, passionate and extraordinary adventure.

All courage – and our best wishes. Niklaus, Greg and Patrick.

As always, they were negotiating hard on our behalf. As we were leaving the Caribbean, the New York Oceanic controller told Niklaus that he had heavy traffic outbound from the area and asked him to bring the balloon down from its altitude of 35,000 feet. When Nik made a counter-suggestion – that the aircraft should fly lower – he was amazed when the American promptly agreed, saying, 'That's a good idea.'

But things soon became more difficult. At that time of the evening the area we were going to pass through next was heavily used by commercial aircraft, flying north and south, and New York told Nik that it was impossible for the balloon to continue eastwards at 35,000 feet. He was surprised because he had never expected to have any problem with the Americans. Now he said that he could not stop the balloon and that it had to stay at its present flight level because that was its most economic height.

New York Oceanic quoted a letter of agreement, which it had received from Breitling in advance of the flight, saying that we would be travelling between 31,000 and 33,000 feet. 'Stick to the agreement,' said the controller – and hung up. Nik waited a few minutes, called again and said, 'Listen – we have to talk about this a bit more.' He explained that the letter had been written two months earlier and that the jet stream had turned out to be higher than expected.

'Yes,' said the American, 'but what about all these other pilots? They can't stop their climb at 290 – it's not economic.'

'Surely you can discuss it with them?' Nik persisted. 'Ask them to stay at 290, or go up to 390, just for one night. Why not?'

'Well, we'll see. Maybe we'll try.'

'You do realize,' Nik added, 'that if our guys have to descend to 310, they won't make it. They'll ditch in the Atlantic – and you know who'll have to get them out? That's you, because they'll be in your control region.'

After a full thirty seconds' silence, the American said, 'Listen – I'll call you back.' Half an hour later he gave us clearance.

BRIAN

In going for the Atlantic we knew we were taking a calculated risk. Even if we failed make the coast of Africa, we would get more than three-quarters of the way across the ocean and would then be in fairly easy reach of rescue helicopters based at the American airfields on the Azores. If we ditched the chances of dying were quite small.

Down in the control room Alan was thinking ahead:

Our best guess at the moment is a landing in Mali on Sunday at sunrise, but that might change. Mali is mainly desert and has lions, leopards etc . . . Getting to you could be a problem. We are going to fly in by private jet, but we might then have to get four-wheel-drive vehicles and drive across the desert because there do not seem to be any helicopters in Mali . . . If we miss Mali, the Nigerians are not being particularly helpful, and we can't get any aircraft into Libya. If you have the fuel, Egypt is still the best bet.

James Manclark has been on the phone. So has Kevin Uliassi. Both offered congratulations on the flight so far and wished you success.

Acknowledging his fax, I returned to my facetious mode:

Thanks for your thoughts on landing in Mali. You keep adding another twelve hours on to our journey.

One thought which may help us get to Egypt, and might save your bottom in the rear of a four-wheel drive: do you think there would be any chance of pre-positioning a couple of *Orbiter 2's* fuel tanks along our route – after the finish meridian, of course? We could simply tape them on and continue out of trouble.

To speed us on our way we got a wonderful message from Pierre Blanchoud, our aeronautical advisor, addressed to both of us:

Luckily we have the prospect of a fast, high-altitude flight, in a blue sky, without fear of CBs, because in winds of this speed CBs cannot form, and if one does climb almost to your height, it will soon disperse. Our maps show us a jet stream which will take you to Egypt without any problem.

Brian – Your dream has become a reality, and you may well land in the vicinity of the Pyramids.

Bertrand – Profit from these unforgettable moments of the flight. You should talk to the wind, your ally, and thank it, just as the sailor thanked the dolphin which saved his life. Observe how the clouds scatter from your route to let you pass, and how the cirrus above you shows you the route to follow, the jet stream . . .

You must remain concentrated and vigilant, both confident and receptive of what your intuition tells you. Visualize your landing in the sand – and until we meet again, may God hold you in the palm of His hand.

CHAPTER ELEVEN

LAST LAP

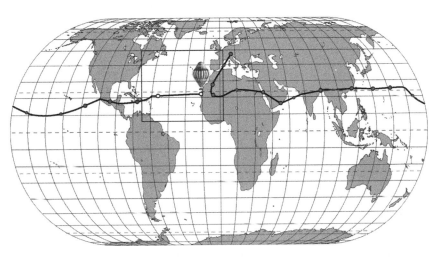

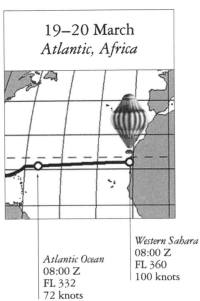

19–20 March
Atlantic, Africa

Western Sahara
08:00 Z
FL 360
100 knots

Atlantic Ocean
08:00 Z
FL 332
72 knots

BERTRAND

We went out over the Atlantic like a rocket. At 05:00 Zulu on 19 March – still for us the middle of the night – we were doing 80 knots, on a true track of 078, heading for Africa but also edging towards the centre of the jet stream. Dreadful as it had been to be ejected from the jet over the Gulf of Mexico, it was fantastic to be pulled back into it now. The cold was intense: outside the capsule the temperature was 50 below, and inside it was minus 2°C. One of our heaters had failed completely and the pilot light on the other had been reduced by ice to a pathetic flame an inch high. If I put a hand in front of the fans that were supposed to circulate warm air from the heating units, I felt only a cold draught.

When Brian woke me and I went back to the cockpit, it was still completely dark; and when the sun came up I saw that we were surrounded by cloud – a thick layer, probably alto-stratus, moving at the same speed as us. Inside the layer there was no sunlight, bringing the danger of condensation freezing on to the envelope and icing it up. To climb above the cloud I had to burn what seemed an appalling amount of propane, aware that every push was one less in the tanks. I forced myself to stop calculating precisely how much fuel might be left. Then at last we came out into full sunlight and our speed went up to 85 knots.

With frozen fingers I added a few words to my diary: 'I'm praying that the jet stream keeps us in its centre and doesn't eject us.' Every time I spoke to Pierre or Luc on the phone, I asked the same question: 'Are you sure we're not going to be ejected again? We just can't afford that.' And every time they answered, 'Don't worry. You're right in the centre. But if you could fly even higher, you'd go even quicker because the core is still above you.'

When I heard that the control centre had become a forest of parabolic antennae and that the media were going crazy with excitement, I noted:

> I just cannot allow myself to think about things like that – because if I did, I would start to believe we'd already succeeded. I'm just not allowing myself to think of all the hopes of our team and our families and friends. I'm really starting to think we're going to do it, but I'm not allowing myself to believe it. And I think that even if we do succeed, I still won't be able to believe we've done it.

Everything had become unreal. For the past two days we'd been experiencing the extraordinary sensation of knowing that we were on the point of pulling off one of the greatest achievements imaginable and yet not being able to believe it. It hardly seemed possible that all those people in the control centre could be working on our behalf, and it seemed equally incredible that hundreds of journalists had become obsessed by what we were doing. We felt that suddenly the eyes of the entire planet were on us.

Time seemed to have stopped. There was no time any more. The beginning of the flight was both yesterday and an eternity ago. We had to count on our fingers to decide what day it was and enter the date in our log book.

In those moments of suspension I made a couple of promises to myself. One was that, if we succeeded, I would not take revenge on anyone who disparaged us during the project. I would not even hit back at critics like the self-styled aeronautical expert who had been briefly involved in another round-the-world balloon attempt that never got off the ground. The man appeared on Swiss German television saying that Breitling was mad to send off these two pilots, who were bound to fail. The balloon was too small, he claimed; it did not carry enough fuel, its crew was not properly trained, and it had taken off only for publicity purposes. Now I thought, let him and a few others eat their words.

During that afternoon the flight was smooth, the balloon was well balanced at 35,300 feet – just below the ceiling – and was making from 84 to 90 knots. Everything looked so promising that after Brian took over from me I was too excited to sleep. All the same, as I lay in the bunk listening to the burners, I was completely at ease. My body was so relaxed that I felt I was outside it: I had the impression that although my mind was awake, my body was asleep and refreshing itself.

That night was in any case made shorter by the fact that we were speeding eastwards and would cross the finishing line next day. Also, we were cutting down on our rest periods because we wanted to be in the cockpit together when that great moment came.

BRIAN

I couldn't believe how cold I was when trying to sleep. I was inside my sleeping bag, which was supposed to be effective down to Arctic temperatures – minus 35°C – but I never did get my feet warm. When I took over from Bertrand in the cockpit I was wearing every garment I had, including three pairs of trousers and several tops, with the whole lot inside the sleeping bag. Part of the trouble was that it was almost impossible to get one's circulation going by exercising. After the advice from Bertrand's father, I did try some push-ups – just possible in the central corridor if you kept your elbows in; but after getting out of bed one morning and doing thirty or forty squats, I found I could hardly move – so after that I gave exercise a miss.

The tension was affecting everybody. Having sent Control several messages and got no answer, I found that in my anxiety I'd been using the wrong fax. 'Sorry, must be the excitement,' I wrote. 'Am now on Capsat 2. No wonder you weren't talking to me.' Twenty minutes later I faxed:

Flight level 360, with 95 knots. Desperate to see 100 knots, but don't worry – I'm not desperate enough to go through the ceiling – unless there's a lady's boudoir above. We did flight level 365 earlier. How close is that to Per's record?

Control replied that, according to Alan, our pressure altitude must be about 38,000 feet, 'so all that noise must be these records breaking'. By then, after some jokes about how much alcohol was being consumed on the ground, I was addressing Smiffy as 'Squiffy':

Hello, Squiffy and C, How are you? Looks as if it may be the last night I sit here and freeze me diddlies in this seat. I suspect that if we're still flying tomorrow night, we'll both be at the helm. Another degree west, and I'll be able to fold the map so I can see land ahead. The back of my hand has swollen up, for some strange reason. Thought I must have knocked it, but it's starting to look like an infection. Won't it be absolutely typical that I'll be on antibiotics and therefore not able to drink anything for a week. You'll have to drink it for me. There – have you just seen his eyes light up, C?

Little did I realize what a huge web of people was helping us. When I asked Smiffy if he could find out the sea state in the Atlantic, he called his friend Mickey Dawson at New York Oceanic. After a chat, Mickey asked how he could help, and when he heard the request he exclaimed, 'Holy cow! Is he going to ditch?'

'No, no,' said Smiffy. 'He's just a Brit, and a bit cautious.'

'OK,' said Mickey. 'Give me ten minutes.'

When he called back, he said, 'Now! I've been talking to this really nice lady of the San Juan coastguard in Puerto Rico, and here's the weather at the surface: wind 310 at ten knots, one metre waves . . .'

Messages from our met men were consistently reassuring. 'Congratulations – you are in the middle of the jet stream,' Pierre faxed at midnight Zulu. 'However, the higher, the faster.' Urging us not to fly below 34,000 feet, he predicted a steady increase in our speed to 120 knots and concluded:

This leads to an entry into Egypt at 03:00 Zulu [on 21 March]. If you fly higher, it will be even faster. Flight level 380 gives 01:00 Zulu, for example. But save your fuel.

On the ground things really were going crazy. Control started to send us more of the Internet messages that were coming in from all over the world, especially America. 'Incredible!!! Keep it up and land safe,' wrote one man in Seattle. From California came, 'Go, cats, go', and from New Jersey, 'Doing a great job, guys. You're almost home.' What we did not know at the time was that Andy Elson had gone on television in the UK and claimed that, having done all the fuel calculations, he knew we were not going to make the coast of Africa.

BERTRAND

When Brian went to bed, I promised to wake him an hour before we reached the finishing line. As we sped towards Africa it was still fully dark. At that moment we were on tank pair No. 5 – a good omen for me. When I pressed the button on the instrument panel to see what sort of crazy figure the weighing mechanism would give, it read: 55 kilos. I remained completely still, overcome by an immense feeling of thankfulness. The sight of those magic figures made me cry and pray, both together. Afterwards I noted in my journal:

I love those signs. I don't know where they come from – but I'm happy to accept them as one of the mysteries of life. Many people don't even recognize such signs, and I am sure I myself miss a lot of them. The best moments are those at which you recognize a sign as it appears. Such coincidences cannot happen by chance. Once again I really have the impression we're being guided.

In a later entry I continued:

During our three-week flight in our own magical world of the gondola, there has been no let-up in the suffering of the people on the planet on which we've been looking down with so much admiration. There must be something we can do to alleviate all this suffering, using the celebrity that we are bound to get. It would be nice to start a foundation of our own, which could give help every year to some charity that promotes greater respect, tolerance and harmony between people, and between people and nature. We don't understand why we have so much luck up here. But let's do everything we can to spread it around us.

That led me to think about the prize of one million dollars which the American brewing company Budweiser had offered to the first crew round the world. The company had stipulated that half the money should go to a charity, and during the flight Brian and I had often thought how nice it would be, when the time came, to choose a recipient.

In the control centre the Smiths were on duty. 'Hello, my friends,' I faxed. 'When we cross the finish line, you will all be in the gondola with us. It will be the victory of passion, of friendship and of endurance – that's why it will be the victory of all of us.'

'Thank you for your message,' the Smiths answered. 'We've been with you all the way along, and we're not going to let you cross the finishing line without us. You may be in range of Canaries Control: 124.7, 119.3 or 126.5.' A few minutes later Cecilia came through again:

Dear Bertrand,
This will probably be my last message. It now feels like the lull before the storm in here! I don't suppose I'll be able to get to the keyboard after this.

Just wanted to say what a great honour it has been working with you both on this very special project. Smiffy and I have both said from the start how much we hoped the good guys would win. We felt it was so important that, as Jo has said so often, the prize must surely – HOPEFULLY – go to two balloonists who feel passionately about ballooning. Now it seems that dream must come true.

Much love from us both – Cecilia and Brian.

At 05:56 I faxed Control again to say, 'Hello, approaching the coast' – but there was absolutely nothing to see. The GPS indicated we were about to make landfall, but I had no visual evidence of it. That part of Africa was uninhabited and there was not a light to be seen – a big difference even from the west coast of India, where we had spotted Porbandar from miles away. From Geneva Jo answered:

Good morning, Bertrand and Brian. According to our calculations, you should be crossing the coast now. Welcome to Africa! I hope you will have a beautiful sunrise and a glorious day. Much love – and we are thinking of you both.

I replied:

Dear Jo, Your calculations are right. We are just coming back now to the Western Sahara after almost three weeks around the world. The hours before the finish are probably the longest of my life. First light of day just coming now. Best XXX – Bertrand.

Dawn was fabulous. At 06:15 the sun came over the horizon dead ahead, and I saw again the desert I had loved so much twenty days earlier. The finishing line was still 500 kilometres away, but, at the rate we were travelling, we would take only three hours to reach it. I wondered what could still stop us, when suddenly both burners blew out. I tried to re-ignite them without success. I whispered to myself, 'This is unbelievable, we are going to fail by just a few kilometres.' I took a deep breath to relax and finally managed to re-ignite the flame. A moment later I got a call to say that a chase plane with Terry Lloyd of ITN on board was coming up to film the balloon and conduct interviews.

The sun was barely up when I saw the small private jet come past. We were so high up that the pilot could not use his flaps and gear to slow down but had to keep going at high speed, leaving a huge white trail of condensation around us. As he went screaming past, Terry came on the radio, demanding that I wake Brian for an interview.

'Terry,' I said, 'throughout the flight we've kept our rule of never waking the other unless there's an emergency.'

'*Please*, Bertrand,' he pleaded. 'I absolutely need Brian for British TV.'

'All right,' I said. 'All I can do is talk loud enough over the radio so that, if Brian happens to be awake, he'll hear me and get up.'

'Talk louder, Bertrand! Shout!'

'Don't worry – I'm shouting.'

My raised voice soon took effect. Brian stuck his head out through the curtain of the bunk and staggered into the cockpit practically naked.

BRIAN

As the balloon sprinted towards the finishing line, we both put on our Breitling fleeces for the benefit of the video we planned to make and sat in the cockpit, counting the degrees of longitude downwards. Our speed was creeping up above the 100-knot mark.

But the flight was not over yet. As ever, our ground team were working away on our behalf. In the control room Brian Smith was exhorting everyone not to get carried away but to keep their eyes on the ball. Patrick Schelling faxed to say, 'We're almost there, but we still need to coordinate with air traffic control.' When he spoke to the tower at Dakar, which controlled Mauritanian air space, the man on duty said, 'Oh – so you're coming round again!' He said he would rather we flew at 35,000 feet but would accept our level of 36,000. Clearance had already been arranged for Libya and Egypt.

We knew that the main problem now confronting the control centre was that of recovering us when we came down. They didn't want us to land in Mauritania or Mali: apart from the leopards that Alan had mentioned, there were apparently mines scattered all over the place; and there were no helicopters. The next available country was Algeria, but the Algerians weren't very keen to have us and would not guarantee our safety. After that came Libya: Bertrand really wanted to land there because he'd heard that Gaddafi has a 200-strong, all-female bodyguard. But even if the good Colonel had given us a friendly welcome, he wouldn't have let the press planes in – and he might even have denied access to Breitling's private aircraft, which was bringing the recovery team.

That left Egypt – and towards the end of the flight the advice from Control was simply to stay as high as we could and keep going as fast as we could for as long as possible. I began to feel a bit stupid, because

After nearly three weeks of flight, the *Breitling Orbiter 3* crosses the deserts of North Africa for the second time. Inside the balloon nothing has changed, the same concentration is still required, but on the ground champagne is overflowing in the control centre (*Bertrand Piccard and Brian Jones*).

Half an hour before landing in the Egyptian desert, the ice falling from the balloon envelope has collected on the red capsule as it flies low over the eroded terrain (*Bertrand Piccard and Brian Jones*).

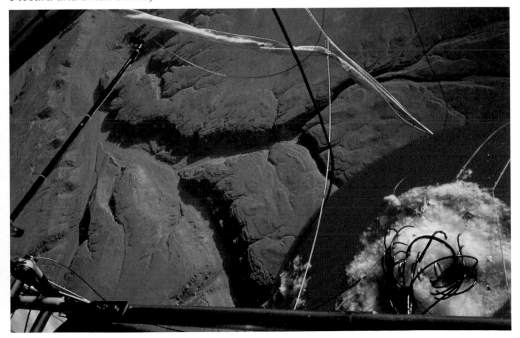

The first encounter with the Breitling aeroplane, taking pictures and filming as the balloon comes in to land in the Egyptian desert (*Popperfoto/Reuter*).

Seen from the Breitling jet plane, Brian and Bertrand try desperately to deflate their balloon as it turns into a vast sail which drags the capsule across the sand (*Sygma*).

Waving and cheering at the aeroplane: having landed safely in Egypt in the middle of nowhere, Brian and Bertrand start to realize that their dream has come true (*Martin Rütschi*).

As three hundred journalists desperately tried to get transport to the landing site, the only way to take a celebration picture was with a remote control camera. Note the ice on the tanks which shows how little fuel was left (*Bertrand Piccard and Brian Jones*).

Brian washing his hair with the only warm bottle of water (*Bertrand Piccard and Brian Jones*).

After seven hours in the desert, an Egyptian rescue helicopter finally arrives (*Bertrand Piccard and Brian Jones*).

As the news of the successful landing reaches the control centre, Alan Noble, flight director, sprays the rest of the team with champagne (*Associated Press*).

The two weather gurus, Pierre Eckert and Luc Trullemans, worked in synergy during the whole project. Together they were greater than the sum of their parts (*F. Wichser*).

The ground control team were almost as excited as the pilots after the success of the mission. Left to right (back): John Albury, Debbie Clarke, Brian Smith, Sue Tatford, Cecilia Smith. Front row: Joanna Jones and Alan Noble (*Cecilia Smith*).

The real moment when Brian and Bertrand could express their pleasure and their joy was when they were able to share their triumph with the rest of the team, with their families and with the thousands of people who had come to Geneva to welcome them as heroes (above – *Edipresse – Di Nolfi*; left – *Sygma*; below – *Popperfoto*).

Bertrand and Brian receiving the Olympic Order from Juan Antonio Samaranch, president of the IOC, beside the Olympic flame in Lausanne (*IOC Olympic Museum – Maeder*).

Her Majesty Queen Elizabeth II gave Bertrand and Brian the Charles Green salver at Cameron Balloons in Bristol, where the Queen also met the other team members (*PA*).

Bertrand and Brian at the monument erected in Château d'Oex to celebrate their successful flight (*Yvain Genevay*).

Back to Paris, where the book belonging to Jules Verne is returned to Jean-Jules Verne, the great-grandson of the famous writer (*Sygma*).

'We took off as pilots, flew as friends, and landed as brothers' (*Keystone*).

Symbolized by this frozen hatch in front of the rising sun, the greatest adventure of all is probably life itself (*Bertrand Piccard and Brian Jones*).

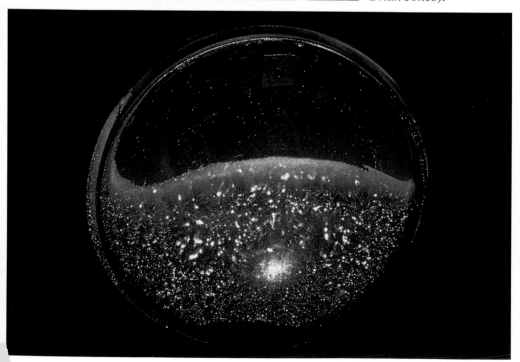

ever since Puerto Rico I'd been saying in faxes and interviews that I wasn't sure we had enough fuel to reach the African coast – and suddenly here we were proposing to carry on for several thousand kilometres. The reason was that our speed had tripled over the last leg – something we could not have foreseen.

Both of us had a feeling of invincibility, that we could do whatever we damn well pleased. Go to the Red Sea? Carry on to Saudi Arabia? All sorts of silly notions flashed through our heads. Yet one idea loomed large for me.

At the first press conference I faced after Bertrand invited me to fly with him, somebody asked me where I hoped to land if we made it round the world. Off the cuff I answered, 'By the Great Pyramids in Egypt.' Now that this seemed a real possibility, the press latched on to it and turned it into a major theme. As it turned out, however, we had to fight to keep ourselves away from Cairo because the wind there was too strong for a safe landing. We didn't want any more than four or five knots of wind at ground level, but around the Pyramids the wind was blowing at twenty knots; to attempt a landing in that would have been almost suicidal.

As we drew near the finishing line at 9 degrees 27 minutes West, Alan – ever the practical organizer – rose to unprecedented heights of politeness and emotion. He faxed:

Gentlemen: What you are going to achieve today is an historic event of world proportions. Consequently it has to be stage-managed.

I propose the following, which has been agreed by Breitling:

1. When you have crossed the line, you phone the usual number at the control centre to confirm time of crossing. I will briefly congratulate you (and probably burst into tears). That conversation will be covered by a single live TV camera crew that will send the image world-wide.

2. When that conversation ends, please wait two or three minutes while I fight my way into the press centre. Then please call 717 7999. This conversation, which I will conduct, will be live before a huge crowd of journalists. I would like both of you to speak and say what you feel. (Bertrand – please persuade

Brian: the media say they have not heard enough from him.) I will then pass just a few questions to you from journalists. To save time, I propose Bertrand answers them in French, Brian in English – but please be brief. After a few minutes please say that for reasons of power you cannot continue, but that you hope to see them all when you return to Geneva.

3. Then please call back on the control centre number to talk with Michèle, Jo and Thedy in private.

We expect you to cross the line at approx 10:30 Zulu. I will come back to you later to discuss landing, but at the moment we are assuming Egypt. I'm proud of you both. Alan.

BERTRAND

As we were coming up to the finishing line the phone went dead. The antenna had frozen again, so we could not call Control, and nobody could call us. We crossed the line without knowing the precise moment because we were travelling so fast that when we looked at the GPS we found we were already past the mark.

We stood up and embraced, shaking hands, slapping each other on the back, and shouting, 'It's incredible. We've done it! We've done it!' We gave the little football a push, and off it went: *'Olé! Olé! Olé! Olé!'* For the first time its parrot cry of 'We are the champs! We are the champs!' was appropriate. Nineteen days had passed since Brian had given it to me a few thousand feet above the Alps.

In the control room the assembled throng was waiting desperately for news. When no call came through, Alan faxed:

According to our poll report you crossed the line at 09:54 Zulu. Congratulations, guys. You did it. Well done from everybody here at Geneva. Love you both. Alan.

Brian and I had been discussing how we could describe the feeling that we had been helped on our way by some higher force, and now we hit on the idea of calling this agency – which had guided us through so many obstacles – an 'invisible hand'. Without wanting to appear naively religious, we were keen to float an idea that people could interpret in any way they liked. And so we formulated a joint message:

Hello to all our friends in Geneva.

We can hardly believe our dream has finally come true. We almost got lost in political problems, in the slow winds of the Pacific, the bad headings over the Gulf of Mexico. But each time, with God's help and great teamwork, the balloon got back on course to succeed.

We are the privileged two of a wonderful and efficient team that we would like to thank from the bottom of our hearts, now that we are sharing with Breitling the results of five years' work. We are eternally grateful to the invisible hand that has guided us through all the obstacles of this fantastic voyage.

Soon after we had sent our fax the satphone came alive again, and we had our pre-arranged press conferences, with Alan holding the fort at the other end. We could hear, live, the fantastic scenes taking place in Geneva. Champagne was flooding and being squirted everywhere. People were laughing, crying, cheering, embracing. All the journalists were so swept up in the emotion, so conscious that they were witnessing a great event, that they could not stop talking. Many of the world's leading networks continued transmitting the proceedings live not for five or ten minutes, but for a whole hour.

Among the crowd in the control room was my father. I knew quite well that he would not be able to relax until the flight was over. Instead of giving vent to his delight like everybody else, he remained very rational and kept his emotions hidden. 'Bertrand,' he said quietly over the telephone, 'it's fabulous, what you've done. But you still have to land, and I want to remind you of something very important. Probably you've thought of this, but in case you haven't, when you land, *you must bend your knees.*'

As a teenager it had sometimes hurt me to be treated as a little boy, but now I knew how important it was for my father to give any advice that would help to keep me safe. It was also a way for him to cope with his emotions. I myself find it so much easier, so much more natural, to let feeling show, to let it out. But that is not my father's style. He had broadcast live on Swiss radio every day and made frequent visits to the control centre, but although he had been terribly afraid for us all through the flight, all he did was to reassure others, saying there was nothing to worry about. For three weeks he slept badly and probably suffered more stress than Brian or me.

Others were less restrained. Stefano Albinati and I had a wonderful conversation, but then he was so overcome that he plunged the top half of his body into an open cupboard and stood there, with his head in his hands, back to the room, convulsed by sobs.

BRIAN

In the balloon we soon felt a sense of anticlimax. We were still flying. The same desert was still below us. And the gondola was just as cold. When a journalist asked me over the satphone, 'What are you going to do now?' I answered, 'When I can get through to my wife on the phone, I'm going to tell her I love her, and then I'm going to have a cup of tea.'

The great British reaction! But we did bring out our precious *pâté truffé* – the only tinned food on board. We had meant to eat it to celebrate crossing America, but things had gone so badly between Mexico and Honduras that we hadn't felt like it then. Instead, we attacked it over Mauritania. The cans were of the old-fashioned type, which you open by peeling off a strip round the walls with a slotted key. One of the keys was missing, so Bertrand set about the can with his yellow Swiss Army knife, specially made for Breitling. (It is a tradition in the Piccard family that its male members have a Swiss Army knife in their pockets at all times: Bertrand's father and grandfather both kept the knives which they had taken with them into the stratosphere and to the bottom of the ocean, and Bertrand had brought three knives of his own on the flight.) The tin resisted his efforts so strongly that he had to give up, and we opened the other can instead. We spread the *pâté* on some digestive biscuits which had originally been provided – irony of ironies – by Tony Brown.

Our ridiculous wrestle with the *pâté* tins made us laugh, and that broke the feeling of anticlimax. Thereafter, we just got on with the flight. The cold was worse than ever because we had accidentally blown the element of our second kettle by switching it on with no water in, leaving us no means of heating water. For food we were down to a few biscuits and *panettone*, some smoked emu, Etivaz Gruyère cheese, pumpernickel and margarine. In the storage space beneath the floor our bottles of water had frozen solid: to get a drink, we had to bring up a bottle at a time, crack the plastic and melt lumps of ice by putting them into cups and cradling the cups in our hands.

Another empty fuel tank hung up, and then a third. I thought the rogues might be held on by large accumulations of ice, and that we were going to have to be careful when we descended to lower altitudes as they would probably start to drop off when we reached warmer air at about 10,000 feet.

On the ground, the Breitling reception committee was about to set out for Egypt: Alan faxed to say that he would be leaving in two hours' time with Thedy Schneider and a rescue team. Meanwhile he gave us some instructions and advice:

> I propose a high-speed, high-level flight over Libya. Once well across the border into Egypt, commence a gradual descent down to, say, 5,000 feet, keeping air traffic control advised of your intentions. As you go down, your track will change from 92 to 98 degrees true. We are looking to land you 26 to 28 North, 29 East, but the exact position is beyond our abilities to predict at this time. There are some large open areas and a few ranges of hills which appear to be no higher than 1,200 feet.
>
> Suggest you have items ready for immediate use as ballast, with the usual provisos about not killing anybody below. You will need to decide how you are going to deal with the hung-up tanks. If they fall off as you touch down, the loss of weight will send you up again. It might be better to go outside and cut them free before you stabilize at low level.
>
> Despite the fact that we will reach Cairo late tonight, and have helicopters that are supposed to be able to take off at first light, I think it unlikely we will be with you for the landing. Don't be tempted to leave the balloon inflated for too long – we don't want a repeat of the problems we had in Burma.

BERTRAND

We spent the whole of 20 March crossing the desert at very high speed. Three weeks earlier we had flown slowly over these huge expanses, full of hope that we might succeed. Now we were above them again, with success behind us, and I found that immensely satisfying. For safety reasons we were covering an extra 4,000 kilometres, yet that seemed nothing but a pleasure. The balloon was going easily and, apart from the cold, everything was fine.

Inevitably, before take-off, we had sometimes talked about the possibility of establishing new records – for distance, duration and altitude. Every time we started on that tack, one of us said '*Shhhh!*' because we didn't want to tempt fate. After bagging the absolute distance record we had also broken the absolute duration record during our crossing of the Atlantic: in the whole history of aviation nothing had flown longer or farther than we had without refuelling.

But still, out there, was the altitude record. Until the last lap we had never thought seriously about going for it, because an attempt on it would be a huge extravagance: we would burn a lot of propane and risk venting helium if we pushed the balloon through the ceiling. But now that we were in sight of touchdown, it was a different matter.

BRIAN

I said nothing about records to Bertrand when he went to bed, but at 16:05 I faxed John at Control to say:

> I hope the barograph is working. This is our last chance to get altitude for very little fuel, so we are going close to the ceiling to see if we can put the altitude record in the bag. FL 371, 113 knots.

That brought a sharp retort:

> You arrogant little git! More records indeed! If you go for altitude, do NOT lose your track, as you need to stay as far south as possible, due to possible 18-knot winds at the surface near Cairo tomorrow a.m. Also, do not lose helium.
> Alan reminds you that you have a radio altimeter, which will help your descent to low level.

His last sentence was too much: the radio altimeter was our largest instrument, right in the middle of the panel. We'd been sitting looking at it for nearly three weeks, and it was hardly possible for us to forget it. I couldn't let the remark go without a sarcastic riposte:

> Thank Alan very much for the flying lessons. The radio altimeter – is that the one with the three little white hands, or the sexy yellow one with the orange button? Would he like to be Training Officer next year?

With short burns I pushed the balloon gingerly upwards, and for two or three minutes I scanned the bottom of the gas cell constantly with a big torch. When I saw it go really tight, I decided, 'Right – that's it.' In due course Control confirmed that we'd taken the record with a corrected altitude of 38,500 feet. When Bertrand woke up, he emerged from the bunk saying, 'Brian! You know, it's a pity we didn't go for the altitude record, and this was our last chance.' I gave him a big smile and said, 'Don't worry. I did it while you were asleep.'

Next on the fax was Jo, addressing us lavishly as 'my heroes!' and saying she had given a bag of my clothes and shaving equipment to Alan, *en route* to Cairo. She sent love and congratulations from the family, then handed over to John, who added:

> The Queen (yes, the proper one) and Tony Blair, as well as Jacques Chirac, have sent congrats. Juan-Antonio Samaranch has announced you will both receive the Olympic Order. Will you still speak to me?!

I replied:

> Hi, Sweetheart (not you, Albury),
> Did the Queen give the message over the phone? I hope the old git didn't try to sell her a balloon. I've got to bring the beard back to Geneva, so Bertrand doesn't look too grubby. I assume the plan is to bring us straight back? Nobody tells us anything. Do you think they will let us stop at a hotel to clean up? They should insist on it, otherwise it'll take a week to get rid of the smell. Tell John he can still use my Christian name when we are on our own.
> FL 365 and doing 130 knots.

BERTRAND

My last night at the controls was the most wonderful of the flight. A slender crescent of new moon rose ahead of us, born of the desert. Once more I was living the intimate and loving relationship that we had established with our planet, but this time I was totally relaxed, thanks to the feeling of success. I had the impression that I had left the cockpit and was flying among the stars, which had swallowed our balloon. I felt so privileged that I wanted to enjoy every second of that world of the air.

Soon after daybreak *Breitling Orbiter 3* would have to land in the Egyptian sand. Brian and I would be lifted away from the desert by helicopter, and we would immediately have to find words to satisfy the curiosity of the public; but at that moment, as I sat muffled in the down jacket, the bite of the cold brought home to me that I was living one of the best moments of my life. 'The only way I can make this instant last,' I wrote, 'is to share it with others. We'll have to write a book, and we'll sign it together, Brian and I, as a reflection of the wonderful spirit of this flight.'

My mind was ranging ahead, thinking of what would happen in the next days and weeks and years. Every now and then the intensity of the cold brought me sharply back to the present, but for the first time in twenty days I had no fear of failure and I found it a huge pleasure to fly the balloon without worrying about what would happen if I made a mistake or if we were on the wrong track.

Watching the stars, I thought about the invisible hand and found myself wondering about God. Neither Brian nor I are conventionally religious, but we both believe there is a God. I believe in the God that has created human beings, but not at all in the God that humans have created.

It seems to me that most religions have created the God that they would like to have – a human projection, not a mystical reality. Officially I am a Protestant, but I hate to say I'm either Protestant or Catholic – or anything else. Rather than belonging to any one denomination, I am Christian, because I find that Christianity is a good way to explain life and to find a path to God. In its original form Christianity is a completely tolerant religion, and the same is true of Islam or Judaism or Buddhism or Hinduism: all these religions originally allowed people to open their hearts to others, and to God, and to make a space for divinity inside themselves.

But instead of speaking about 'religion,' I prefer to speak of 'spirituality' – a means of admitting God to our hearts, rather than a system of ideas worked out to prove that one god is better than another. My most important quest is for a sense of the essential. I do sometimes go to a place of worship, but it may be to a mosque or a Buddhist temple as often as to a Christian church, depending on where I am. I remembered intently how, during my last trip to China, I got down on my knees in a Buddhist lama temple to pray for the success of my flight. The guardian obviously found it a little strange to find a foreigner kneeling in his temple, but then I saw in his eyes that he realized how important this moment was for me.

Very often we are lost in life, swept up in automatic thoughts and reactions, and lose sight of the essential: most of the things we pursue are trivial – we cannot take them with us when we die. I think it important to have moments in which we perceive the essential, deep inside our hearts. Sometimes I find such moments in churches, but I have also found them in meditation and in flight: my hang-glider or my balloon has sometimes been my church.

There were many such moments during the flight of *Orbiter 3* – and not only when things were going well. Often they came when things were going badly – for instance, when we were over the Pacific, flying slowly, frightened and racked by doubts; for me those were fabulous moments, when I felt the essential of life, of just being alive and aware, and seeing what really matters. Confronted by the Pacific, by water, air and light, I sensed that the earth is alive in a mineral sense (as I had over the desert), and I knew I had to accept things as they were. Once I did that, I found great serenity and confidence.

This is not a fatalistic outlook; rather, it is a philosophy of accept-ance. Many elements in life can be controlled, but some cannot. One is the direction of the wind; others are death, disability, accidents and illnesses. You cannot change them – you simply have to accept them. Acceptance is very important – and ballooning is a philosophy of acceptance which helps one go through life.

Late in the night I discovered that the jet stream contained many layers of wind, each separated from the other. The layers were so

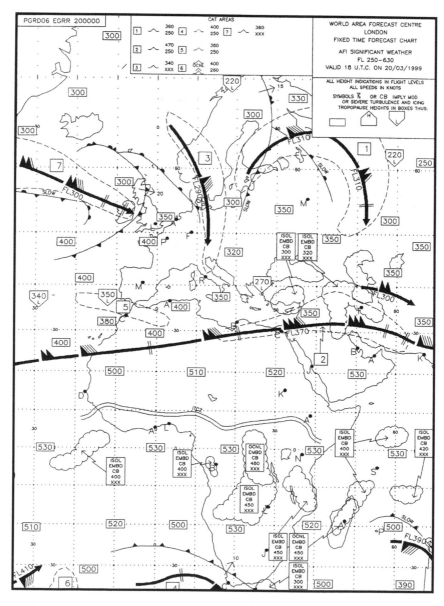

Weather chart for Africa on 20 March 1999, the final day of our flight. The thick black lines show the jet streams. It was the beautifully straight one across Africa that carried us to Egypt; those over northern Europe were fragmented, and would not have brought us across the Atlantic. Each thick arrow indicates 50 knots of wind, each slanting line 10 knots.

sharply defined that, every time we moved up or down, or from one to the other, the envelope changed shape, billowing out at one side like the sail of a boat and tucking in at the other. By watching the compass and the GPS, and glancing up to see which side of the balloon was being inflated or deflated by the gradients of the wind, I could tell if the new layer we had entered was better or worse than the one we had just moved out of. Our aim was to keep as far south as possible; so when the left side of the envelope bulged, I knew the wind was pushing us to the right and tried to keep in that layer. Physically as well as visually, flying the balloon became just like sailing a yacht — for I could hear the Mylar fabric of the envelope slapping in the wind and see its shivering silver in the light of the burner flames.

Sometime that day Don Cameron had flown over from Bristol to stand in for Alan at the control centre. Now he sent a message congratulating us on our 'magnificent achievement' and giving us advice for the morning: we were to begin our descent as we crossed the Egyptian border and should aim to land near a village called Mut soon after sunrise. I responded:

Thanks for your landing suggestions — and also a lot of congratulations to you and your factory for having built such a wonderful balloon. It was (and still is) a real pleasure to fly it through the skies of this planet.

Soon, more emphatic orders came up from John: 'DO NOT LAND IN THE GREAT SAND SEA, as you will be there for weeks. It is not good at all, and even helicopters do not go there.' I replied that I understood the problem, but asked why, in that case, we couldn't carry on for 150 miles beyond Mut and get close to the Nile valley? John's answer was that we should not fly for more than a couple of hours after sunrise because the wind always gets up in the desert as the sun climbs and hot air starts to rise off the sand.

Don could well have given the press more information about what was happening. Three hundred reporters and cameramen had massed in Cairo, where they were waiting for us in the middle of a sandstorm. Everyone at Control knew we were going to land a long way to the south, where conditions were much calmer, yet there was no contact between those who knew where we were heading and the press.

In the small hours of the morning, exhaustion overcame me before the end of my stint and I asked Brian if I could have two more hours' sleep. He kindly got up – and it was this changeover that messed up our plans for landing.

BRIAN

Once again our controllers in Geneva were talking their way through a problem. The Egyptians had given us permission to overfly the country but not to land. Our team argued over the telephone: 'Listen – the balloon is running out of fuel. If the pilot doesn't have permission to land, he'll have to declare a full emergency, and you'll be obliged by the international rules to deal with it' – whereupon the Egyptian controller said, 'OK. In that case, I give you permission.'

Our maps, which seemed very accurate, showed a green area that looked like a river valley or oasis near the place formerly called Mut, now Dakhla. We thought the green could be cultivated fields, and a better bet for landing than the desert, so we decided to go for that. Soon after I had taken over for my final stint, I faxed Control:

> Hello boys and girls. Brian back in the driver's seat for a while so that Bertrand can put on a face pack and get his rollers in. If you could send up a cup of tea, it would be preferable to even one of Smiffy's jokes now.
>
> If it's going to be a Jones landing, then it will probably be one bounce in each of the villages/towns mentioned. Tell Alan we don't need advice about checklist items, how to fly the thing or what lines to pull. Leave us a little pride. However, all other assistance regarding landing strategy, balloon performance and forecasted winds is gratefully accepted.

Then at 02:23 I faxed:

> Fuel state (and what a state). Both pairs 5 and 11 showing 26 [kilos] on contents gauge. What this means, I don't know, but it should equate to about six hours' burn time, so should be OK.
>
> If calculations are wrong, we have been told not to land in the

Great Sand Sea, but not why. Is there a chicken farm, or is it a quicksand-type surface? What we don't want to have to do is descend to a level with too little wind, and have to use fuel to climb back up to find the winds again. So an educated guess at a wind profile from Luc would be nice.

Switching back to tank pair 5 now. They are on the leading edge, and will probably be dropped before landing. Isn't it exciting!

John swiftly put me right:

The Great Sand Sea is not to be landed in because it is deep sand, you daft old fool. It will be days before they get you out. There are airfields at ASYUT, NEW VALLEY (AL KHARIJAH) AND DAKHLA (MUT), and roads that look OK. Alan is heading for Mut, so see what you can do.

I faxed back:

There's so much ice in here that when we start our descent it's going to be like the Nile in the gondola, rather than the other way round. We just may lose comms. If so, assume we are OK unless we really cock it up, in which case we will start up the EPIRB [emergency beacon]. Otherwise we will avoid using distress comms equipment and try hand-held Icoms for comms with rescue craft and ground.

Thanks for the message [about the sand]. Hasn't anybody got shovels down there? I really don't think we are going to make Mut . . . Anyway, according to my map there is rising ground immediately after the road, which could make life difficult on an overshoot, and winds unpredictable. Al Kharijah is a good place for Alan *et al.* to start, but don't put your dosh on Mut.

Later still I added:

Typical balloon pilot – can't make a decision. I think we may now do better to consider a possible approach on the road to the northwest of Mut. Next road could be 180 nautical miles on, and would put us well into the morning sun. So considering initiating descent at 26.45 East. What do you think?

That message crossed an up-coming one from the met men, which suggested the same thing: that we should begin our descent at sunrise and aim for Mut 'or track leading from it to northwest'.

'Everyone here is very concerned for your success and safe landing,' Luc continued. 'Please make every effort to report your safe landing to us as soon as it has happened.' Still on a high, I responded: 'Don't worry. If at all possible, you'll be the first to know we're down safely. Then I'll tell Bertrand.'

CHAPTER TWELVE

HARD LANDING

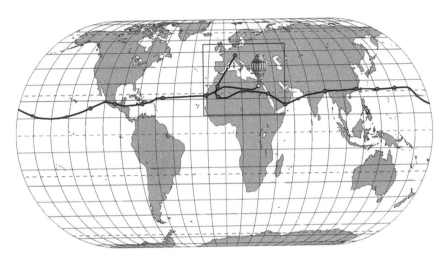

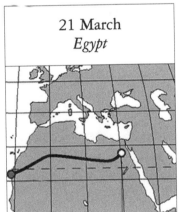

21 March
Egypt

Dakhla
06:00 Z
Landed

BERTRAND

We had trained for the landing on the supposition that I would be flying the balloon as we came back to earth and that Brian would carry out all the tasks that needed to be done outside. This made sense, as I had landed a big Rozier balloon twice before, and he had specialized in the external systems, practising on the release mechanisms that needed to be operated in sequence from on top of the gondola. But when he woke me for the last time he had already started the descent and was in full control of the balloon's flight, speed and direction.

He wasn't having an easy time, but he'd got the feel of it, so there seemed no point in taking over from him. We therefore switched jobs, and when the time came I was the one who went outside. It wasn't the most sensible arrangement because we kept having to give each other advice about what to do next, but at the time it seemed the sensible option.

BRIAN

We started our descent from 32,000 feet as we crossed the border from Libya into Egypt, our plan being to come gently down at about 300 feet a minute, progressively losing speed. By then we were doing

130 knots, and we had worked out what our trajectory should be from the winds that the met men had predicted for various levels. But it turned out that Luc and Pierre's forecast was quite wrong, and we continued to travel much too fast. Nor could we bring the balloon down at the rate we wanted. At first I found I could lose height simply by keeping the burners switched off; but the heat of the sun rapidly intensified, and at around 20,000 feet the sheets of ice that had formed on the inside of the hot-air cone started to melt and smash down on the gondola.

The noise inside the capsule was tremendous – thumps and bangs and slithering crashes – and the envelope was shedding so much weight that the balloon no longer wanted to descend. The only way we could continue down was by venting helium. I opened one gas valve and kept it open for what seemed ages, but still we were not descending. From his position under the hatch Bertrand called, 'Open the other!' I did so, and suddenly we found ourselves dropping out of the sky at 800 feet a minute – far too fast. Then another load of ice fell off, and we started up again.

BERTRAND

On our way down, while Brian was at the controls, I saw an opportunity for a fabulous photograph. The red, rising sun was glowing through the frozen porthole, and the effect was so striking that I simply had to take a picture. 'Brian,' I said, 'I'm sorry. I know it's not really the moment, but could you just move out of the way . . .'

Because of the bombardment by falling ice, I had to wait some time before I could open the top hatch – and when I did, sheets of ice and gouts of water cascaded in. Until that moment, for twenty days the gondola had remained dry and in good order; now suddenly it was awash, an absolute mess, with water and ice everywhere.

When I climbed out on top of the gondola I was suddenly in the sun. The air was warm, and ahead of us lay dark, rocky hills eroded into deep gullies. I shovelled masses of ice overboard with my hands and prepared the fifty-metre-long guide rope, setting it in position for deployment. The rope was made of hemp and weighed nearly 100 kilos; the idea was that in the moments before touchdown it would drag along the ground and keep the gondola side-on to our line of advance. Then I took out the safety pins from the release mechanism at each corner of the load-frame so that we could fire off pneumatic charges to separate the envelope from the gondola if we had to. I also filmed everything – the envelope, the ice, Brian in the cockpit. I felt it was important to record everything. But when I tried to pull up the dangling solar panels, I found that after three weeks' inaction I had become incredibly weak, and the array felt so heavy that I had to call on Brian for assistance. With him standing under the hatch, holding the end of the rope, and me calling out, 'One, two, three – pull!' we heaved in unison. Another job was to release all the lines connecting the gondola to the envelope and cut the thermocouple wires with bolt-croppers – altogether a lot of work.

BRIAN

There was no way we were going to land in the river valley: we missed it because we simply couldn't get the balloon down fast enough. At 3,000 feet, instead of the fifteen knots predicted, we still had twenty-eight, and not until we were down to 1,000 feet did we at last slow down.

The Breitling party which had flown out to meet us was already in the area and had been trying to call us on the emergency frequency, 121.5, from their Canadair jet. After a fruitless search for the balloon, the pilot was on a final approach to Dakhla airfield when suddenly, ten seconds from touchdown, he heard my voice in his headphones calling, 'Any station – this is *Breitling Orbiter* balloon. Do you read us?' Instantly he shoved the throttles forward, overshot the runway and climbed away. Stefano Albinati rushed up to the cockpit, and once the aircraft had gained height found he could talk to us easily. I gave him our GPS coordinates and he headed in our direction.

Dakhla was less than a hundred kilometres away, so we knew the aircraft would be with us in a few minutes. Bertrand took his camera on to the roof to film it coming – and a tremendous moment it was when we saw it. As the white jet began to circle us, low over the desert, rocking its wings as a sign of victory, Alan Noble came on the radio. I told him we'd missed the river valley but that we would try to land close to a road marked on our maps some eighty kilometres ahead.

'OK, then,' he said. 'Why don't we go and spot it for you?'

'Fine,' I agreed, and the plane disappeared ahead of us. Within minutes it was back and Alan was saying, 'Believe me, there is no road out there. You might as well land as soon as you can.'

Bertrand, back inside, started to stow all the loose equipment. We needed to keep the laptop out for communication with the control centre, so we left it on the desk. I was still struggling to steady our descent, standing in the corridor for quick access to the burner control panel and peering out through the portholes, which gave very poor downward visibility – particularly as at that moment the gondola happened to be flying backwards. Ridiculous as it must sound, we failed to use the famous radio altimeter about which Alan had pestered us the day before.

Just as I was thinking, 'We must still be about 150 feet up,' I glanced down through the curved glass of the front hatch and saw stones. They looked extremely close. I was wondering whether convex glass could have a magnifying effect when Bertrand, who was watching through the rear hatch and therefore looking forward, shouted, 'Brian – look out! We're not even ten metres up! Hold tight! We're going to hit!' Immediately I switched on full burners. We both stood clutching the top rail of the bunk with our knees bent to absorb impact. Seconds later there was an almighty *BANG!* as we hit the ground.

We were down for no more than a second. With the weight momentarily taken off it, the balloon snatched us back into the air. Up we went again, bouncing straight to 300 feet, where another blast from the burners stabilized us and stopped us coming down.

Looking out, we realized it was the most horrendous place in which to try to put down a balloon. We were approaching a plateau of sand, but beneath us, running up to the edge of the flat ground, was a steeply sloping mass of eroded rocks – and it was these we had struck. Fortunately the polystyrene blocks which I had failed to cut away after the launch took the brunt of the impact and saved the capsule from significant damage. More important, they prevented our remaining four fuel tanks from striking the rocks: had one split, the consequence might have been a catastrophic fireball. Fate had played its hand once again.

Over the radio came Alan's cynical voice, awarding us five out of ten for our attempt at touchdown. Bertrand went back on the roof and saw, a mile or two ahead, a flat plateau that looked perfect for landing. 'Give it five minutes,' he advised. 'Then we'll be over a suitable area.'

We were travelling at five or ten knots, with the Canadair plane still circling. Members of the party were filming us – among them the official observer from the Fédération Aéronautique Internationale, Jakob Burkard, whose job was to record the precise moment of our touchdown.

When we reached the level stretch of ground, Alan called, 'It looks good. Take it.' Bertrand, inside again, apparently told me to put my helmet on, but I was so busy I never heard him. He pulled on his own helmet and, seeing a single red light on the instrument panel showing that only one of the gas valves was open, he suggested I open the other as well, and leave them both open, to vent a substantial amount of the helium. This is the way to land a Rozier, as it effectively transforms the balloon from a gas balloon into a hot-air balloon.

Now at last *I* was flying *it*, rather than having it fly me, and I brought us in with a few careful final burns. At the last moment we again both clutched the rail, but there was hardly any impact, and after one more tiny bounce we finally came to earth, with the capsule travelling lengthways. The gondola slid along on its belly for a few yards, then stopped. For a moment we looked at each other, speechless with the realization that we were safe. The flight was over, and we were surrounded by utter silence.

Then Bertrand cried, 'Check the time! Check the time!' I did so. It was a few seconds after 06:00 Zulu on Sunday, 21 March. Quickly I retrieved the laptop, which had shot off the desk and flown across the cabin, giving me a hefty clout on the side of the thigh, and at 06:01, seeing that we still had a signal on the Capsat, I hurriedly faxed to Control: 'The Eagle has landed. All OK. Bloody good. B.'

With hindsight, I feel slightly embarrassed to have used what seemed a rather unoriginal phrase, but it was completely spontaneous: the sight of the desert must have triggered a subconscious memory of the moon landing. I wanted Control to know we were safely down, but I didn't have time to type anything longer or more poetic.

In fact Control knew we were down, for three successive sets of figures from our GPS had been the same. Quickly Sue came back: 'Is the plane with you? Or anyone on the ground with you? Please advise status.'

BERTRAND

My ears were hurting because in the rush of preparing to land I had dragged my helmet on in a hurry and nearly ripped my ears off. As soon as the gondola settled, we both pulled the red rope of the rip panel through the top hatch to release the main body of helium, but the envelope stayed up, held aloft by the gas in the little tent balloon at the top.

Imagine the scene. The sun was fully up. We were absolutely in the middle of nowhere: the fluorescent red gondola on the ground, the silver envelope overhead, and a white three-engined jet plane circling us only forty or fifty feet off the ground. We learned later that in the plane's cockpit the automatic ground-proximity warning was screaming, 'PULL UP! PULL UP!', but the pilot was on such a high that he ignored it.

Grabbing still and video cameras, I opened the rear hatch and scrambled outside to film the scene before the balloon collapsed. As I put my left foot down on the sand it left a print, and I had the same thought as Brian when he faxed that echo of Neil Armstrong's famous message from the moon. Like the lunar surface, the desert was unmarked, and when I saw my own footprint, I thought, 'Well, for Armstrong and Aldrin, it was wonderful to set foot on land so far *from* the earth – but for me, now, it's a thrill to stand *on* the earth again.'

As I went out I was almost overcome by emotion. Determined to film the balloon while it was still inflated, I ran away from the gondola and immediately found I was out of breath from the unaccustomed exercise. The envelope was leaning at an angle of maybe forty-five degrees, with wind already blowing into its mouth and making the Mylar billow. While I filmed I kept talking – to no one in particular – to heaven, perhaps – saying, 'This is fabulous! Thank you! Thank you!' Then the Breitling plane came by on a really low pass, and I filmed that too, holding the camera in my right hand and waving with my left.

Over the radio Stefano told Brian that he had to go back to Dakhla to refuel, but that they would send people to rescue us. Now that I had at least some pictures in the can, I asked Brian to pass out the first-aid box. I put it down on the sand, stood the video camera on it, set it up and left it running. Then I went back into the gondola, closed the rear hatch and said to Brian, 'OK – now we can make the official exit!' So we emerged again and had ourselves filmed as if by an invisible cameraman. The relief and joy of getting down safely made us turn the whole thing into a celebration.

We stood there, alone in the silent desert. I was still wearing my flying suit, with three layers of fleece beneath it, and soon began to sweat – but there was so much to take in and film that for the moment I didn't bother to strip off. Into my head there came again that strange dream from a couple of nights before – about how Brian and I had completed our journey round the world but hadn't been able to tell anybody about it. Now, in a curious way, the dream had become reality: we had made our circumnavigation, but there was nobody on the scene with whom we could share our joy.

BRIAN

When we scrambled out through the rear hatch, we realized how lucky we had been. The plan had been to jettison the remaining fuel tanks on one side of the gondola while we were still well off the ground and to come in to land with the denuded flank of the capsule leading. With the high workload, we simply hadn't had time to cut away the tanks; the trail rope slid ineffectively over the sand, but by a miracle we had landed end-on, so that the presence of the tanks made no difference.

Now we could see all too clearly how little fuel we had left. The remining liquid propane was so cold that even on the ground in the desert ice was forming on the outside of the cylinders and showed the level in each plainly. We reckoned that if we had put all our remaining stock together, it would have filled one tank less than a third full and given us only a few more hours of burning. That was how close we had run things.

The Canadair jet circled overhead for about ten minutes before it flew away. On the emergency radio frequency Alan told us he was going to try to reach us overland with four-wheel-drive vehicles. That made us both furious. We thought that in a last-minute burst of meanness he was trying to save money by not hiring a helicopter, and the last thing we wanted was a five-hour wait, followed by a five-hour drive through the desert, before we got to a hotel where we could have a shower and a meal. In fact the trouble was not cheese-paring on Alan's part: there was another reason altogether.

At Control in Geneva a call came in from some sort of agent in Cairo whose name sounded like 'Zigzag'. Mr Zigzag – as he instantly became known – was demanding double the amount budgeted by Breitling for a rescue helicopter: he wanted 30,000 dollars, or else the helicopter already on its way would be ordered back. This threw the controllers into a panic because all the main decision-makers had gone off to Egypt; but after some debate, they resorted to their list of confidential telephone numbers, and Brian Smith called the private number of the Swiss Foreign Minister. The response was instantaneous – so quick that it took Brian by surprise. The Minister listened courteously and said he would see what he could do. No one in the control centre is sure what happened next, but four hours later Mr Zigzag rang back to say that the problem had been resolved: two helicopters and a C-130 Hercules transport plane were on their way. Furthermore, there would be no charge.

Back inside the gondola, we activated the satellite telephone and called Control to confirm that we were down in one piece. But after thirty seconds communication was cut, and we couldn't get through again. Instead we sent a fax:

06:39 – We are absolutely in the middle of nowhere. Possible five-hour wait now for pick-up. Kept the envelope, but next time, Don, let's have a method of ripping out the top tent balloon. Anybody want to buy some sand? Thanks, gang: see you soon. Bertrand and Brian.

Sue replied:

Please keep this on so that we can communicate. Someone will be here until your rescuers get to you. However, we have all been up all night, and have now had champagne for breakfast . . . Don't build too many sandcastles.

We could have built any number – and they would have given a bit of variety to the scene. The desert around us was totally flat, as flat as anything could possibly be, in every direction. The surface was of soft, yellow-brown sand with a scattering of pebbles, and there was no vegetation, no insect life, no birds or animals – nothing. Apart from the envelope shifting in the wind, the only thing moving was the heat haze round the horizon. It was as if we had landed on another planet, and somehow it felt entirely appropriate that after such a marathon flight we were alone in a world of our own, instead of landing live in front of CNN cameras.

Soon, though, we heard engines again, and another plane appeared – a turboprop Pilatus PC 12, which some journalists had rented and brought over from Switzerland. This one flew desperately low – no more than fifteen or twenty feet up on its last pass – as we stood waving and holding our arms aloft in a victory sign. Then a third visitor came into view – a tiny red and-white four-seater plane, whose pilot announced himself by radio as Peter Blaser, a Swiss balloon pilot and a friend of Bertrand's. Deciding he wanted to witness our landing, he had flown all the way from Switzerland with his wife and a friend, stopping in Malta, Cyprus and Cairo – and even if they missed the landing itself, they had beaten all the 300 journalists still stranded in the Egyptian capital to the site of our touchdown.

The little plane flew off, and again we were alone – except for a couple of swallows and dragonflies which materialized out of the desert, appearing from nowhere, and skimmed round and round the silver fabric of the envelope. Thinking they might be thirsty, we put out some water – but of course they paid no attention.

Because we'd been hoping for a quick airlift out, we had already started unloading essential equipment that we wanted to take with us: survival packs, first-aid kit, radios, computers and so on. Bertrand was responsible for the films and I took charge of the data-logging units and the barograph. We piled this stuff outside.

We also brought out some bottles of water, not only to drink, but to enjoy a treat which I'd been looking forward to for days – washing our hair. The bottle we'd been drinking from during the night had only a little ice in it, but the rest were frozen solid, so we laid them in the hot sand to thaw and carried on with other tasks. When the great moment for a shampoo came, I stripped to the waist, selected the bottle I knew to be the warmest and handed it to Bertrand so that he could pour its contents over my head while I soaped and rinsed. Then we changed places and, with the warm water gone, I doused his head with water so icy that he yelled in protest.

'Don't be such a cissy!' I told him.

'But it's freezing,' he protested – and I chuckled, because I knew he wasn't exaggerating.

BERTRAND

With the planes gone, we were left in silence, except for the sound of the Mylar envelope rustling in the breeze. Then, as the surface of the desert warmed up, the wind began to rise and the balloon became fully inflated by air blowing into its mouth. Not wanting to lose the envelope – now an important piece of history – we decided to try bringing it down; so we put the safety pins back into the release mechanism and blew open one corner after another to release the flying cables one by one. The balloon leant over more and more, but it was still exerting such a pull that it tugged the gondola over on its side and dragged it across the sand for about ten metres, breaking the communications antennae.

A minor panic set in. A moment earlier, we'd felt perfectly safe – and both our control centre and the Breitling party thought we *were* safe. But, suddenly, we had no contact with anyone. It was extremely hot and, with both of us on the verge of exhaustion, we now faced the possibility that the envelope might drag the gondola not for a few metres but for hundreds. If the fuel tanks struck a rock, the whole thing could explode in an instant. Disaster threatened.

'For Christ's sake, let's cut away the envelope completely,' said Brian – but I was determined to keep it. So we attacked it with our survival knives, running round it, waiting till a gust forced it down towards us, then slashing at it and twisting the blade sideways in an attempt to puncture the gas cell. Besides billowing up and down, the envelope was rolling sideways, and we kept having to jump out of the way as it bore down on us. The rubbery membrane of the gas cell proved incredibly tough: we were stabbing with all our strength, but our knives seemed to make little impression on it, and Brian's only reward for his efforts was a sprained wrist.

BRIAN

We didn't seem to have got anywhere with our knives, so I suggested we try firing emergency flares at the gas cell. We had a pack of mini-flares, with a pen-type gun, powerful enough to go up two or three hundred feet before they burst in stars. We fired three, but they simply bounced off the thick skin.

Then I said, 'I know what'll do it — our distress rocket.' Designed for use in the jungle, it was supposed to penetrate the tree canopy and climb to 1,500 feet — a fairly major firework, and we had only one. So I stood in the mouth of the balloon, holding the tube in my hand, and aimed the rocket straight upwards. I suddenly wondered if this was such a good idea, and glanced at Bertrand for reassurance. The recoil was so powerful that it pushed me back a couple of metres. A ball of fire burst into the mouth of the balloon, shooting up to hit the gas cell — and bounced off, then ricocheted around the inside of the balloon until it fell and burnt its way through the side of the hot-air cone, setting fire to the Mylar. Bertrand was holding a bottle of water and rushed to pour it over the flames, while I made a dive back into the gondola for a fire-extinguisher.

Between us we put out the blaze, but the struggle left us feeling shattered. We were standing there defeated, not knowing what to try next, when natural forces again came to our aid. Up swept a huge gust of wind, which twisted the balloon sideways and brought to the top all the cuts we had made in the gas cell. To our intense relief the envelope collapsed of its own accord — so fast that it caught Bertrand by surprise and came down on top of him. Suddenly he found himself forced to the ground, half smothered by heavy fabric. The weight of it drove him down on to his knees, and he thought he was going to be suffocated. He shouted for help, but he was so well muffled that I didn't hear him, and because I was standing on the far side of the huge, crumpled heap, which in places was still twenty or thirty feet high, I didn't realize what had happened. The result was that he had to cut his way out by slashing upwards with his knife.

By then I'd had enough. Feeling utterly exhausted and wanting only to lie down, I climbed back into the gondola through the top hatch, which was now on one side. The bunks were uninhabitable because they were nearly vertical, and the whole inside of the capsule was an awful mess. Not only had we shipped ice and water, but our kit had fallen out into a jumble, and as I scrambled in my boots left sand all over the formerly pristine white insulation on the walls. I was so worn out that I flopped down on one of the pilots' seats, which was lying more or less horizontal. It was incredibly uncomfortable, but all I wanted was to shut my eyes: apart from everything else, I think I had a touch of heatstroke.

BERTRAND

With the envelope down, I sat with my back against the keel of the gondola, letting sand run through my fingers, reflecting that we had flown over deserts for seven or eight days and were now safely down, in physical contact with one of those desolate wastes. I could have stayed there for a long time — except that the wind kept increasing until sand started to fly through the air.

Reaction set in. Like Brian, I felt exhausted and badly wanted to lie down, so I too climbed back inside and looked for a place to rest. The only thing I could think of was to cut through the safety harness in the bunk to release the mattress and to lay it on the face of the shelves along one side of the corridor, which had been vertical but was now horizontal. On that makeshift bed I stretched out and soon fell asleep.

BRIAN

I was so uncomfortable twisted down on the pilot's seat that I couldn't stay there very long; so I took a piece of foam rubber, which we had planned to strap around our bodies in the event of a nasty landing, and laid it next to where Bertrand was lying. I could only just balance on it, but at least it was better than the chair, and I lay there with my head right next to his.

All at once he began to swear atrociously in French — the first time I'd ever heard him cursing — because drops of water were falling on his head. Where they were coming from he couldn't make out, but it seems that ice must have formed inside the Kevlar shell of the gondola, behind the foam insulation. Every minute or two he would grab a cloth and wipe irritably at the surface above his head — only for the process to start again. Soon he was going full blast —

'*Merde! Quelle est la saloperie qui me tombe sur la tête?*' — but I couldn't help seeing the funny side of it and lay there giggling.

BERTRAND

Because we'd lost our main communications system, we retrieved our hand-held radios and switched them on. Of course, their range was much more limited than that of our bigger sets, and at first we couldn't get any contact. Unable to go back to sleep, because drops of water kept falling on me, I lay there awake until suddenly I heard voices talking half in Egyptian, half in French. I jumped outside and tried to call them on the VHF emergency frequency, but although I could still hear them talking I couldn't make them hear me.

At last, at around three o'clock local time — seven hours after touch-down — through the dust haze I saw two Hercules C-130 transports heading in our direction. Finally the crew responded and said they were being followed by a helicopter, which would reach us in five minutes. The Hercules began to circle us, a thousand feet up, and guided a huge Russian military MIL-17 helicopter, with space for thirty people, to our position. It landed next to us in a storm of sand.

The six-man crew was an Egyptian medical rescue team — very friendly and ready to give us all sorts of assistance. I couldn't help thinking that if we'd needed *medical* assistance we'd probably have been dead long ago, but we were delighted when they helped us carry our equipment into their aircraft. We kept a close eye on everything because all the items were very important to us: the official mail which we'd carried round the world, the computers with all the messages stored in them, the barograph and pieces of the envelope. As souvenirs, Brian and I had each cut out a piece which included the balloon's registration, HB-BRA.

Inside the helicopter, one of the Egyptians asked, 'Have you got everything you want to take?' Even though I said yes, two men jumped out, ran across to the gondola and grabbed everything they could. I protested that we didn't need the stuff immediately and that our team would come out to fetch it later, but they brought it anyway. Much of it never emerged from the helicopter. We lost half the mail, one of our flying suits, one survival pack, a life raft and more besides.

The pilots told us they proposed to fly to Asyut, refuel there and go straight on to Cairo, which would have taken three hours. That was a tough prospect as the machine was extremely noisy and vibrated severely. But after less than half an hour, when we came overhead Dakhla, we saw the Breitling plane on the ground and told the air crew that our friends were down there – whereupon they said their orders had changed and they were going to land there anyway.

So we came in towards this big oasis surrounded by thousands of palm trees, with some small pyramids of its own and, we heard later, hot springs that gush up from 5,000 feet or more beneath the surface of the earth. During the approach we realized that this was our return to the real world – for there on the tarmac was a swarm of people, obviously waiting for us. The helicopter came in down a glide path, like a fixed-wing aircraft, and taxied to the apron. Before we had even put our feet on the ground we were hemmed in by a rush of more than a hundred journalists, literally fighting to get in front of each other to take photographs.

Because of the struggling human barrier it was some time before we could reach our friends from Breitling and greet them. Eventually, with huge emotion, I reached Thedy and threw my arms round him. He had put so much into the project – not just money and energy but enthusiasm and his company's reputation – that I couldn't find words to thank him enough. I felt that, by succeeding, we had paid back some of the trust that Breitling had put in us, but in the heat of the reunion it was impossible to express such thoughts clearly. Also there was Thierry Lombard, a private banker from Geneva and a great benefactor of charitable organizations, a good friend who had always been in the right place at the right time to help and reassure us.

Ceremonies began at once. We were presented to the Governor of Dakhla and his officials. The Swiss ambassador, who had come from Cairo on the Breitling plane, handed me an official letter from the President of our country – a moving document which congratulated us on persevering through all difficulties, and said that the whole world had followed the flight, which had been a wonderful triumph for Switzerland. Caught up in such a surge of joy and emotion, Brian and I were constantly between laughter and tears. A journalist handed me a satellite phone to call Michèle in Cairo. When I heard her voice I found it difficult to speak, but I know my first words were, 'Can you imagine, *Chérie* – we made it!' These were the words I had dreamt of saying for five years, and I am sure the power of the moment will stay in my mind and my heart for all my life.

BRIAN

Two notable absentees were Stefano Albinati and Alan Noble. By the time we flew in, they had set off in a convoy of four-wheel-drive vehicles in search of us. Somebody called them back by iridium phone (which works through a satellite), but as they were already five hours out into the desert we had to wait all that time for them to return.

Meanwhile, the Governor invited us to his office to have a shower and a gigantic lunch of Egyptian specialities – stuffed tomatoes, chicken, lamb, rice, cucumber in yoghurt. After three weeks without a proper wash the shower was a rare delight, and after days without fresh fruit or vegetables the food looked wonderful, but I was so tired that I could hardly eat. Bertrand, on the other hand, pitched in with his usual gusto. As the meal did not begin until four o'clock and we'd had nothing to eat all day, he was starving.

Our gracious hosts could not have been kinder; but unfortunately, once we had eaten, they absolutely insisted that we did some sightseeing. There was nothing on earth we wanted less: our only desire was to get into the luxurious Breitling jet and fly off home. But the Governor took us in his air-conditioned car to see a water-pumping station – clearly his pride and joy – and we drove through the town with an escort of two police cars, their sirens wailing. Everything had become quite surreal: Bertrand and I still wearing our heavy flying suits and boots, punch-drunk with fatigue, keeping glazed smiles on our faces as details of hot-spring technology washed over us.

We were supposed to fly to Switzerland the same day, but it was already dark when Alan and Stefano returned from the desert, so plans were changed and it was decided that we would stay the night in Cairo. After yet another emotional reunion, we all jumped into the Breitling plane and just an hour later landed in Cairo in the midst of an incredible scrum. From every side people charged at us with microphones and cameras, and it was some time before Bertrand could even see Michèle and the children. Then the girls rushed at him and he swept them up into his arms, crying *'Bonjour, les filles!'* They were in a state of high excitement as they had seen the pyramids during the day and were now being reunited with their father.

The first individual I spoke to was the British ambassador, Sir David Blatherwick, who came up in an immaculate pinstripe suit and insisted on carrying my bags.

'You can't do that,' I protested.

'My dear boy,' he said. 'That's what I'm here for.'

I thought, 'This is great! I could really get to like this game.'

The next person I bumped into was Terry Lloyd, from ITN, who thrust a microphone in front of my mouth and shouted, 'How d'you feel?'

'Knackered!' I answered. Then I turned to the ambassador and asked, 'Can I say that on television?' He replied, 'I think you can say whatever you like.'

Our next move was to the Swissôtel, in town, and Sir David pressed me to travel there in his car, rather than in the official coach. When I said I thought I should stay with the rest of the team, he said, 'No, no, I must insist' – so off we went in a splendid black Rolls-Royce, with a Union Jack pennant flying from its bonnet. 'Such style!' I thought.

I soon saw why he wanted me on board: he was determined that his car should arrive at the hotel first and that the first pictures the TV cameras got would be of me descending from the British Embassy Rolls. Much as I enjoyed being fêted, after spending so long sealed in our private bubble in the sky I found it a shock to be plunged back into the harsh reality of the world, where politics ruled the roost.

BERTRAND

Because of the time difference, our arrival in Cairo coincided exactly with the television news in Europe. The airport was a madhouse, with everybody thrusting microphones and cell phone telephones at us, demanding live interviews. Luckily, the Swiss ambassador realized that I would need some time alone with the family before the official press conference at the Swissôtel. So, most gallantly, he put us in his big black limousine, alone with his Egyptian chauffeur, for the twenty-minute drive into the city, while he himself went in the bus full of journalists.

At the hotel, pandemonium reigned. Outside there were camels, local musicians playing Bedouin music, and three hundred journalists wrestling with one another to get pictures. Brian and I each had five bodyguards forcing a passage for us through the crowd. It was an exotic and exciting scene, but by then we were both on autopilot, wearing fixed smiles and going wherever we were led.

In the big ballroom of the Swissôtel we sat at a table and gave our first proper press conference. We thanked Breitling for its inestimable support, praised the work of our team, and so on. One question made Brian bristle: 'What do you say to those who describe your flight as frivolous and a waste of money?' Brian answered, 'Before anyone asks questions of that nature, I suggest he looks at the history of the flight – and I think he'll find the question superfluous.'

Nobody asked technical questions; instead, interest quickly turned to the philosophical aspects of the flight. The reporters wanted to know how we had felt – what the human experience had been like. I had a chance to explain how lucky we had felt to be flying in a bubble of peace above a world in which so many people were fighting, suffering and committing atrocities. This, I think, immediately created an attractive image of the flight: the first articles described how we had been pushed gently round the earth by the wind, accompanied by the spirit of peace, without trying to control nature or prove ourselves stronger than the elements. Our message, the writers said, was one of tolerance and respect, as much for human beings as for the natural world. They seemed to catch the spirit of our flight extraordinarily fast.

The Egyptian Minister of Tourism came to congratulate us and said he was sorry we hadn't landed by the pyramids, because he had installed a whole lot of chairs for spectators to watch us come down and had laid on local musicians to serenade our descent. I tried to explain that the wind round Cairo had been too strong, but I don't think he really understood much about ballooning. Then, again, we had something to eat – another wonderful meal laid out in the Swissôtel. The moment we finished dinner, Michèle and the children had to board the journalists' plane for the flight back to Geneva because the Breitling aircraft was full.

Brian and I went off to snatch a few hours' sleep. In the middle of the night I woke up, terrified because I could not hear the roar of the burners. The room was pitch dark, and in my panic I thought, 'Brian's supposed to be flying the balloon. He must have fallen asleep.' I called out, 'Brian! Brian! The burners! Keep the balloon in the air!' I was convinced we must be going down. At last I sat up in bed, found the light switch and started to laugh out of sheer relief.

BRIAN

In the morning the whole team was in a state of euphoria. We woke quite early, had breakfast and boarded a bus for the airport. The Breitling aircraft was exceedingly luxurious: big enough to carry forty passengers, it was fitted out to seat only twelve. All the seats were upholstered in cream leather. The four at the front — two on each side — swivelled through 180 degrees. Behind them on one side was a sofa with two single seats opposite, and behind these were two more pairs of singles. During the flight a stewardess called Sandra served us a delicious meal of lobster and fillet steak and some incredibly good claret, Château Cheval Blanc. She also won my heart by coming up to me and saying, 'I've carried every kind of celebrity and pop star on this plane, and I've never asked for an autograph, but I'd be honoured if I could have yours.' So Bertrand and I both signed one of the menus and gave her a signed photograph.

The only jarring note was struck by the doctor whom Breitling had brought out in case we urgently needed medical treatment. Sitting down beside me, he quizzed me about my health. When he asked if I had any problems, I showed him the swelling on my hand and dropped my trousers to display the lump caused by the impact of the laptop. He dismissed those as mere contusions and pressed me for details of any other ailments from which I might be suffering. Shortness of breath? Giddiness? Rashes? Oedema? Anxiety? My answer to everything was no because there was nothing whatever wrong with me, but at the end of the consultation I began to wonder if I wasn't feeling ill purely as a result of all his suggestions.

There was so much to talk about that the four-hour flight seemed to pass in a flash. With all our friends — Thedy, Stefano, Thierry, Alan — we went through every stage of our voyage round the world and discussed our ideas about creating a foundation.

CHAPTER THIRTEEN

HEROES' WELCOME

BOTH-OF-US

We flew round the world in pursuit of adventure, not of celebrity. We flew for the passion of flying, of exploring all the skies of our planet. Of course we knew that the first people to succeed would enter the history books, but when we came back to earth we were astounded by the excitement that our circumnavigation had aroused. The hysterical reaction of the media in Cairo gave us a taste of what lay ahead: we were surprised to see that for many of the journalists this was the greatest adventure. Yet when we landed at Geneva at 12.30 p.m. on Monday, 22 March, we still had no inkling of what lay in store.

First came a fleeting moment of doubt because the airport seemed to be deserted. As we touched down Bertrand said, 'What a pity we didn't get back yesterday, at the weekend, because a lot more people would have been free to come and meet us.' While the plane taxied past the terminal building we had our faces glued to the windows — and saw not a soul. 'They could have given one of the cleaners a Swiss flag,' Brian muttered, 'and she could have come out on the balcony and waved it.'

The aircraft taxied for a long way, and then, at the far end of the airfield, to our amazement we realized that the tarmac was covered by an immense crowd. As the plane came to a halt we could see thousands of people waving – incredible numbers. Rain had been falling and umbrellas were still up, but as we arrived the downpour was stopping. Later we heard that the airfield had been thrown open to the public for the day, that the facility had been advertised on television and radio and in the press and that there had been a colossal security operation to screen such numbers, but in the heat of the moment we had no time to wonder how everyone had got there.

When the door of the aircraft opened, we heard a roar of cheers. We looked at each other as if to say, 'Do we really dare go out?' A moment later we were standing side by side on the top of the steps, waving furiously to communicate our joy. Below us, a sea of faces, all laughing and cheering; a forest of Swiss and British flags waving wildly. At the bottom of the steps on one side were our team, our wives and Bertrand's children, all with tears in their eyes, all waving and calling out. The noise was so great that we couldn't hear what they were shouting, but their delight and excitement were electrifying. We stayed at the top of the steps for what seemed an eternity, just to savour the moment.

When the time came to walk down the narrow ladder, Brian gestured and said, 'After you.' Bertrand replied, 'No – we'll go together.' So we put our arms round each other's shoulders and off we went, step by step, side by side, down the ladder. As long as we were walking down we were still on the flight, but already we felt that our lives would change for ever once we hit the tarmac.

Our feet touched down simultaneously – whereupon our families rushed at us. Bertrand's father came up and embraced him. Adolf Ogi, the Vice-President of Switzerland, whom Bertrand had only met on formal occasions, hugged him, congratulated him and addressed him by his Christian name. We had intensely emotional meetings with the staff from the control room, some of whom, extraordinary as it may seem, Bertrand had never met. John and Debbie, for instance, were quite new to him – and yet he knew their voices, their humour, their style, their personalities. It was equally wonderful for Brian to be able to thank his old friends for everything they had done. We took them all in our arms, overjoyed that we could associate them with the team's triumph.

The same was true of our magic weathermen, Luc and Pierre, who had become popular heroes in their own right through television and newspapers. Whenever the gondola's antennae froze up, preventing us transmitting pictures from the air, cameramen had gone to photograph the weathermen in the control centre, so their faces became well known – and before our plane came in they had gone round the crowd in a lap of honour. The whole scene was fantastically moving. There were so many people to thank.

BRIAN

My own reunion was overwhelming. Bertrand had met Michèle and the girls in Cairo, but this was the first time Jo and I had seen each other. I wasn't just meeting my wife again after a three-week separation: Jo had been an integral part of the Orbiter project. She had put up with all my bad moods during the difficult periods of *Orbiter 2*, and for months we had worked together all the hours that God sent on *Orbiter 3* – so that on top of our natural delight at seeing each other we were swept up by a tremendous feeling of joint achievement.

For me, our homecoming was the most emotional part of the whole flight. Never before in my life had I played a part in an undertaking on this scale. Ever since crossing the line I'd realized that what we had done would mean nothing until we were able to share the achievement with others. The emotion of the event lay in the sharing of it. So for me, our return to Geneva was the time when everything came to a head – the most extraordinary moment of my life.

Of course I had been desperately keen to be with Jo and our closest friends – John and Debbie, Brian and Cecilia. But I was also intensely moved by the obvious joy of all the Swiss who had come to greet us. Their faces were lit up with excitement and pleasure, and I felt they were really sharing our triumph. The fact that so many people were joining us in spirit lifted the experience to a higher plane.

BOTH-OF-US

The public had been corralled behind fences, but they all wanted to shake hands, so we allowed ourselves to be pushed – almost carried – into an open-topped car. Standing in the back, we were driven along the barrier, shaking as many hands as we could. Probably none of the crowd realized why our vehicle was a Peugeot – but behind the make there lay a little saga. The Peugeot car company had booked the VIP suite in the airport for an important meeting in the middle of March, but because our balloon was still flying and the control operation had to be maintained, the firm graciously withdrew and found another venue. In return, the airport manager, much relieved, asked them to lay on one of their cars for our homecoming. Even if the team's official cars were Chrysler Voyagers, this was no moment for petty rivalry.

It would have made no difference if we'd been in a dustcart. People were thrusting flowers at us, handing us drawings of the balloon done by their children, offering photographs of the take-off. After a tour of the crowd our driver carried on into an enormous hangar, and we realized that all the people in the open were just the ones who could not be fitted inside.

When we climbed on to the stage and saw Don Cameron, we hugged him, and Bertrand exclaimed, 'You built the most wonderful balloon ever made!'

'Well!' he retorted. 'We had the two best pilots in the world to fly it.'

As we took our places, confronted by thirty microphones, every-body was waving and shouting – so we stood on our chairs, holding hands aloft, overwhelmed by the excitement. Even the journalists were cheering. The applause seemed to go on for ever, and it was a long time before either of us could start to speak. Then Brian made a brilliant remark which deflated some of the tension: 'What an amazing coun-try,' he said, 'where nobody has to go to work on a Monday!'

Every television station in the world seemed to want to interview us. Our homecoming went out live on CNN, NBC, BBC, Sky News, TF1, Swiss Television – everywhere. People seemed surprised that, instead of boasting of how many records we had broken, we spoke about how we had gained respect for human life and nature. Soon the atmosphere was the same as in Cairo: rather than worry about technical details, everyone wanted to know what had been going on in our minds.

'What was the best moment of the flight?' someone asked.

'The time between take-off and landing,' Bertrand told him. 'It was a dream lasting twenty days.'

'What were you thinking all the time?'

'We didn't need to think,' said Bertrand. 'We just felt. We felt incredibly respectful for the miracle of life on the planet. We felt enormous admiration for the quality that human beings can achieve if they're not fighting rivals for more power, more territory, more money.'

'What about this invisible hand you mentioned?'

'We'd be dishonest if we claimed that we succeeded on our own,' Brian replied. 'We had the best balloon, the best possible back-up team and the best possible morale, but all that wasn't enough to account for our success. "The invisible hand" was the only name we could think of for the mysterious force which seemed to come to our aid so often.'

Bertrand picked up the theme. 'We also felt we were being helped on our way by the good wishes of millions of people. That's why we decided to dedicate the flight to the children of the world. They'll be the adults of tomorrow, and they must know how important it is to have peace and tolerance on earth.'

'Now you're heroes and famous all over the world,' somebody else asked, 'what are you going to do with your celebrity?'

During the flight we had never dared consider such matters, but now Bertrand answered openly, 'Yes, we do seem to be famous – otherwise you wouldn't be here! But it would be futile to use our fame just to promote ourselves. Rather, we want to use it to spread the message of peace which we conceived in the air. We're going to use the prize money from Budweiser to form a foundation which will promote the spirit of peace.'

Again and again we tried to emphasize that ours had been a team effort. Our balloon could well have been called *Team Spirit*, we said, because it was exactly that which enabled us to succeed. 'Without Breitling, we would have had nothing. Without Don Cameron and his team we would have had a lousy balloon instead of a wonderful one. Without Alan Noble and the control team, without Luc and Pierre, the flight would never have come off. Without the Swiss diplomats, we never would have been able to cross China.'

Then someone asked, 'Honestly, how did you manage to survive together for three weeks in such a small capsule?'

'By respecting each other and talking through every problem that came up,' Brian told him. 'We never got the slightest bit irritated with each other. We're both professionals, and we left our egos in the car park when we took off.'

Bertrand added, in a phrase that became famous, 'We took off as pilots, flew as friends, and landed as brothers.'

Then Richard Branson appeared on the platform with a magnum of champagne, which he shook up and squirted over us as if we were Grand Prix drivers. The meeting broke up into individual interviews, and these lasted until 11.30 p.m. – by which time we were both utterly exhausted.

Our phrase about the invisible hand set off a tremendous debate. Journalists began discussing what it was, or who it was, that had sped us on our way. Good, rational people said, 'Of course, they mean their two weathermen.' But later several people wrote to the newspapers saying, 'It's not the meteorologists. It's God.' Other people thought it was their prayers which had helped us. Obviously, all these factors contributed.

BRIAN

The joy of ordinary Swiss people was brought home to me when I got away from the crowd and walked down to the control centre for a cup of tea. Outside the door I noticed a fair-haired young man standing around and smiling at me nervously. When I came out, after nearly an hour, the boy was still there, and because he half-moved towards me as if wanting to say something, I stopped and talked to him.

'Mr Jones,' he said, 'can I have your autograph?'

'Yes, of course,' I replied, and I signed my name in a little book that he produced. As I was writing, his eyes filled with tears and he said, 'Mr Jones – you've made my dream come true.'

My eyes, also, were moist in that extraordinary moment, which summed up the way the flight had gripped people's imagination. There was no envy or jealousy: the success belonged not just to Bertrand and me, but to the nation, and somehow to the world.

At the first opportunity – in the shower at the Holiday Inn – I shaved off three weeks of beard. Bertrand had jokingly suggested that we should not shave before returning to Switzerland because he thought that if we came back looking fresh and shaved people would just think we'd been for a picnic. Anyway, in the event we had no opportunity to shave; but I hated my beard, and I lost no time in getting rid of it.

BOTH-OF-US

While all this was going on, the balloon was still lying in the desert, guarded — if that's the word — by a troop of the Egyptian coastguard. Melvyn James, head of the retrieve crew subcontracted by Breitling, remained overnight in Dakhla, and the next day he organized an expedition to rescue the gondola and as much as he could of the envelope. Several vehicles drove out, and he told his helpers not to touch anything before he arrived; but by the time he came on the scene they had already started stripping equipment out of the capsule — not least the toilet, which they had completely dismantled.

A powerful helicopter lifted the gondola back to Dakhla, where it was put on a truck and driven to Alexandria. Thence it came by sea to Marseilles. By the time it reached Switzerland a good deal of equipment had disappeared from it. Sadly enough, one casualty was the little singing football that had hung in the cockpit throughout our flight.

Later the gondola was put on exhibition in the fine transport museum in Lucerne; but its final home is the National Air and Space Museum at the Smithsonian Institution in Washington, where a big hall houses many milestones in aviation: the Wright brothers' *Kitty Hawk*, Lindbergh's *Spirit of St Louis*, Chuck Yeager's *X 1* (the first plane to break the sound barrier), and the Mercury, Gemini and Apollo space capsules. The Swiss Government would have liked to keep our gondola at home, but when it was suggested that the capsule should join the illustrious assembly in the United States, we felt it was the greatest honour anybody could confer. The gondola is the only piece of equipment in that fabulous display which is not American, so it constitutes a magnificent advertisement for Switzerland and Europe.

In the first few days after our return the Piccard household was deluged by bouquets of flowers, presents, bottles of wine, letters by the thousand. People were not only congratulating us: they were also expressing their thanks at having had the opportunity to dream with us.

As if to show how friendly the race had been, our competitors sent us moving letters – Steve Fossett, Richard Branson, Colin Prescott, Jacques Soukup, Dick Rutan, Kevin Uliassi. Barron Hilton, who had sponsored many round-the-world attempts, was also full of enthusiasm. One phrase of Dick Rutan's has stuck in our minds ever since: 'In some time, when the excitement is over, you'll both have the opportunity to sit down and realize how magnificent your achievement has been.'

Many letters contained invitations to events taking place over the next few days. In a single, unbelievable first week we went to the Aéro Club in France; to Belgium, for an audience with Crown Prince Philip; to New York, to receive the medal of the Explorers' Club; and to England to meet the Queen. There was also a ceremony in Bern, at which almost the whole Swiss Government gave an official welcome to our team – including Alan, the weathermen, the air controllers and representatives of Breitling. Breitling itself invited the fifty people most closely involved in the project to Rochat, the best restaurant in Switzerland, in the Hôtel de Ville in Crissier, where the firm gave us a wonderful evening and presented each one of us with a specially engraved watch.

In Paris, at a beautiful ceremony organized by the Jules Verne Adventure Association, attended by Buzz Aldrin, we gave back our treasured copy of La Vie, which both of us had signed, to Jean-Jules Verne himself. Then we received the Gold Medal of the Aéro Club of France – the oldest such club in the world. The presentation was made by the Club's President, Gérard Feldzer, but the arrangements were extraordinary, for the address was given by Jean-Pierre Haygneré, the French astronaut then orbiting the earth in the Mir space station. He performed the ceremony by remote control, speaking from space directly above France; Bertrand already knew him from former contacts, and it was wonderful to hear him congratulate us from such a god-like altitude. We also received the Gold Medal of Youth and Sport from the Minister, who said that she was giving it not because we had gone round the world but for the sentiments about peace and friendship which we had expressed when we returned.

In England, the Queen and the Duke of Edinburgh came to Camerons' factory in Bristol on 1 April. Because of the date we had thought the whole thing was a joke, and even when all the factory staff

lined up we were fully expecting Don Cameron to say, 'April fool!' But
the royal couple really did come, and on behalf of the British Balloon
and Airship Club the Queen presented us with the Charles Green
Salver, a splendid silver tray first given to the balloonist of that name in
1839. We were delighted that she took the trouble to have a few nice
words with every member of the team.

That was also the first time we had seen Andy Elson and Colin
Prescott since our flight. They were as friendly as could be: there were
no hard feelings of any kind, and Andy said that, disappointed as he was
not to have succeeded himself, he was glad it was us who had done so.
He explained that it was the lack of spare batteries that had forced him
to ditch, and altogether was very honest about his failure.

We cannot report every ceremony or transcribe every tribute that was
made, but one speech caught the atmosphere of all the events. This was
the one given by Max Bishop, General Secretary of the Fédération
Aéronautique Internationale (FAI) at the splendid new Olympic
Museum in Lausanne, where the main hall was packed – not least with
dozens of children, sitting on the floor in front of the seats and on the
stage. Before we received the Olympic Order from Juan Antonio Samaranch, President of the IOC, who had given us unfaltering support
throughout the project, Max spoke first in his native English, then in
perfect French, reducing both of us – and many others – to tears:

Mr President, Distinguished Guests, Ladies and Gentlemen,
We are here today to honour two great aviators, two outstanding
sportsmen and two remarkable human beings. Bertrand Piccard,
Brian Jones, we are all proud of you. We feel that we too have
taken part in your adventure. We were with you in spirit when
you soared up from your Alpine valley in Château d'Oex, not far
from here; when you tiptoed through the Chinese Corridor;
when you floundered over the Pacific; and when you finally sped
over the Sahara to touch your balloon down, a symbol of late
20th-century technology, in Egypt, the cradle of an ancient
civilization that fascinates you, and so many others. We all shared
emotions with you: joy and fear, optimism and frustration,
doubt, gratitude, and the final elation that you described so
eloquently. Your balloon, on its three-week voyage round our

fragile planet, was a beacon of hope for all the world's peoples, and particularly for its children.

In your characteristically modest and unassuming way, you reminded us that hard work and perseverance pay — that not everything can be obtained instantaneously. You taught us that what some thought impossible could be achieved with patience, skill, courage and dedication. You showed us that, in this last year of a dark and turbulent century, incredible adventures are still possible, and that these strike a chord in the hearts of people around the world of all ages, inspiring us all to cast aside empty cynicism and set ourselves higher goals.

Your flight was an example of all that is best in the Olympic movement, an ideal that we in the FAI share. By drifting unobstructed over so many national frontiers, you showed these to be insubstantial barriers, dividing people who in reality share common causes and aspirations. By competing with your fellow round-the-world balloon contenders in an open and friendly fashion, you demonstrated fair play and respect for other competitors. By dedicating your flight to the world's children and establishing your charitable fund 'Winds of Hope', you have shown that great sporting achievements should not be selfish acts, but dedicated to others.

This last great aeronautical exploit of the 20th century ranks with the greatest in the archives of the FAI, which was founded in 1905 and which, by a happy coincidence, moved its headquarters from Paris to the Olympic capital, Lausanne, just a few months ago.

Among the records that the FAI has had the honour of ratifying we find:

Louis Blériot who, in 1909, crossed the Channel from Calais to Dover for the first time.

In 1910 George Chavez made the first crossing of the Alps.

In 1927 Charles Lindbergh succeeded in crossing the Atlantic, solo.

In 1931 a certain Auguste Piccard achieved the absolute ballooning altitude record.

Then Chuck Yeager beat the sound barrier in 1947.

Yuri Gagarin first flew in space in 1961, and Neil Armstrong walked on the moon in 1969.

The first non-stop, unrefuelled circumnavigation of the earth in an aeroplane was Dick Rutan's, in 1986.

And now we can add two names to the FAI's scroll of honour, to our cavalcade of heroes: Piccard and Jones.

But these are no ordinary heroes. Even in the company of the distinguished names I have mentioned, Bertrand Piccard and Brian Jones stand out for their humility and generosity of spirit, their ability to communicate their feelings to ordinary people, and their determination to help others. The men that you, Mr President, are honouring today are not only great airmen and athletes. More importantly, they are distinguished ambassadors for our air sports and for the Olympic ideal. Most important of all, they are excellent examples for the children of the world to look up to.

On behalf of all air sportsmen and women the world over, I salute you, Bertrand Piccard and Brian Jones. This is an honour you richly deserve. We wish you well in the important work of education, encouragement and support of others that lies ahead of you.

For both of us it was fascinating to be associated with the heroes of our childhood, with the explorers and aviators we had so much admired all our lives, and to receive the same honours and the same medals.

In Brussels we had a grand ceremony at the Royal Institute of Meteorology, where Luc normally worked, and we were officially welcomed by Prince Philip, Crown Prince of Belgium. Prince Philip's father and grandfather had been friends of Bertrand's forebears, so this was something of a Piccard family occasion.

For Bertrand, to acquire an Explorers' Club medal was a particular thrill because his father had been awarded one: he kept it in his living room, and as a child Bertrand was always looking at it. Now he was given the same prize. We flew to New York on Concorde because it was the only way to fit the trip in, and at the dinner 2,000 people gave us a standing ovation. We sat at the same table as the astronaut John

Glenn, who had given Bertrand his autograph at Cape Kennedy when he was a boy of eleven.

Another trip was to Washington, where we collected the Budweiser cheque for one million dollars. The company had specified that half the total should go to charity; we shared the rest with Breitling, who presented their share to the same charity. The presentation ceremony was held at the Smithsonian Institution, to which we rode in a carriage pulled by eight gigantic shire horses: we started in the park next to the Capitol and went up Independence Avenue to the museum, where a red carpet had been rolled out. A makeshift stage had been arranged underneath Lindbergh's *Spirit of St Louis* and in front of the Apollo 11 capsule – an amazing setting.

Yet another ceremony took place in Château d'Oex. Exactly two months after our landing we returned to our launch point in a special panoramic train. Thousands of people were waiting for us at the station. Together with Luc and Pierre, we rode in the basket of a balloon set on a trailer, and paraded through the village to inspect the monument created to commemorate our flight: a pyramid of light-coloured stone, surmounted by a bronze globe showing our trajectory, with little bronze balloons standing proud over our take-off and landing sites and an inscription recording details of the circumnavigation. Such was Brian's feeling for the local people that he got Bertrand to teach him one special sentence of French, which he spoke over the microphone to tremendous applause: '*Aujourd'hui, ma femme Joanna et moi, nous sommes rentrés à la maison.*' ('Today my wife Joanna and I feel we've come back home.')

BRIAN

Many people have asked how the flight changed us. There was an obvious physical effect in that we both lost weight: Bertrand shed nearly five kilos, dropping from 62 to 57 kilograms, his lowest for years. I lost about the same – 10 pounds. The difference between us was that I was happy to be lighter, whereas he was not. Part of the loss was due to the fact that we ate relatively little, and part to the fact that our muscles withered from lack of use. Our worst problem immediately after our return was exhaustion: the schedule of appearances was so hectic that we had no chance to recover.

While I was project manager for *Orbiter 3*, and during the lead-up to launch, I was totally focused on getting the balloon built and ensuring that its systems would operate as designed. I gave little thought to what it might be like to fly round the globe. The depth of my relationship with Bertrand, and all our talks about the wellbeing of the planet, elevated the whole experience to another plane.

There is no question that the flight changed my life. It made me more extrovert: the feeling that I wanted to share our story and tell everyone about it brought me out of the relatively private way of life I had followed before. The urge to spread the word is such that I now positively enjoy giving lectures about our circumnavigation. The flight got rid of some of my typically British reserve and brought my emotions closer to the surface. I feel closer to nature, and cry more easily now. Before my first British TV appearance, which went out from a London studio some ten days after our return, I was put in the green room to wait. The television news was in progress, showing scenes of the conflict in Kosovo. Before that moment we had been on the move so much that I had hardly been aware of the war; but now I found that the sight of refugees leaving their homes, and the evidence of massacres, brought tears to my eyes. Before our flight I would not have been so moved: I'd have taken in the refugees' plight, but then switched my attention to the next item on the programme. Now I was more deeply affected — and no bad thing, either.

To go from total obscurity to celebrity status in twenty days was exceedingly strange, but soon I began to see that most people in high places are no different from the rest of us. After our return Bertrand and I met a number of important personalities — from royalty to heads of state, former astronauts and film stars — and to my surprise I found all of them, without exception, incredibly nice. They had no affectations and gave themselves no airs: on the contrary, they were natural and friendly, and had time for us. It was a revelation for me to find that a hero like John Glenn, revered in aviation circles, has heroes of his own.

Another result of the flight was that it brought a new dimension to my already deep friendship with John and Debbie, Smiffy and C, and the other people on the team. Three weeks of shared danger, excitement and tension created a unique bond between us. Whenever we meet now and talk about the flight, there is a greater depth to the conversation than the mere words convey. We scarcely have any need to discuss what we were feeling at the time, or how close we came to each other: we all know, and the unspoken knowledge itself reinforces the bond.

As for Bertrand: the fact that the two of us shared such an experience certainly created a deep and lasting friendship. I always look forward to seeing him and enjoy his and Michèle's company. I love his children, and have promised myself that I will learn French so that I can communicate with them better. His phrase about our becoming brothers was accurate as well as memorable. He will always have a special place in my life.

BERTRAND

For me, the most striking fact about the whole flight was that we had such extraordinary luck. Why was the honour of succeeding granted to us? Why, when people were suffering all round the earth, when atrocities were being committed and wars fought, should we have been having the most fabulous time of our lives? We looked down on the planet with awe and admiration, and yet many questions remained unanswered.

Now, whenever I see a globe or a map of the world, I have an almost proprietorial feeling about it. Before the flight, I associated globes and maps with geography lessons. Now when I look at a globe and turn it on its axis, or observe every detail on it, I get a tremendous feeling of pleasure and strong emotions as memories of the flight flash through my head. I feel far more closely involved than before with the life of our planet and of those countries that we flew over. When King Hassan of Morocco dies, when starvation hits the Sudan, when war breaks out between Pakistan and India, I think, 'Well – I've been there. I know what the country looks like, and I feel closer to the people. In some way, flying round the world is like taking it in our arms.'

I emerged from the flight with much greater respect for life and for mankind. I now feel far more deeply concerned about ecology and wildlife as well as about the way people behave. When I say 'ecology', I don't mean fanatical attempts to rid nature of human beings in order to turn the world into a nature reserve. I mean the deep respect everyone should have for every form of life – from air, sand and water to trees, animals and humans. 'Respect' means the realization that there is valuable life, though in different forms, all around us and inside us. Neither is the goal to get rid of the high technology which we have been able to develop: instead the aim is to use it to understand nature better, rather than wanting to extend our power. For me such subjects are not just theoretical any more but completely practical concerns. I am so thankful at having had my dream come true that I feel I must pay back something to the planet.

One way of doing this has been to form our Winds of Hope charitable foundation. Our plan is to use the interest from the Budweiser money and other donations to make an annual award, every 21 March – the anniversary of the landing. This award will fund projects which provide concrete, lasting assistance to child victims of catastrophes, diseases or conflicts, whose sufferings are unreported by the media or forgotten by the general public.

We hope we can exploit the status we have achieved by meeting high-level officials and politicians, as well as thousands of ordinary mortals, so that people will listen to what we say. To give money to worthwhile projects is one thing, but we feel we can also promote selected projects personally by offering them the backing of our celebrity. We know that during the flight school classes all round the world were following our progress. Even in countries that we had no chance of overflying, children's attention was focused on the balloon. So, wherever we go, we should have an immediate affinity with the children, and through them with their teachers and government officials. We should also be able to score from the fact that we will have no secondary agenda: we will not be looking for further publicity – just for results.

I am not a professional adventurer. I have now returned to my job as a practising psychiatrist, and I enjoy giving talks and lectures about the flight. But what I have realized is that the whole flight turned out to be a metaphor for life. In life many people are afraid of the unknown, afraid of losing control, with the result that they try to over-control everything. Many of their problems arise from the fact that they expend a lot of energy seeking to control events over which they have no power. On the other hand, they fail to control those things which are within their power.

During the Breitling *Orbiter 3* project we learnt what we could control and what we couldn't. We could control the construction of gondola and envelope, the building of the team, the technical training of the crew. Once in the air, though, we could not control the weather or the wind. The only way to change our heading was to change our altitude.

On earth the situation is very similar. People become prisoners of their problems, their lives, their fate, as the balloon is prisoner of the wind. Exactly as in the balloon, if you want to change direction in life, you have to climb: by deliberately reaching upward, through philosophy, psychology or some spiritual discipline, you can achieve a different trajectory.

What I do with my patients now is exactly what we did in the balloon – except that in psychotherapy I'm not the pilot: I'm the weatherman, always trying to help the patient find the altitude at which he or she will discover the most suitable track. If you have the wrong altitude and the wrong heading, you get lost in storms, you get lost in suffering, you get lost in pain. So, although university taught me the theory of psychotherapy, ballooning has taught me a new, practical approach to the subject.

It is now very important for me to help my patients, or the people to whom I give talks, to realize that life itself is a great adventure. In life you have the same kind of storms that can destroy you when you are ballooning and you are anxious about the future. There are moments when you have no wind and you are depressed by your stagnation; at other moments, everything seems so easy and smooth that you wonder why other people find life (or ballooning) so difficult. When people are healthy, young and handsome, of course they think life is simple – but that's a mirage. In fact life is a huge and difficult adventure because you are facing the unknown: by definition, you never know what will happen, and the only ability you need to develop is that of adapting yourself to whatever happens. Although you cannot control what will come, you can control your reaction to it. When each new problem comes along, you have to dig inside yourself to find the resources to go further and learn new strategies for survival and evolution.

So now, although I am no longer in the round-the-world balloon, I feel myself in exactly the same situation in life. Just because we landed safely, the adventure is by no means finished. Our descent into Egypt was a practical return to earth, but the flight continues in life. That's why the greatest adventure of all is not flying around the world in a balloon: the greatest adventure is travelling through life itself.

Looking ahead, I expect that somebody will make a solo round-the-world attempt — and the most obvious candidate must be Steve Fossett. I also anticipate a round-the-world race, with all competitors taking off from the same place at the same time. They will try to fly faster than we did, and if they succeed their pleasure will be more short lived. Brian and I will not take part in such a race, but we will be glad to support it.

We are happy and proud that our team's achievement has become part of the history of aviation. But all the honours we received were no more than the icing on the cake. The cake — if I can put it like that — is the opportunity our flight gave us for constructive action in the future.

Meanwhile, I very often like to bring back into my mind how I sat in the Egyptian desert with my back against the gondola, feeling the wind get up. I remember how the warm wind blew on my face for the first time in three weeks, how the wind increased until I could feel it with my entire body. This was the wind — the wind of providence — which had carried Brian and me round the world, in harmony with nature. Henceforth, and for ever more, I will think of it as the Wind of Hope, and I will do all I can to hasten it on its journey round the earth.

ROUND-THE-WORLD ATTEMPTS

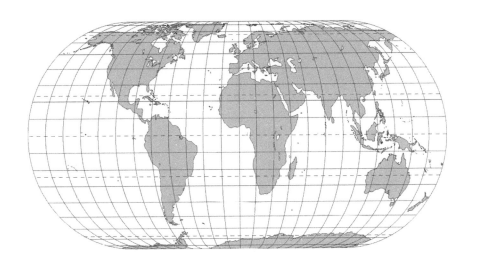

Year	Pilots	Balloon	Country of Origin	Take-off	Result
1981	Max Anderson	Jules Verne	USA	Egypt	Landed in India. Flew 2,763 miles, 47.30hours
1993	Henk Brink	Unicef Flyer	Holland		Never took off
1993	Larry Newman Don Moses Vladimir Dzhanibekov	Earthwind 1	USA	Reno, USA	Crashed shortly after take-off
1994	Larry Newman Richard Abruzzo Dave Melton	Earthwind 2	USA	Reno, USA	Frozen valve, landed same day
1995	Larry Newman Dave Melton George Saad	Earthwind 3	USA	Reno, USA	Anchor balloon burst during initial climb
1996	Steve Fossett	Solo Challenger	USA	S. Dakota, USA	Landed in Canada. Flew 1,819 miles, 51.13 hours
1997 7 Jan	Richard Branson Per Lindstrand Alex Ritchie	Virgin Global Challenger	Britain	Morocco	Flew 19 hours, landed in Algeria

Year	Pilots	Balloon	Country of Origin	Take-off	Result
1997 12 Jan	Bertrand Piccard Wim Verstraeten	Breitling Orbiter	Switzerland	Château d'Oex, Switzerland	Came down in Mediterranean after six hours
1997 15 Jan	Steve Fossett	Solo Spirit	USA	St Louis, USA	Landed in India. Duration record – 146.44 hours; distance record – 11,265 miles
1997 Dec	Richard Branson Per Lindstrand Alex Ritchie	Virgin Global Challenger	Britain	Morocco	Envelope broke away and flew on its own
1997 31 Dec	Kevin Uliassi	J-Renée	USA	Illinois, USA	Balloon burst after one hour
1998 1 Jan	Steve Fossett	Solo Spirit 2	USA	St Louis, USA	Landed in Russia. Flew 5,802 miles, 108.23 hours
1998 8 Jan	Bertrand Piccard Wim Verstraeten Andy Elson	Breitling Orbiter 2	Switzerland	Château d'Oex, Switzerland	Aborted take-off: envelope not inflated

Year	Pilots	Balloon	Country of Origin	Take-off	Result
1998 9 Jan	Dick Rutan Dave Melton	Global Hilton	USA	Albuquerque, USA	Balloon burst. Pilots parachuted
1998 28 Jan	Bertrand Piccard Wim Verstraeten Andy Elson	Breitling Orbiter 2	Switzerland	Château d'Oex, Switzerland	Landed 7 Feb in Burma. Flew 5,266 miles. Absolute duration record – 233.55 hours
1998 7 Aug	Steve Fossett	Solo Spirit 3	USA	Mendoza, Argentina	Crashed in Coral Sea, off Australia. Distance record – 14,236 miles
1998 Winter	John Wallington Dave Liniger	Remax	Australia	Alice Springs, Australia	Take-off announced but never made
1998 18 Dec	Richard Branson Per Lindstrand Steve Fossett	ICO Global Challenger	Britain	Morocco	Flew seven days. Ditched off Honolulu. Flew 12,404 miles, 177.57 hours

Year	Pilots	Balloon	Country of Origin	Take-off	Result
1999 Jan	Jacques Soukup Mark Sullivan Crispin Williams	Spirit of Peace	USA	Albuquerque, USA	Never took off because of Chinese block
1999 Jan	Kevin Uliassi	J-Renée	USA	Illinois, USA	Never took off because of Chinese block
1999 18 Feb	Andy Elson Colin Prescott	Cable & Wireless	Britain	Almería, Spain	Ditched off Japanese coast with power failure. Flew 11,495 miles. Absolute duration record – 425.41 hours
1999 1 Mar	**Bertrand Piccard Brian Jones**	**Breitling Orbiter 3**	**Switzerland**	**Château d'Oex, Switzerland**	**Three absolute world records: first round the world; distance record – 25,361 miles; duration record – 477.47 hours**

TECHNICAL TERMS

AERAD	High-altitude flight navigation chart
AFTN	Aeronautical fixed telecommunications network
ATC	Air traffic control
Capsat	Satellite telefax system
CB	Cumulo-nimbus cloud
Comms	Communications
EPIRB	Emergency personal identification radio beacon
ETA	Estimated time of arrival
EVA	Extra-vehicular activity
FIR	Flight information region
FL	Flight level
GPS	Global positioning system (navigational aid)
HF	High-frequency radio (long range)
Knot	Nautical mile per hour. One knot = 1.16 miles per hour
UTC	Universal time code – same as Zulu
VHF	Very high frequency radio (short range)
Zulu	Zulu time = Greenwich mean time